21737

CLA has

D1237026

TYLER, TEXAS, C.S.A.

OTHER BOOKS BY
WILLIAM A. ALBAUGH III
AS AUTHOR OR CO-AUTHOR

The Handbook of Confederate Swords.
The Original Confederate Colt.
The Confederate Brass-framed Colt and Whitney.
Confederate Arms.

TYLER, TEXAS, C.S.A.

By
William A. Albaugh III

THE STACKPOLE COMPANY
HARRISBURG, PENNSYLVANIA

L. C. Catalog Card No. 58-12307

*Printed and Bound in the United States of America
by* The Telegraph Press, *established 1831
Harrisburg, Pennsylvania*

*This book is dedicated
to
my beloved wife,
Lucille.*

ACKNOWLEDGMENTS

The author would like to thank the following for their assistance in preparing this work:

Bill L. Hendricks, Burbank, Calif.
Col. Leon C. Jackson, Dallas, Texas
B. G. Miller, Tyler, Texas
James F. Moser, Jr., Falls Church, Va.
National Archives, Washington, D. C.
Carl Pugliese, Yonkers, N. Y.
Edward N. Simmons, Kansas City, Mo.
W. Thomas Smith, Richmond, Va.
Bernard N. Snyder, Hudson, N. Y.

Map of *Tyler, Texas* and Vicinity

Scale of miles
0 5 10 2₀ 3₀

Fayetteville

AR

Fourche R

Arka

SALINE RIVER

INDIAN TERRITORY

RED RIVER

Paris

Bonham

TEXAS

RED RIVER

Ft Worth

Dallas

Jefferson

CADO LAKE

Marshall

Greenwood

Shreve

TYLER ☆

Carthage

Henderson

Waxahachie

Corsicana

Palestine

RUSK

Waco

Nacogdoches

SABINE RIVER

L

Temple

Huntsville

CONTENTS

FOREWORD

What a change our Country has undergone since this date last year.

The storm of war then hovering over our heads is now breaking with all its fury upon us. Our once beloved Country at that time was but partly disrupted and had the proper conceptions and laws been enacted we perhaps would not have been engaged in deadly strife.

During the past year a terrible Civil War has been inaugurated, the end and evils of which are beyond human perception. Brother has met brother in bloody conflict. The father and son from the Kennebec have met with savage ferocity, son and brother from the Rio Grande.

Men in the South whose hospitality the ingrates of the North have partaken of, and from whose hands they have received much kindness and innumerable favors, have seen their homes burned by, and themselves flee the sword of their former guests. This too because these men of the South knowing their rights dare defend.

It seems the old motto of the Romans, "Vae victis" has been fully adopted in the present contest.

Out of the old Government a new one has been formed, all of its parts put into active and vigorous operation. Never has there been in so short a time formed one so perfect in all its parts, and founded on so sure a basis.

A large army of a half a million has been raised, clothed and fed, and this without one cent to begin with. So far, the omens seem to be good for the success of our new gov-

ernment and the people of it more united than ever and determined to resist to the bitter end the encroachments of an insolent foe.

There has been quite a change in the old U. S. Government. The masses are wild with fanaticism and urged on by still more fanatic leaders.

The Federal Constitution, once held sacred and binding, has been violated more openly and flagrantly than ever. An army has been raised by the President without the authority of Congress. The habeas corpus act suspended, citizens imprisoned without charge or hope of trials. Ladies subjected to injuries and insults entirely unbecoming a civilized nation. These and other acts have been performed, not only disgraceful and dishonorable, but proof of the imbecility of the government. So far the aspects of affairs in the North seem fast tending to a military despotism and whether they avoid it or not, the government will never command the respect with nations it did before the rupture.

The South as yet has acted entirely upon the defensive. The plunder-seeking vandals of the North have been met at every point on land with success and our homes and firesides have been defended from devastation and their polluting touch. Our arms have been victorious at the battles: Bethel, Bull Run, Manassas, Springfield, Oak Hill, Lexington, Carnifex Ferry and in other lesser engagements.

The enemy have as yet accomplished little more than the capture of two small seacoast batteries at Fort Hatteras and Port Royal. This is doing but little after one year has expired in which this rebellion was to have been crushed in three months. It is time the people of the North had made the discovery that the Southerners were terribly in earnest and that the cry of Palefox at Saratoga; "War even to the knife!" is their cry. We are entering upon a new year. What it may bring forth, mortals know not, but God still being our helper, although we may sustain reverses, we will at last be victorious.

Our ship of State has been launched. Though upon a troubled sea, we have a brave and skillful Pilot and with Jeff Davis at the helm we may expect to weather the storm and ride safely into the haven of peace and prosperity.

From the diary of Will Clegg, Private, Co. "F", Second Louisiana Regiment

INTRODUCTION

THE CONFEDERATE STATES ORDNANCE
WORKS, TYLER, TEXAS

THIS is the story of the Confederate States Ordnance
Works, Tyler, Texas, during those long-ago days
when the red and starry blue-crossed flag flew from the
capital of every State south of the Potomac River. This is
a story of how desperate men took antiquated fowling
pieces, double-barreled shotguns, and using ingenuity in
place of material and equipment, turned these makeshifts
into muskets and rifles to arm the all-too-thin gray line
of the Confederate army.

Who were those men and how did they operate?

An air of mystery hangs heavy over a number of
Southern ordnance activities, and as their written records
dissolved with the Confederacy, what they made and how
is usually determined only by the Sherlock Holmes process
of putting two and two together.

Although following no particular pattern, the survival
ratio of Confederate weapons is not as low as might be
supposed; and any establishment of sufficient size to have
produced even as few as 50 stand of arms usually has
several specimens extant, testifying to the existence of that
enterprise. For those that doubt, we point to the firm of
Schneider & Glassick of Memphis, Tenn., whose total output of revolvers is believed to have been fourteen, of which
two (possibly three) have survived the years; or of less than
one hundred handguns made by Thomas W. Cofer of
Portsmouth, Va., at least eight are known to the author.

It would seem reasonable to suppose that the larger the establishment and the longer it remained in operation, the more arms would be produced, hence, more weapons which might survive to give mute proof of their maker's existence and enterprise. The Richmond Armory and Arsenal, main source of supply for General Lee's army, bears us out on this theory. Weapons made there are still reasonably plentiful.

The Tyler, Texas, plant was in continuous operation from 1862 until even after the war's close. We might then expect specimens from this armory to be fairly common; but in the case of Confederate ordnance, comparison with other establishments usually leads the thinker to disaster, for just as their methods of operation were highly irregular, so is the survival ratio of the weapons they produced.

Today, 90-odd years from 1865, we have as the sum existing total from Tyler, Texas, C.S.A., a handful of lockplates and only four complete guns. This is a meager monument to the ingenuity and bravery of those men who were the main source of ordnance supply for the Confederacy in the southwest. The Armory and its products seem to have disappeared into thin air. Such a conclusion is not too farfetched, and might be remembered at the end of this story.

SURVIVING RELICS FROM TYLER

What is the surviving physical evidence of 1861-1865 at Tyler? Of the Armory itself which was located about one mile south of town near the southeast corner of Mocking Bird Lane and the old Palestine Rd., no trace remains.

We can turn then only to the relics themselves; to this pitifully small collection which symbolizes that Texas which was Confederate. What went into their being? As heartaches can not be measured, nor tears counted, our story must concern itself with the more material things such as production figures and mode and method of operation. *These* can be reported with accuracy.

According to *Firearms of the Confederacy,* twenty-nine Tyler, Texas, lockplates came to light in 1931 when an old Grand Army of the Republic post was dissolved. These are described as follows:

Three lockplates marked, "Texas Rifle, Tyler, Cal. .57." These bear the serial numbers #46, #679 and #472.

Two lockplates marked, "Texas Rifle, Tyler, C.S." with serials #409 and #458.

One lockplate marked, "Texas Rifle, Tyler, Cal. .57, C.S., 1865," serial #802.

Eight lockplates marked, "Enfield Rifle, Tyler, Cal. .57, C.S." with serials #60, #63, #64, #170, #196, #244, #261 and #262.

Six lockplates marked, "Enfield Rifle, Tyler, Tex., Cal. .57, C.S., 1865" with serials #460, #462A, #469, #479, #484 and #500.

Two lockplates marked, "Hill Rifle, Tyler, Tex., Cal. .54, C.S." with serials #12 and #301.

Two lockplates marked, "Hill Rifle, Tyler, Tex., C.S." with serials #192 and #229.

Three lockplates marked, "Austrian Rifle, Tyler, Tex., Cal. .54, C.S., 1865" with serials #26, #42 and #49.

Two lockplates marked, "C.S." with serials #133 and #274.

Even a casual study of the serial numbers on these lockplates reveals such an overlapping that it seems obvious the numbers found thereon had nothing to do with total output. Rather, they must have applied only to that particular gun or model of gun. This is not unusual, as a weapon's serial reflects its sequence in a particular model and not the overall output of a factory which might produce a number of different type arms—each with their own set of serials.

The discovery of so large a number of lockplates without a corresponding number of guns naturally gave rise to considerable speculation. One theory was advanced that Confederate authorities had put into operation a system of manufacture wherein the various component parts of firearms were made at different points, later to be assembled into a complete arm at some central armory.

Such a system was vaguely contemplated by the South and even reached the point where the Armory at Macon, Ga., supplied both Richmond, Va., and Fayetteville, N. C., with gun stocks. That is about as far as the Confederacy proceeded along this line; and with the case in question, we will determine that the surplus of lockplates resulted from a procedure common to Confederate ordnance establishments of "doing the best with that which was at hand." When armories lacked material to make a complete gun, all workers turned to and made whatever they could from whatever was plentiful at the moment. At Tyler, this happened to be lockplates.

Tyler, was by no means alone in this practice. At other armories on various occasions, we find all hands engaged in fabricating brass buttplates, bands and trigger guards—there being no iron for gun barrels, steel for bayonets, nor wood for stocks. These components would be made later on—when and if the iron, steel and wood were forthcoming. Meanwhile the workers must be kept busy.

In this present day and age of the specialized worker, such procedure seems fantastic. It would be hard for us to conceive of all General Motors' employees making fenders for automobiles while awaiting the material from which to make engines, but let us remember that the mechanic of 1860 was not so specialized. Most could work as easily on one part of a gun as another.

THE FOUR TYLER, TEXAS, GUNS

From the lockplates we pass on to the balance of the known physical relics of Tyler. These consist solely of four complete guns—each different from the others. They are:

1. A crudely made arm of the typically Austrian pattern, caliber .54, with an overall length of 53 inches. The barrel is 37½ inches and is provided with a regular U. S.-type model 1861 rear sight. The mountings are all of iron, two bands with sling swivels attached to the trigger guard and to the top band which also acts as a nose cap. The lockplate is marked, "Austrian Rifle, Tyler, Tex., Cal. .54" forward of the hammer, and, "C. S., 1865," to the rear.

As in all Tyler arms, the lock is attached to the stock with one screw. Serial #11 is stamped on *all* lock parts, the barrel, the buttplate, and trigger guard.

2. Patterned after the Enfield rifle, caliber .57. Overall length 48½ inches with a 33-inch barrel (5 groove rifling) provided with a lug for sabre bayonet and a two-leaf rear sight. The mountings are all of brass. The trigger guard is shaped like that of an Enfield but the bands are flat and are retained in place by regular band springs. The lockplate is marked, "Texas Rifle, Tyler, Cal. .57," in three lines forward of the hammer and "C. S." to the rear. It is also marked "C. S." on the barrel and buttplate tang. The serial number of this weapon (as in the one preceding) is #11, which is to be found on *all* lock parts, barrel and buttplate. Sling swivels are on the stock to the rear of the trigger guard, and on the top band. Weight of the arm is eight and one half pounds.

3. Enfield-type rifle with Mississippi-type rear band. Overall length 43½ inches with a 27-inch barrel, .54 caliber. Front and rear sights are of inlet brass. Iron mounts. No provision for bayonet. Sling swivels are on trigger guard and top band. The lockplate is marked in front of the hammer, "Hill Rifle, Tyler, Tex., Cal. .54," in four lines, and "C. S., 1865," in the rear. Serial #337 is found on 10 different places, including *all* parts of lock, barrel, etc., and even on screw heads.

4. Overall length of 43¼ inches with a 28-inch barrel, fixed rear sight. The barrel is held to the stock by two spring type barrel bands. Mountings are all of iron. The lockplate is marked, "Texas Rifle, Tyler, Cal. .57," to the front of the hammer, and "C. S." to the rear. The serial #24 is to be found on all parts of the lock as well as on the barrel (just slightly to the rear of the front sight), and other parts of the gun. The sling swivels turn slightly to either side, possibly because the rivet type attachment is loose, but more probably having been made that way so they could turn one quarter turn either side with the movement of the sling. According to the owner of this gun it is well made, although it shows marks of hand manufacture. The barrel is rifled, 3 groove. Bottom of the barrel under the front sight is noted to have a small dove-tail cut out, which might have held a lug for a swivel ramrod.

It takes no student of arms to note the wide difference between these four guns. Which then is the standard, or are all four standard, each representing a different type gun, each to be used for different purposes?

The one point in common to all four—and all of the lockplates—is the single screw-hole method of securing lockplate to stock. Although this method is entirely commonplace in a shotgun or sporting rifle, in a military piece this is a peculiarity.

Having examined all of the physical remains of Tyler, we turn now to the written records.

For part of the story that follows, the writer is deeply indebted to Lawrence D. Satterlee. His article on Tyler, Texas, which appeared in Theodore Dexter's *A.R.C.A Arms Quarterly* (Vol. 1, No. 3) is the only real information on this subject to date. It covered activities at the Armory from its inception in May 1862 under private management, until purchased by the Confederate government in the fall of 1863.

While on the subject of Satterlee and Dexter, I wonder if collectors are aware of the debt owed to them and to other early historians? Satterlee, Dexter, Bowie, Standish, Quick, Keighley-Peach and Steuart—most present-day research takes up only where these gentlemen left off.

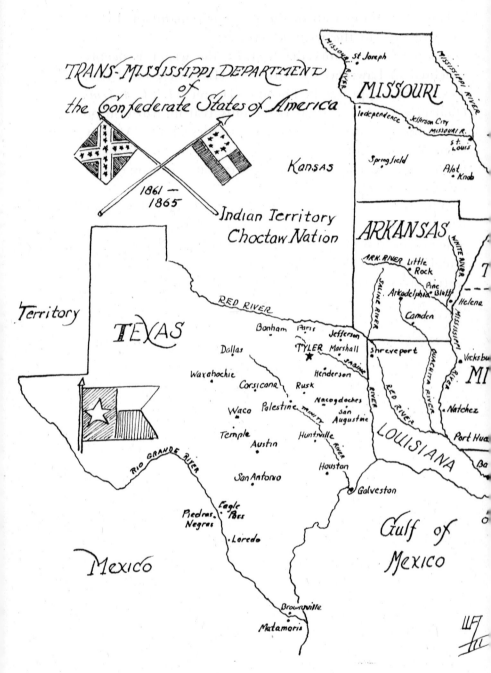

PART I

THE ARMORY OF SHORT, BISCOE & CO.

and

CONFEDERATE ORDNANCE ACTIVITIES IN
ARKANSAS

THE ARMORY OF SHORT, BISCOE & CO.

TYLER, Texas, was named for John Tyler, tenth
president of the United States, and came into being
as the seat of Smith County, organized in 1846. The town
was incorporated January 29, 1850, when it was enacted
that "the limits of said corporation shall extend over one
hundred acres of land, in a square, laid off so as to leave
a public square in the center of said Corporate limits."
(Laws of Texas, Special Laws of the 3rd Legislature, Vol. 3,
page 60.)

According to *A History of Tyler & Smith County, Texas*,
the 640 acres of land which now compose Tyler sold
originally for a total of $100 on October 2, 1846; but
by February 6th the following year (1847), land values had
so increased that one hundred of the original acres (including the Public Square) brought $150!

As might be expected, the town grew up around the
Public Square. "By 1847, there was a log house on the
southeast corner of the Square where the occupants sold
whiskey, tobacco, powder and lead. There was at this time
another log house situated on the northwest side of the
Square. It was a one-story house made of hewed pine logs,
20 feet wide by 30 feet long, facing south. This old house
was used as a kind of camp where newcomers would make
their headquarters until they could get a permanent one.
It was also used as a courthouse until sometime after 1850
when another log building 20 by 20 feet was erected in
the center of the Public Square for that purpose. Thick
timber was on the Square and small paths or trails lead

through the woods from one part to another." *(A History of Tyler & Smith County, Texas.)*

Other log houses lined the square, there being no brick buildings until 1855 when five brick stores were erected. In 1858, a three-story brick building was built by Col. George Yarbrough which he used as a dry-goods store.

By 1860, Tyler had a population of 1,024 persons. *(Hist. of Texas & Texans, Vol. 2, page 900.)* The entire Smith County had only 13,392 white and 4,982 negroes within its confines. *(Handbook of Texas II, pages 629 and 814.)*

The town is not hard to visualize—log houses scattered around a large tree-grown square, wherein deer were frequently observed and shot, with possibly a half dozen brick buildings. The southwest was filled with such towns. A small dusty Texas town of no particular importance. It was typical of its day, age and locality. Properly patriotic, its citizens made no bones as to their standing on the questions of the North, the South, States' Rights and the negro.

Tyler could boast of no railroad, but it did have a newspaper, the Tyler *Reporter,* which in 1860 was edited by Samuel W. Warner and Maj. James P. Douglas. *(History of Tyler & Smith County, Texas, page 120.)*

On August 1, 1861, there appeared in this newspaper the following advertisement which probably occasioned no undue comment, one way or the other:

To Arms! To Arms!

J. C. Short would respectfully return his thanks to the public for their liberal patronage heretofore extended to him, and inform the Southern people that he is still manufacturing some of those fine Kentucky Rifles, warranted to kill an Abolitionist at 400 yards.

He also manufactures superior Double Barrel Rifles and Shot Guns, and has just opened a fine lot of Colt's Repeating Pistols, English Repeaters, Deringer Pistols, and a variety of single Pistols, Bowie Knives, Shot Bags, Powder Flasks, Game Bags, Patent

Wadding, Dram Bottles, etc. Also keeps on hand a good lot of double and single shot guns.

A fine lot of Caps, Powder and Lead, and everything usually kept in the Gun-Maker's line, all of which will be sold to suit the hardtimes.

Repairing of all kinds in the gun lines, attended to with neatness and despatch, and all work warranted. Shop on the East side of the Square, Tyler, Texas.

1862

The following spring, Mr. Short's desire to furnish arms came into official notice, being brought to the attention of the Military Board of Texas. Whereupon he was written by P. DeCordova, Secretary of the Board:

I am instructed by the Military Board of the State to correspond with you on the subject of the manufacture of arms.

You have been highly recommended by Judge Roberts as a very competent man, and the Board wish to engage all such in the service of this State.

I am directed to ask if you will undertake the manufacture of Mississippi Rifles, at what price, and if you are fixed as to manufacture any quantity quickly?

If willing to make a contract with the Board on the part of the State, you will please communicate with the Board all these particulars as well as the probable price you can afford to make these guns for, and also what amount of material fit for the purpose is within your reach?

Any information on this subject that you may think proper to communicate to the Board will be thankfully received.

Here then was an opportunity to eradicate Abolitionists —not singly at 400 yards as heretofore, but on a wholesale basis, and upon receipt of the above, Short directed his enterprise toward making a Mississippi-type rifle. Being accustomed to sporting and hunting arms (lock attached to stock with one screw), it is not unusual that the military rifle he devised also had the same type lock.

[13]

As the armory he planned was larger than his own means would permit, he interested another local gunsmith (William S. N. Biscoe) in his project, and the company of Short, Biscoe & Co. was formed. Also connected with the firm as a partner was George Yarbrough, already mentioned as having built the first brick three-story building in Tyler. It was probably this latter partner who furnished the bulk of the necessary financial outlay. He is said to have been involved to the extent of $80,000.

At any rate, the partnership between the three was formed in May 1862, and the firm began their preparations of supplying the State of Texas with rifles.

For this purpose they purchased one hundred acres of land one mile south of Tyler, built a large brick house, and set about initial operations, which included purchase of material, machinery, etc. (*Confederate Military History.* Vol. 11.)

The three partners decided that it was not beyond their capabilities to manufacture five thousand stand of arms (with or without bayonet) and formally submitted their proposition to the Texas Military Board. They received a reply dated Austin, Texas, Aug. 14, 1862, from F. R. Lubbock, the Board's President, and also Governor of the State.

Messrs. Short, Biscoe & Co., Tyler.

Gentlemen—Your proposition to build for the State of Texas, 5,000 stand of arms after the model of the Mississippi Rifle, has been by me placed before the Military Board for their action, and I am instructed by the Board to say that they will close a contract with you upon the basis laid down with some immaterial alterations. As I said to you, we wish the bayonet of the model furnished us some longer to suit the gun, giving it a point of about 5 inches of steel, the rest of good iron as well tempered as possible. The price of the gun and bayonet to be $35.00 instead of $30.00 as proposed by you without the bayonet. I have assured the Board that you would commence work in about 4 or 5 months and deliver the guns as rapidly as possible. The great object, of course, is to get the arms as speedily as they can be had.

In your proposition you required 1/3 of the contract price advanced, but I understood you to say that you thought from 5 to $6,000 would be as much as you would require at one time, and it would be several months before you would need that amount.

We will be pleased to hear from you at your earliest convenience and trust you will proceed with all dispatch in getting ready for the work. As soon as we hear from you, we will prepare the contract and make arrangements for the necessary advance.

To the above, Lubbock adds a postscript to the effect that he had received a letter from the Confederate Ordnance Officer advising that all government guns would be .577 inches in bore. Texas was asked to confine their arms to that caliber. "If it makes no material odds to you," says Lubbock to Short, "we would like yours to correspond with that size."

Shortly thereafter (Oct. 27, 1862) Lubbock sent Short, Biscoe & Co. a rifle gauge prepared by Condederate Ordnance with the advice that the War Department had recommended all guns to be made by the different States to be of .577 caliber. According to Lubbock, the gauge was stamped ".5770." The wish that Short & Biscoe would conform to this caliber was reiterated.

Caliber .577 was set as standard for all Confederate infantry arms by Col. J. Gorgas, Chief of Ordnance, on June 9, 1862, who on this date issued a circular which read:

It has been determined to adopt the calibre of the Enfield rifle .577 for all infantry arms made here-after at the various government establishments. (Gen. orders, Conf. Army, page 234.)

Following the above, Gorgas wrote the Governor of Texas; July 5, 1862.

Your Excellency:

It seems advisable to inform the various States that the Confederate Government is now manufacturing arms of the calibre .577 exclusively, and it is hoped for obvious reasons that the States will adopt the same calibre for any guns they manufacture. Gauge plugs for the calibre named will be prepared and distributed if desired.

At the time of this correspondence, the Post Office in Tyler was located in a two-story frame building on the north side of the Square, having replaced a log house located at the southwest corner of the Square which burned about 1859.

From the Tyler *Reporter,* Sept. 5, 1855, we gain some information as to mail in those days. According to this source, a stage-coach line extended from Tyler to Waco, and from there to Austin. Mail leaving Tyler at 7 a.m. on Monday, Wednesday and Friday, would arrive in San Augustine on Tuesday, Thursday and Saturday.

During any study of Civil War records, we must disassociate ourselves from any comparisons with present-day method of communications, for although time was most decidedly of the essence to the Confederacy, the way of life then was leisurely, and there were no rubber stamps indicating "Urgent," "Top Priority," etc. Letters received were answered only when the receiver got around to it, which in the case of Lubbock's letter of Aug. 14th to Short, Biscoe & Co., was Sept. 6th.

Hon. F. R. Lubbock:

Your favor of the 14th August came to hand by due course of mail. We have delayed writing you as our Mr. Yarbrough was in Austin. After the writing of the letter above referred to, and being informed of the action by the Military Board, informed you that you could at your convenience prepare the contract papers, and forward them, which as yet have not reached us. We are now preparing with all possible energy for the work, and have secured all the necessary iron and steel for the gun and bayonet, a portion of which we have already here, and the balance is on the road. The only difficulty presenting itself to us so far, is in the way of hands (gunsmiths). Col. Hubbard and Roberts and Lt. Col. Lott (commanding C.S. regiments) have refused to let us have any (men) out of their respective commands, their excuse being that it is a private enterprise for the State and that they are not to be benefited by it, and that you as Governor of the State, had refused to let them have arms belonging to the State to arm their regiments, etc. We have about 20 hands already secured and believe we shall be able to secure enough by the time we are fully under way. We have made application to Gen'l Holmes for the men Col. Roberts and Hubbard refused us.

Here we have a classic example of the age-old struggle between States Rights and Central Government. The State of Texas refused arms to the Confederate Government, so the Government in turn would refuse to release gunsmiths from the army to make guns for the State of Texas. The temptation to explore this further is strong, but along with heartaches and tears, States Rights has no place in this work. We are concerned only with rifles and Tyler, Texas.

J. C. Short in his letter of Sept. 6th, made note that he had made application to Gen'l Holmes for the men refused the firm by Colonels Roberts and Hubbard. On Sept. 30th, the Military Board of Texas also wrote Major General T. H. Holmes, C.S.A., Commanding Trans-Mississippi District;

The Military Board of the State having entered into contract with Messrs. Short, Biscoe & Co., of Tyler, Smith Co., Texas, to manufacture for the State of Texas five thousand stand of Arms after the model of the Mississippi Rifles, these parties have expended a large amount of money in purchasing machinery and stock to enable them to turn out these arms with expedition, find themselves much pressed for workmen to enable them to comply with their contract, a failure which may work much agony to the State. I am instructed by the Board to request that you will detail the following named men from those under your command for work in the armory of Messrs. Short, Biscoe & Co., Tyler, Smith Co., Texas:

S. R. Clay, T. M. Kidd, Asa W. Longfellow, of Capt. Sharp's Company—Hubbard's Regt.

M. B. Behiller, George W. Hager of Anderson's Company.

D. M. Sparks—Eryledon's Company.

A. Tights—Robert's Regt.

J. H. Brown—Rupel's Company, Lane's Regt.

W. W. Churtran,—Mone's Company, Sweet's Regt.

Henry Flore—May's Company, Speight's Regt.

Messrs Short, Biscoe & Co., expect to pay parties full wages for their work, and will report should they leave their employment.

The Board requests your favorable consideration of the subject of this letter.

Actually at the time of the above letter, there was no contract existing between the State and Short, Biscoe & Co.

The terms for the contract were drawn up as of Nov 5, 1862, but included a provision that bullet moulds were to be supplied with each rifle. The contract read as follows:

This agreement made and entered into by and between J. C. Short, Wm. S. N. Biscoe and George Yarbrough, doing business under the name and style of Short, Biscoe & Co., of Tyler, Texas, of the 1st part, and the Military Board of the State of Texas, composed of F. R. Lubbock, Governor, C. R. Johns, Comptroller, and C. H. Randolph, Treasurer, of the 2nd part, WITNESSETH, that the said Short, Biscoe & Co., do hereby agree to make and manufacture for the Military Board of the State of Texas, five thousand (5,000) stand of arms after the model of the Mississippi Rifle, length of barrel to be 33 inches, bore of the size to carry ball of half ounce in weight, walnut stocks, iron mountings, iron ramrod, two bands with loops, double-sighted and single trigger, with the improved bayonet invented by Mr. Short, somewhat longer than the model furnished to the Board, so as to suit the Gun. The bayonet to have a point of five inches of steel, and the remainder to be of good iron, well tempered.

Said Guns to be in all respects, good substantial war guns, to be furnished with wipers and moulds and to be made and finished in 1st class workmanlike style at the price of thirty-five dollars for each gun, complete as above described. To be delivered to the agent of the Board at Tyler in lots of one hundred or more, and at least five hundred guns complete to be delivered by the 1st day of June A.D., 1863, and the whole number of guns contracted for to be delivered by the 1st day of January 1864. Provided that the party of the 2nd part shall not be compelled to take, except at their option, a larger number of Guns after the 1st day of August than have been delivered up to that time.

It is agreed and understood between the parties that the party of the 2nd part shall test these guns according to the prescribed rules for testing army guns.

The party of the 2nd part agrees to advance from time to time as may be wanted in sums of five thousand dollars, the sum of Thirty thousand dollars. It being understood and agreed that for every advance made, the party of the 1st part shall furnish security to be approved by the party of the 2nd part in double the amount so advanced and further that fifty percent of the price to be paid shall be deducted towards repaying the advance and also that not more than ten thousand Dollars shall be advanced by the party of the 2nd part, until after the delivery of the 1st five hundred guns.

The broken contracts for arms between individuals, the various Southern States and/or the Confederate Government, if laid end to end, would assuredly reach from Fort Sumter to Appomattox. None were able to fulfill their hopes, and few the promises that were agreed upon by either party of the 1st or 2nd part. Although the lack of steel, iron, brass, and wood played an enormous part in this unfulfillment, the efficiency of the United States Army can be considered the main common denominator.

Out of all those who contracted to the Government for any sizeable amount of arms, and who actually did what he said he would, the name of Samuel Griswold, of Griswoldville, Ga., stands crystal clear. Slightly ironic it is that the one man on whom the South relied most heavily for revolvers (we are of course excluding Samuel Colt) originally came from Vermont. Old Sam Griswold allowed as how he could furnish the Confederacy with about 100 revolvers a month. The thirty-six hundred (plus) brass-framed products from Griswoldville, over a three-year period, attest to the integrity of at least one Yankee.

The arms contract with which we are concerned was signed by Short, Biscoe & Co., although exception was taken to the provision which required the furnishing of a bullet mould with each gun. In a letter appended to the contract, the firm set forth their objections.

P. DeCordova, Esq., Sec'y of Military Board.

We herewith return contract for manufacture of Guns, signed as sent, making one exception, that is, moulds, which if our recollection serves us, we did not propose to make, in as much as ammunition for army purposes is always prepared, and there would be but little or no use in having moulds for each Gun having that kind. In making our estimate we omitted the moulds in the proposal. The making of Moulds for 5,000 Guns is an item of considerable importance, would be worth $2.00 each for a round ball, or $3.00 each for a long ball of the size that these Guns are to be made. Refer again to the original proposal and we think you will find that the moulds were omitted.

The mandril for giving us the size of the bore came to hand opportunely for which we are much obliged. As yet we have heard nothing of the hands asked for from the Texas regiments in Arkansas, neither have we heard anything from the two asked for in Conscript Camp at this place. We are pushing everything along as rapidly as possible, and think by 1st January, we shall be able to begin on the Guns. It takes a large amount of preparation to commence the manufacture of Arms.

Just about this time, the Texas Military Board was shocked at the reply they received from Gen'l Holmes, in answer to their request for exemptions for certain

Texas gunsmiths. Writes Gen'l Holmes, through his Asst. Adj. Gen'l. T. G. Anderson:

In answer to your communication of the 30th inst., I am instructed by Major Gen'l Holmes to say, it is out of his power to grant your request to have certain men detailed to work for Messrs. Short, Biscoe & Co., Tyler, Texas.

The Military Board lost no time in their attempt to set straight this obvious violation of States Rights, for the day after receiving the above (Nov. 7th), DeCordova wrote directly to no less a person than Hon. G. W. Randolph, Secretary of War, Confederate States of America.

I am directed by the Military Board of the State of Texas to state to you, that in obedience to the law of the last Legislature, which created the Board and defined its duties; a portion of which was to procure arms and ammunition, they have entered into contracts with several parties to erect armories and manufacture guns. They have also erected a State Foundry at this place (Austin), all of which has caused the expenditure of large sums of money, and now that the armories and foundry are both in operation they find difficulty in procuring workmen, most of the mechanics who are proficient, having volunteered and joined the army, some at the 1st sound of the tocsin, and others to avoid the conscription.

It being the opinion of the Board that competent mechanics would be of more use to the Confederacy in these workshops than in the army, they had no hesitancy in addressing Major Gen'l Holmes, commanding the Trans-Mississippi District, a request that he would detail certain men in the various Texas regiments, now in Arkansas, to work in the different Armories, now under contract with the Board. Very much to their surprise the following answer from Gen'l Holmes reached here this morning. (Here, Anderson's letter is quoted.)

Under this aspect of affairs, the Board respectfully requests that you will issue such orders as may be best in your judgement, that will enable Gen'l Holmes to comply with the request of the Board for men to work in the different armories and the State foundry already made or may hereafter be made by the Board.

The Board is composed of the Governor, Comptroller and Treasurer of the State, which will be a sufficient guarantee to you that no man will be improperly applied for.

In connection with this application and further to show the necessity of the request contained herein, being favorably responded to, I would state that the soldiers who have left the State have taken with them their private arms, and left the State nearly bare, rendering it incumbent on the Board to leave nothing undone that can by human exertions be done to have arms ready for the people left in the State, to protect themselves if invaded by the Northern vandals, or the wily Indian, assisted and incited by our slaves, if such should happen.

Nov. 24th, the Board got around to writing Short, Biscoe & Co., noting the exception in the arms contract relative to the bullet moulds. The Board was of the opinion that the firm should furnish one mould with every eight or ten guns, this being "absolutely necessary to make the guns efficient, because fixed ammunition may not always be had in these times."

The Military Board was entirely correct in their assumption that fixed ammunition would not always be at hand.

Other firms supplied moulds of the proper caliber for their weapons. Spiller & Burr was one such, and an unfinished bronze revolver mould recently dug up at Griswoldville, Ga., and presently in the author's collection, shows conclusively that moulds were also made by the firm of Griswold & Gunnison.

If bullet moulds were needed and used, what of a container to carry the powder? With such a wide variety of private arms which embraced fowling pieces, double and single shotguns, flintlocks, etc., it was necessary for many Confederate soldiers armed with these obsolete weapons to carry some form of powder flask or horn all through the war.

A few powder horns can be classified as Confederate by

[22]

the inscriptions carved upon them, but strangely, to date, no one has ever come up with a powder flask which can be positively identified as having been made either by the Confederate government or by private manufacture under contract.

The question then arises, were any such made? The answer to this is a very definite "yes." The "Captured Rebel Ordnance Records" in our National Archives is full of references to both manufacture and issuance of powder horns and flasks. To quote a few: G. W. Fall & Co., Nashville, Tenn., on Nov. 1, 1861, was paid $48.40 for eleven powder horns at 40¢ each and forty-four powder flasks at $1.00 each. On the same date, Sam Vanleer & Co., furnished twenty-seven powder flasks at 75¢ per and fifty-two powder flasks at $1.00 per, plus thirteen powder horns at $1.00 per. Nov. 5, 1861, J. H. Horton received $31.83 for twenty-one powder flasks. Volume #108 of these Captured Records, showing invoice of supplies sent to various ordnance stations from Richmond, shows the following regarding flasks:

Jan. 13, 1862, 465 bullet pouches were sent to Lt. Col. George Gant at Camp Maury.
Jan. 14, 1862, 100 bullet pouches, 100 tin powder flasks were sent to Capt. N. R. Chambliss.
Jan. 20, 1862, Capt. R. W. Ayres of Danville, Tenn., had 800 tin powder flasks and 800 slings for same sent him.
Jan. 27, 1862, Capt. I. W. Feltz was sent 24 tin powder flasks and slings.
Jan. 28, 1862, Capt. I. F. McCutcheson was sent 52 powder horns and slings, and on the same date, Lt. P. McClung was sent 274 tin powder flasks and slings and 260 powder horns and slings.
Feb. 6, 1862, Col. Dearing was sent 390 powder flasks with slings, and 310 powder horns and slings.

In March 1864, M. H. Wright, Comdg., C. S. Arsenal, Atlanta, Ga., wrote "Lt. S. P. Kerr, on Ordn. Duty" as follows:

You will proceed to Columbus, Ga., and see what arrangements can be made to get canteens and powder flasks of tin.

You will first call on Capt. F. C. Humphreys, Ord. Off., and act in accord with him . . . Get Capt. Humphreys to make such contracts if he will, for 10- to 15,000 powder flasks . . . (Vol. 77.)

These are just a few, but it must be obvious from these that tin powder flasks were commonplace in the Confederate army even as late as 1864. Like the Tyler, Texas, rifles, they seem to have disappeared.

To return to Texas: Upon receiving the letter requesting one mould with each eight or ten guns, Short, Biscoe & Co., advised the Military Board as follows on Dec. 5, 1862:

Yours of the 24th ult. is at hand. I have to say in relation to moulds, that we can not consent to inserting moulds unless at a fair remuneration. We can make them, and will say that you may insert the number you want to the hundred guns, or one mould for eight or ten guns, as the Board may desire, for a round ball at $2.00 each is the proposition we first made. We made our estimate without including the moulds. To make any considerable number of them would be attended with considerable expense, and could we have foreseen the circumstances now surrounding us, we would not undertake to put up the Gun at the price that we have agreed to do it, simply for the reason that everything has advanced in price to such an extent that it will cost us double what we first anticipated it would to start this armory. We shall have to pay hands sound prices for work. We should like to accede to what you say the Military Board think we ought to do; but when they know the circumstances, we are satisfied they will readily see they ought not ask it. Laborers have been scarce and difficult to get since we commenced this work, and today is the first day that we can say we have had a sufficient force of common laborers. We are now running up the building (brick) and hope to have it up and covered in the next four weeks, with anything like good weather, as it is now.

As of 20th Dec., 1862, the State of Texas and Short,

Biscoe & Co., reached an agreement and the modified arms contract between the two was finally signed.

The following spring was spent in erecting their plant, machinery, etc. We do not hear of the firm again until June 8, 1863.

State of Texas, County of Travis.

Know all men by these presents, that we, J. C. Short, Wm. S. N. Biscoe and George Yarbrough, doing business under the firm name of Short, Biscoe & Co., as principals, and L. P. Butler and John Dewberry as securities, are joined by and severally bound unto the State of Texas in the sum of fifty thousand dollars upon the following conditions, to wit: J. C. Short, W. S. N. Biscoe, and George Yarbrough, doing business under the firm of Short, Biscoe & Co., did on the 5th Day of Nov. A.D. 1862, sign a contract with F. R. Lubbock, Governor, C. R. Johns, Comp-troller, and C. H. Randolph, Treasurer of the State, composing the Military Board (created by law) to make 5,000 stand Arms, which contract was afterwards, to-wit, on the 20th Dec. 1862, signed on behalf of the Board by F. R. Lubbock, President of the Board, and whereas the said Board have at the request of said parties modified the contract so far as to advance upon their request the sum of twenty-five thousand dollars upon the agreement that the said Short, Biscoe & Co. are to furnish 500 stand of Arms on the 15th day of August, and 500 more on the 15th day of October next ensuing and that on the payments due on delivery for these guns, shall be deducted fifty percent towards the reimbursement of the said sum of twenty-five thousand dollars, and the balance that may be due shall be deducted from the payment of the next lot of Guns delivered hereafter.

Now, therefore, if the said Short, Biscoe & Co. comply with the agreement as modified, and deliver at the dates mentioned the number of specified of Arms, then this obligation to be null and void, otherwise to be in full force and effect

In testimony whereof, the principals and securities have herewith set their hands at Austin, this 8th June, 1863.

Five hundred stand of arms were to have been forthcoming on Aug. 15, 1863. Three weeks after this date had past (Sept. 8th), DeCordova inquires:

I am instructed by the Board to inquire of you whether the 500 Guns that were to be ready by the 15th of last month are ready for delivery? Also, all information as to the delivery of the balance. The necessity of having these arms is so great, that we wish to be informed how many you will deliver after this time every month.

Should you require any further assistance from the Board to enable you to push the work with expedition, it will be cheerfully afforded.

Arms are required at this time, as you are aware, and the Board trust that your best energies will be exerted to fill your contract.

September 1863! The great victories of 1st and 2nd Manassas, and the various Seven Days Battles before Richmond had been fought and won so long ago they were remembered only by the names on the regimental battle flags, and by the mothers, sweethearts, and widows of the soldiers killed and wounded therein. Chancellorsville was also behind. The great battles of Gettysburg and Vicksburg also had been fought but lost. These were still remembered even so far south as Texas. June 1863, the stars of the Confederate battle flags had reached the height of their arc and by July had begun their descendancy. There would be many more battles, and victories claimed by each side, but for the Military Board of Texas to write Sept. 8th, 1863, that "arms are required at this time" is as classic an understatement as has ever been made.

Sept. 17, 1863, Short, Biscoe & Co., wrote the Board outlining their difficulties.

We can deliver 100 guns in two weeks from this date. We have had much troubles about stock timber and a large number of our hands have been sick. We have been delayed on account of unexperienced hands, having to take such as we could get, as we have invariably been refused gunsmiths from the regular army, and are much annoyed by hands wanting advanced wages, as everything has advanced so much above the usual prices of the Guns. We shall run short of iron soon, as there is a heavy loss on the weight from the raw iron to a finished gun, which will make the iron cost us in a gun from $20.00 to $23.00 to say nothing of labor and other material.

We have 500 barrels bored and turned ready for the stocks, and 250 more bored out and fifty welded, making 800 barrels. We have about 500 bayonets made, and we have nearly all the pieces ready and locks for the 800. We have a lot of timber now seasoning which we will push as we are in need of it, and will put them up as rapidly as possible.

Despite the promise of 100 guns to be delivered two weeks from the above, by Oct. 12th, there were still no guns as evidenced by a letter from the Texas Military Board.

Captain

On the 5th day of Nov., 1862, the firm of Short, Biscoe & Co. signed a contract with the Military Board to make 5,000 stand of arms after the model of the Mississippi Rifle, length of barrel 33 inches, bore of the size to carry half ounce ball, walnut stocks, iron mountings, iron ramrod, two bands with loops, double-sighted and single trigger, with the improved bayonet invented by Mr. Short with a point of 5 inches of steel and the remainder to be of good iron well tempered, at the price of $35.00 to be delivered to the agent of the Board in lots of 100 or more, and at least 500 guns to be delivered by June 1, 1863.

Immediately after the execution of this contract by the parties, they proceeded to the erection of the necessary buildings and to the manufacture of the tools required, and the procurement of material.

The report that has reached the Board from very authentic sources is to the effect that these parties have expended between thirty and forty thousand dollars in the erection of buildings, besides a large sum for material. They did this from their own means, for it was not until the month of June 1863, that the parties concerned asked any pecuniary aid from the Board, who at that date and at their request made an advance of $25,000 to enable them to purchase more materials. Mr. Short is one of the best of men, the best Gunsmith in the State, and the two Guns that have been sent to the Board as a sample will compare favorably with Harpers Ferry rifle, manufactured for the old Government.

The other parties are business men and capitalists and rank amongst the first of our citizens of their portion of the State for loyalty and enterprise. They have had great difficulties to contend with in securing the materials of all kinds, in getting proper workmen for the erection of their buildings, difficulties which the General commanding can appreciate, and know must exist in starting all large enterprises in times like these.

Under the date of Sept. 17th, Short, Biscoe & Co. made the following report to the Board (letter of Sept. 17th quoted).

I had nearly forgot to mention that the contract as to the delivery of Guns was modified so that 500 were to be delivered 15th August, and 500 on the 15 October, and it was agreed that of the Guns delivered, $500 of the price should be deducted towards the reimbursement of the amount advanced and the balance due is to be deducted from the payment of the next lot to be delivered.

I have had to be rather prolix in this statement, so that the whole matter might be clearly understood by the General.

The Military Board suggest whether it would not be as well for the government to take this contract off the hands of the Military Board. Under the direct control of the Government and the supervision of an officer detailed for that purpose, much more despatch in the manufacture of these arms could be obtained, and the Military Board are willing to do so.

It is the opinion of the Board that the hands asked to be detailed by Short, Biscoe & Co. are necessary for the execution of the work or they would not have been asked for. The Board have confidence in the integrity of the contractors and feel assured that they would not ask anything improper.

And so, negotiations for the purchase of the Short, Biscoe & Co. by the Confederate Government were opened by the Military Board of Texas, and shortly thereafter, the purchase was an accomplished fact. (Off. Rec. War Rebel. Series II, Vol. 22, page 1141.)

Having already noted an example of conflict between States Rights and central Government, we see above a basic reason why the former is unsuccessful. If when the going becomes hard the State requests the government to step in, there are few instances when the latter will not oblige, but even fewer when once in they will ever step out, the emergency over. For those that cry "States Rights," and I am loudest among them, let us remember that States Rights can never be maintained when subsidized with Federal funds.

On Nov. 23rd, W. Spalding Good, Captain of Artillery, to whom the Short, Biscoe & Co. arms were to have been turned over for delivery to the State of Texas, notified the Military Board:

There were no guns received at Tyler from the fact that the factory had been transferred to the Confederate States.

Exit Short, Biscoe & Co. except for a brief account of their settlement to the State of Texas.

Short, Biscoe & Co. to Military Board.
June 8, 1863. to cash advanced $25,000
  Interest from June 8, 1863 to Feb. 1, 1864
  5 months, 23 days at 8 per cent $1,294.50
                                                    ————————
                                                    $26,294.50
  This amount advanced on contract to make guns, by act of
Legislature on payment of indebtedness.
                        Credit
One rifle $35.00
Cash paid C. H. Randolph $26,259.50
                                                    ————————
                                                    $26,294.50

The firm came within 4,999 rifles of fulfilling their contract, but left with all accounts squared. They did better than many I could mention.

CONFEDERATE ORDNANCE ACTIVITIES IN ARKANSAS

Because of the close relationship between Tyler, Texas, and Little Rock, Ark., it is necessary to drop back a few years and catch up on what was going on in Arkansas while Short, Biscoe & Co. were preparing their rifles for the State of Texas.

Confederate ordnance records for the State of Arkansas are obscure and for the most part lacking. According to the U. S. War Department records, as of Jan. 21, 1861, this State had on hand in U. S. Forts and Arsenals within its confines, only 1,130 muskets and 54 rifles. Although this figure excludes flintlock arms as well as Colt revolvers and all other patent arms, it would seem safe to conclude that as of Jan. 21, 1861, ordnance activities within the State were of no great importance.

The bulk of the above mentioned weapons were stored in the U. S. Arsenal at Fort Little Rock which also had some machinery for making and repairing small arms.

The Little Rock Arsenal was seized by the State on Feb. 8, 1861. Arkansas seceded from the Union on May 6, 1861, and shortly thereafter, the Arsenal was turned over to the Confederate government on "loan" for the duration of the war.

According to *Confederate Military History* Vol. 10, General T. H. Hindman, C.S.A., created an Armory at Arkadelphia from machinery taken from the captured Arsenal, and "henceforth, Little Rock was used mainly as a depot for the storage of arms."

Says General Hindman:

Machinery was made for manufacturing percussion caps and small arms, and both were turned out in small quanity, but of excellent quality. Lead mines were opened and worked, and a chemical laboratory was established and successfully operated in aid of the Ordnance Dept. and in the manufacture of calomel, castor oil, spirits of niter, the various tinctures of iron, and other valuable medicines. Most of these works were located at or near Arkadelphia, on the Ouatchita River, 75 miles south from Little Rock. The tools, machinery and the material were gathered piecemeal or else made by hand labor. Nothing of this sort had been before attempted on Government account in Arkansas to my knowledge, except for the manufacture of small arms, the machinery for which was taken away by Gen'l Van Dorn and there was neither capital nor sufficient enterprise among the citizens to engage in such undertakings.—

A further supply, together with lead and caps, was procured from the citizens of Little Rock and vicinity by donation, purchases and impressments. This ammunition, and that which I brought with me, was rapidly prepared for use at the Laboratory established at the Little Rock Arsenal for the purpose. As illustrating the pitiful scarcity of material in the country, the fact may be stated that it was found necessary to use public documents of the State Library for cartridge paper. Gunsmiths were employed or conscripted, tools purchased or impressed, and the repair of the damaged guns I brought with me and about an equal number found at Little Rock was commenced at once. But after inspecting the work and observing the spirit of the men I decided that a garrison 500 strong could hold out against Fitch, and that I would lead the remainder—about 1,500—to Gen'l Rust as soon as shotguns and rifles could be obtained from Little Rock instead of pikes and lances, with which most of them were armed. Two days elapsed before the change could be effected. (Off. Rec. War of Reb. Series 1, Vol. 13, page 28.)

General Hindman mentioned the removal of the small arms-making machinery from Little Rock by General Van-Dorn. What happened to this machinery is another mystery of Confederate ordnance. Possibly the following from President Jefferson Davis, CSA, to "His Excellency, H. Flanagin, Governor of Arkansas, July 15, 1863," provides a clue.

Sir:

I have the honor to acknowledge yours—

You can not regret more than I do the injury which has re-sulted from the removal of the machinery for the manufacture of small arms. It had been sent from Little Rock to Napoleon before I heard of its removal. Directions were given to send it back to Little Rock, and afterward, learning that it had been removed from Napoleon before the order was received, though it was promptly given, further directions were given to have it returned, and efforts were being made to do so when, by in-terruption of communication across the Mississippi, the last in-formation I had of it was that it was on the 9th of this month (July, 1863) at Jackson, Miss., and the ordnance officer said he should probably be compelled to send it back to Alabama.

I beg of you to accept assurances of the regard and esteem with which I am, very respectfully and truly, yours. (Off. Rec. War of Reb. Series 1, Vol 22, part II, page 931.)

Despite the esteem and regard of President Jefferson Davis, the machinery for making small arms has never come to light.

General Hindman's account of ordnance activities in Arkansas are rather glowing. There is no question but that he did make something from nothing, which is always an accomplishment. Nevertheless, the probabilities are that the venture into arms-making at Arkadelphia was very similar to that at Holly Springs, Miss., which was more or less a complete fiasco. At Holly Springs, guns were re-paired (and had to be re-repaired), and various component parts were made which would fit no known arm.

The Arkadelphia venture was not so futile as Holly Springs however, and although production was small, some entire arms were fabricated. To date, none have appeared to be identified as such. Despite Gen'l Hindman's com-ments as to the excellent quality of these arms, others dis-agree with his appraisal. Their deficiencies seem to be summed up by Gen'l Cabbell, C.S.A., who says: "The

Arkadelphia rifles with the cartridges sent for them, are no better than shotguns." (Off. Rec. War Reb. Series 1, Vol. 22, page 311, April 25, 1863.)

The ordnance establishment at Little Rock was reactivated in August 1862. Looking around for a suitable person to head this activity, General Hindman turned to the C. S. Navy and borrowed Lieut. John W. Dunnington.

Lieut. Dunnington was formerly gunnery officer of the Confederate gunboat *Missouri* which had slipped into the White River from the wrecked Confederate fleet of the Mississippi. The White River guarded the approaches to Little Rock, and General Hindman had the gunboat sunk to obstruct the channel at St. Charles, the first town above the mouth. Her crew of 79 and two thirty-two-pounder Columbiads and four field pieces were placed under Lieut. Dunnington's command, and in the ensuing battle of St. Charles, against Fitch's fleet of gunboats, so distinguished himself that he came to the attention of the commanding General Hindman.

Dunnington was selected as the person to head the ordnance works at Little Rock, and although he continued to draw his pay from the C. S. Navy Dept., was placed in command of all ordnance matters there with the rank of Lieutenant Colonel.

Lt. Col. Dunnington's "Returns for the month of August, 1862, at Little Rock Arsenal, C.S.A.," are to be found in Vol. 149 Chapt. IV of the "Captured Rebel Ordnance Records." These returns are most enlightening. According to Col. Dunington, "When I assumed command at this Post, all material had been removed to Arkadelphia. There were no persons employed. No shops were open for repair of arms or for fabricating ammunition. Material, tools, etc., had to be procured as well as the employment of laborers. Work commenced the last part of the month."

The Military force at Little Rock under Dunnington's command, consisted of four officers: himself, Major John B. Lockman, Capt. C. C. Green, and 2nd Lt. W. W. Murphy. In addition to these, he had 20 enlisted men and a civilian force composed of a foreman, 2 clerks, 3 gunsmiths (for repairing arms), a laboratorian, 26 laborers in the laboratory and a carpenter (for making packing boxes).

During the month of August 1862, the following work was performed:

Fabricated, one pair of musket bullet moulds, one pair buckshot bullet moulds, 10,000 buck & ball shot cartridges; *repaired*—750 muskets, shotguns and rifles; *received and repaired*—ordnance stores and ordnances; *performed*—guard, office and police duties; *inspected*—Post at Camden and Arkadelphia.

The Post at Camden was under the command of Maj. George D. Alexander. Capt. G. S. Polleys was "Capt. in charge of Works at Arkadelphia." Both of the above play a considerable part in the story that follows.

Col. Dunnington continued to build up his works at Little Rock until November 1862, when Capt. S. C. Faulkner was placed in charge of the Post. Presumably, Dunnington returned to the Navy.

A "Summary of the Work Done for November 1862, Little Rock Arsenal," shows:

Fabrication
75,000 buck & ball cartridges—percussion.
14,000 buck & ball cartridges—flint.
275 paper fuzes.
117 round, 6 pounder canister shot, fixed 1¼.
130 round, 6 pounder ball shot, fixed 1 1/40.
96 ammunition packing boxes.
Repaired
2,236 shot guns and rifles (repaired mostly for troops in service).
23 pistols (repaired mostly for troops in service).

Received and Issued
752 Packages of ordnance and ordnance stores received and mostly issued to troops in service.
Repaired and painted
4 gun carriages.
Performed
Guard, office and police duties.

Perhaps the most interesting point in the above "summaries of work" and those that follow is the reflection that about one-sixth or more of all small-caliber ammunition was for flintlock weapons, from which the conclusion is drawn that no less than one-sixth of the Confederate troops in this vicinity were armed with these obsolete weapons.

The "Summaries of Work done at Little Rock Arsenal, C.S.A.," continue at about the same tempo and scale from August, 1862, until August, 1863. Appended to the "Summary" for August, 1863, is the notation "During the last week in the month, nearly all the stores at the Arsenal have been packed and sent to Arkadelphia, in obedience to orders from Chief of Ord. District of Arkansas." This then marks the beginning of the evacuation of ordnance activities from Little Rock, which city was actually abandoned to the Federals on Sept. 7, 1863.

The reason for this evacuation? President Jefferson Davis in an address to the Senate and House of Representatives of the Confederate States Congress on Dec. 7, 1863, sums it up very nicely:

—Grave reverses befell our arms. —Early in July our strongholds at Vicksburg and Port Hudson, together with their entire garrisons capitulated to the combined land and naval forces of the enemy. The important interior position of Jackson, Miss., next fell into their temporary possession. Our unsuccessful assault upon the post at Helena was followed at a later period by the invasion of Arkansas, and the retreat of our army from Little Rock gave to the enemy the control of the important valley in which it is situated. (Off. Rec. War Reb. Series IV, Vol II, page 1024.)

President Davis said a good bit more, none of which brought cheer to the heart of any good Confederate. There is no need to quote further. Already we get the idea.

The removal of ordnance stores from Little Rock to Arkadelphia was only a stopgap. Looking back over the years, it seems hardly likely those stores were even unpacked at this latter point. What seems more probable is that everything salvagable at Arkadelphia was added to the Little Rock stores, and what was left of Confederate ordnance west of the Mississippi continued on the only route left open—South.

South they went, one hundred miles to set up permanent shops at Tyler and Marshall, Texas. The move was taken under the command of Capt. S. C. Faulkner, formerly "In Charge of Post, Little Rock."

The loss of Vicksburg meant the loss of the Mississippi River, and this loss cut the Confederacy in two large unattached pieces, bridged only by the mutual aims of its peoples. Each piece functioned separately from the other. That portion that lay west of the Mississippi operated as the Trans-Mississippi Department of the Confederate States of America. It consisted of four large States: Missouri (under dual government, North and South), Arkansas, Louisiana and Texas.

Percy Greg in his *History of the United States* Book VI. (page 298) says:

While Grant's enormous force had closed on Vicksburg, General Banks, U.S.A., advancing from New Orleans, had beleaguered Port Hudson. He had made little way, nor was it necessary. As soon as assured of the capitulation of Gen'l Pemberton, C.S.A., (at Vicksburg), Port Hudson was useless and its garrison surrendered. From this moment, though dispatches and individual officers might cross the river (Mississippi), though the Confederates still maintained a vigorous defense in Arkansas and especially in Texas, they were isolated from the government at Richmond and from the main Confederate forces, and were thrown entirely on their own internal resources. Blockade runners brought them arms and ammunition; their forests and prairies were almost impenetrable; and their population, if adverse to discipline, as warlike as any in America; and the army of General E. Kirby Smith, who had been placed in command of the Trans-Mississippi Department was the last that up held the honor of the Starry Cross.

A racial characteristic, or peculiarity, if you will, of Americans has always been their ability to work best under pressure. Despair and defeat does not come readily to such a breed. Thus it was that, cut off from customary supplies, both military and civilian, the Trans-Mississippi Department of the Confederacy, operating from its headquarters at Shreveport, La., continued to wage war through improvisation, substitution, and the will of its people.

After the evacuation of Arkansas, some degree of stabilization was obtained by the Ordnance Bureau of the Trans-Mississippi Dept. whose headquarters were also located in Shreveport, although Chief of Bureau, General Ben Huger, was situated in Marshall, Texas, 40 miles west. Sixty miles still farther west was Tyler, Texas.

On June 16, 1863, Lt. General E. Kirby Smith, Commanding, informed President Davis that his Chief of Ordnance, Major Thomas G. Rhett, had rented (with right of purchase within two years), a tract of land in the suburbs of Shreveport, as a site for an Arsenal. "Machinery has been erected, a foundry established." (Off. Rec. War Reb. Series 1, Vol. 22, Part 2, page 871.) Capt. F. P. Leavenworth was placed in command of the arsenal. Shortly thereafter, Major Rhett, "Chief of Ord. & Arty. TMD," was able to write:

I am putting up at Marshall, Texas, powder mills and cap machines which when finished, will supply all that can be used; and the other works such as gunsmiths' and machine shops, foundries, and etc., are being put up at Marshall and Tyler, Texas, and also at this point (Shreveport). (Off. Rec. War Reb. Series 1, Vol. 22, page 1140.)

Regardless of the Powder mills, percussion cap factory, arsenals, etc. at Marshall and Shreveport, the main source of arms, accoutrement and ammunition was from the Confederate States Ordnance Works, Tyler, Texas.

The removal of supplies and stores from Little Rock had been under the command of Capt. S. C. Faulkner, whose superior officer was Lt. Col. Gabriel H. Hill, Chief of Ordnance, District of Arkansas.

LT. COL. GABRIEL H. HILL, C.S.A.

Because of the prominent part he plays in this story, it may be well to give a little background information on Gabriel H. Hill.

In 1861, Hill held a second lieutenant's commission in the U. S. Army (Off. Recs. War Reb. Series I, Vol. 9, page 107), but following the pattern set by so many other Southern officers, resigned when his native State of North Carolina seceded. He thereupon offered his services to the South and on Aug. 27, 1861, was commissioned a First Lieutenant in the Provisional Army, Confederate States of America, to rank from March 16, 1861.

December 1861 found Hill a major in command of Fort Bartow at Roanoke Island, N. C. (Off. Recs. War Reb. Series 1, Vol. 9, page 107). The following spring he was captured and taken prisoner by the Yankees. Shortly thereafter, the same Major General Thomas H. Holmes, C.S.A., who had refused Short, Biscoe & Co.'s request for gunsmiths, wrote the Confederate Secretary of War Randolph in Hill's behalf, requesting his exchange because,

"He is particularly necessary to me now because of his peculiar experience in this particular field (ordnance)." (Off. Recs. War Reb. Series II, Vol. 3, page 865.) The request was returned to Holmes with the following endorsement: "Individual exchanges can not be effected." But nevertheless shortly thereafter, Hill was released, and on Sept. 28, 1862, was ordered by Lt. Col. Anderson (the Asst. Adjutant General to Gen'l Holmes) "to move from his present camp on Bayou Matoe to a position near Austin." (Off. Recs. War Reb. Series 1, Vol. 13, page 884.) At that time, Hill was addressed as "Major, G. H. Hill, Commanding, Battalion of Light Artillery."

The following month (Oct. 26, 1862), Hill was made General Holmes' Chief of Ordnance & Artillery, and assigned the duty station of Little Rock, Ark. (Off. Recs. War Reb. Series I, Vol. 13, page 899.) He remained here until ordered to Tyler, Texas, on Sept. 13, 1863, (Captured Rebel Records, Vol. 148, order #137), relieving Capt. Faulkner as commander of the post of Oct. 1, 1863. (Order #172.) Faulkner went to Marshall, Texas, to command the Ordnance Depot which was under the jurisdiction of the Arsenal.

Although the Confederacy had been dickering with Short, Biscoe & Co. for the sale of their armory, the deal had not been accomplished prior to Hill's arrival at Tyler. His first official act there was to lease the two largest brick buildings in town. One of these has already been described as the property of Col. George Yarbrough, partner of Short, Biscoe & Co. The other, also of three stories, was rented from Capt. Samuel H. Boren whose property adjoined Col. Yarbrough's to the west.

Each building was leased all through the balance of the war at $150.00 per month. (Captured Rebel Records, Vol.

149.) They were used for purposes which will be described later.

Meanwhile, an agreement with Short, Biscoe & Co. had been reached for the sale of their Armory and early in Oct. 1863, the Confederate Ordnance Department formally took over the premises. The firm was paid $100,000.00 for "125 acres of land including the Armory Building, tools and machinery," the sale being consumated on Dec. 30, 1863. (Vol 149, Captured Rebel Records, Dec. 31, 1863.) Short remained on at the Works as Master Armorer.

Bearing in mind that the entire 150-acre tract that originally comprised the town of Tyler sold for $100 seventeen years previously, it would seem that the firm of Short, Biscoe & Co. did not fare too badly in this transaction.

Shortly after Col. Hill arrived at Tyler, a resident of the town commented upon meeting him and his wife (Nov. 7, 1863). The latter was described as "a waspish, opinionated, little blonde person." The same source was evidently more impressed with the colonel who "is as jolly and good natured looking a 200 pounds as you would ever wish to see." (*Brokenburn*, page 255.) There would be little to make Col. Hill "jolly" in the next eighteen months, or to add to his 200 pounds.

According to Short, Biscoe & Co.'s statement of Sept. 17, 1863, as of that date, in addition to the one gun furnished the State of Texas, they had "500 barrels drilled and turned, ready for the stocks, and 250 more drilled out and 50 welded, 500 bayonets made, and nearly all pieces ready and locks for 800 guns." In other words, the firm claimed to have had just about completed 500 to 800 guns.

Complete records covering the period October 1, 1863, through December 31, 1863, will be found in the appendix of this work. They are not included here because they make for hard reading, but in skeleton form let us see what they have to say.

For the month of October 1863 (1st month under Confederate management), there were employed at the Tyler Works: "2 clerks, 1 asst. storekeeper, 1 chief guard, 1 orderly to officers, 1 sergeant, 15 gunsmiths, 4 blacksmiths, 3 carpenters, 3 harness makers, 2 tinners, 9 guards, and 1 laboratory foreman." These being in addition to Lt. Col. G. H. Hill, Comdg.; Capt. G. S. Pollys, in Charge of Armory, and Lt. W. W. Murphy, Supervising Shops. To the list of persons employed, is appended the note: "Most of the persons above drew rations part of the time, being on the march to Tyler, which accounts for the difference in wages allowed." This means that the evacuation of ordnance stores from Arkansas was still being completed during a portion of the month of October.

The first month at Tyler was spent primarily in getting the Armory and Laboratory ready for operation. Although no new guns were forthcoming, "90 muskets, 2 sporting rifles, 1 Sharp's pistol and 1 Colt's pistol" were repaired. (See appendix for complete record.)

By the end of the following month (November) things had pretty well straightened out, and 100 new rifles with bayonets were turned out. (See appendix for complete record of November.)

The records for December, 1863, showed even more production although only 84 new guns were forthcoming. (See appendix for complete record for month of December.)

January 1864, "130 New Texas rifles" were produced.

February 1864, "92 Texas rifles, 65 Hill rifles, and 39 bayonets" were completed.

March 1864, "36 Hill rifles—long, 40 Hill rifles—short" were the production figures.

In other words for the first 6 months under Confederate management, 547 rifles were produced. It would appear that Short, Biscoe & Co. might have been guilty of slight exaggeration by implying in Sept. 1863 that 500 to 800 rifles were about ready. More probably, they had 500 to 800 underway, but actually only about 100 near the finished stage, and these were the 100 that the records show were completed in November 1863.

A number of important questions now confront us:— What was the difference between the "Texas rifle," the "Hill rifle—long," and the "Hill rifle—short"? The answers to these will be found a little later; and while a number of unanswered questions may still plague the reader at the end of this story as to where the arms made at Tyler may be, nevertheless, there will be no questions as to extent of activity, methods of operation, source of supply, or disposition of arms.

Here then for once is the complete story of a large-scale Confederate ordnance operation, given us not through the third person, or by a veteran long after the war's end, but by the person most concerned in the activity—its commanding officer, Lt. Col. G. H. Hill, Provisional Army, Confederate States of America, Commanding Ordnance Works, Tyler, Texas, and written at the time this history was being made.

PART II

THE C. S. ORDNANCE WORKS AT TYLER, TEXAS

THE C. S. ORDNANCE WORKS AT TYLER, TEXAS

T HE basis for Part II has been taken verbatim from the "Tyler Day Book" which exists only in its original manuscript form in our National Archives, and has never before been printed. The deletion of a few letters has been done only from a standpoint of general interest and will in no way affect the overall picture. Original spelling, etc. has been retained, as have the abbreviations, and the now archaic fashion of capitalizing various nouns—apparently at random.

In charge of the Tyler Ordnance Works was Lt. Col. G. H. Hill, whose letters are interspersed with news events of the day as noted by the author.

The Confederate States Ordnance Works, Tyler, Texas, like all other such establishments, had various accounts and records to keep. Some of these records pertain to production and others to procedures and internal workings. The most interesting record of any Armory or Arsenal is its "Day Book."

The "Day Book" contains copies of all correspondence written at the establishment and signed by its commanding officer. From these letters, we learn of the works' organization, number of men employed, and the type of work each does. Production—amount, kind and type—becomes evident. From the receipts we can ascertain both source and amount of supply, and further, the disposition of articles leaving the plant. Aside from the absolute facts and figures accorded, many personal angles present themselves and give an insight into the personal lives and thinking of the individuals involved. In short, the "Day Book" presents a very clear picture of the entire operation, internal, external and personal.

The "Day Book" of the "Ord. Wrks, Tyler, Texas" opens on Friday, March 4, 1864, with a letter from Col. Hill addressed to Capt. S. C. Faulkner, In Charge, Ordnance Depot, Marshall, Texas:

> I herewith enclose you receipts for stores rec'd. The paper and screws were both badly put up and consequently somewhat damaged by exposure to the weather.

This letter is signed, as are all those that follow; "Very respectfully, G. H. Hill, Lt. Col., Comdg. Ord. Works, Tyler, Texas."

On this same March 4th, Col. Hill writes to "Brig. Gen'l W. Parsons, Comdg. Brig. Texas Troops, Waco, Texas":

> Your request for cavalry bugles has been approved by Major Rhett, Chf. of Arty. & Ord., D.T.M., and I am ready to issue them whenever it may suit you to receipt for same.

Also on March 4th, is a letter to "Maj. Thos. G. Rhett, Chf. Ord. & Arty., D.T.M., Shreveport, La." (this address translated is: Major Thomas G. Rhett, Chief of Ordnance and Artillery, Department of the Trans-Mississippi, Shreveport, La.):

> I enclose you a draft of the castings needed for fan, and also an explanatory letter from Capt. Polleys. You will please have the castings ready as soon as you can, as I will start wagons down with the stores the 1st of next week, and I should like very much to have them sent by them on their return, about the 12th of March. Also as many gun stocks as you can acrue, as I am entirely out.

While Col. Hill was writing the above, the war news according to newspapers of the times, ran something like this:

[46]

The Leonardtown (Md.) *Beacon* noted that 1,000 slaves had stampeded from St. Mary's county within the last few days.

A dispatch from Cincinnati said that members of the 44th Ohio Regt. had wrecked the office of the Dayton *Empire*. In the rioting, a soldier was killed and two wounded and the Home Guards were called out.

Farther South, it was observed that Michael Han was installed as the Union Military Governor of Louisiana at New Orleans.

SATURDAY, MARCH 5, 1864

Hill to Maj. Thos. G. Rhett, Chf. Ord. & Arty, DTM, Shreveport, La.

I made application on the 11th of Feb. last for the detail of Private Martin Horn of Capt. Ed Sharp's company J, 22nd Regt., Haws Brigade, Texas Inf., then absent from his command, and now on his return, I respectfully renew the application and urge his detail as I am greatly in need of his services as a tinner, and almost compelled to have the use of his fine set of tools. Hoping you will make every effort to have him sent me.

It seems hard to imagine the urging of a man's detail because of the need for his "fine set of tools," but such it was in the Confederacy.

Meantime, Baltimore, Md., newspapers published an account of how a Capt. Thaddeus Fitzhugh and 15 men of the Fifth Virginia Cavalry, CSA, made a raid in small boats upon Cherrystone Creek on the Eastern Shore of Virginia and destroyed a quantity of Union government stores and captured the steamer *Iolas,* and the Government steamer *Titan.* The *Iolas* was bonded, but the *Titan* was carried off by the Confederates and later destroyed.

The Richmond *Examiner* reported the first negro soldiers, prisoners of war, captured from General Butler's command as having arrived in Richmond. In commenting upon the prisoners, the *Examiner* suggested that to carry out the theory of racial equality propounded by the Yankees, that each of the negroes be given a white Union officer for a roommate, and added: "The only party likely to be seriously affected either in status or morals, is the negro."

The body of Col. Ulric Dahlgren, killed in a recent raid to release the Union prisoners in Richmond, was received at Richmond. The citizens gave no indication of grief that he had been killed.

TUESDAY, MARCH 8, 1864

On this date, General U. S. Grant arrived in Baltimore from the West on his way to receive his commission as lieutenant general of the Union Armies. He stopped at Barnum's Hotel and was accompanied by his son Frederick, as well as several of his staff officers.

In Richmond, Va., Maj. Gen. Arnold Elzey, commanding the defenses there, issued a general order in which he commended General Bradley T. Johnson and the 1st Maryland Cavalry, CSA, for the defeat of the Dahlgren raiders. General Wade Hampton in his report also gave the Marylanders credit for saving Richmond. When Kilpatrick and Dahlgren made their raid to release the Union prisoners in Richmond, General Johnson with 60 Maryland troopers barred the way so effectively that the raiders were delayed until the Confederates could interpose troops between the Union cavalry and the Southern Capital.

Unaware of either Grant or Johnson, Lt. Col. Hill went about his business in Tyler, Texas.

Hill to Maj. Thos. G. Rhett, Chf. Ord. & Arty., DTM, Shreveport, La.

We are now putting up field ammunition at this Works. We have on hand about 80 yards of flannel, but need 350 additional yards in order to put up what shot, spherical, case and canister I have on hand. You will oblige me by sending it up by return of wagons which carry stores to Capt. F. P. Leavenworth. If possible, send me some linseed or cottonseed oil if you have it, as I am very much in need of same. I also require some spirits of turpentine, and it is impossible for me to get it here. If you can possibly procure me some, please send it up at once.

WEDNESDAY, MARCH 9, 1864

Hill to Capt. F. P. Leavenworth, Comdg. Arsenal, Shreveport, La.

I advised you some days since of a shipment of stores. On their receipt, you will please notify the wagon master that you have return freight for him, and also direct him to call on Capt. S. C. Faulkner at Marshall for stores for me in his charge.

President Lincoln presented to General U. S. Grant the latter's commission as Lieutenant-General in the Army. The presentation took place in the Cabinet Chamber at Washington and in the presence of members of the Cabinet.

Commodore Wilkes of the Union Navy was placed on trial before a court-martial at Washington on charges of permitting the Confederate cruiser *Alabama* to escape. Commodore Wilkes, on the fine cruiser *Vanderbilt*, set out to capture the *Alabama*, but the wily Capt. Semmes, C.S.N., gave the Union commander the slip.

THURSDAY, MARCH 10, 1864

Hill to Maj. Thos. G. Rhett, Chf. Ord. & Arty., DTM, Shreveport, La.

I shall now be in want of more powder. All my rifle powder is now about expended. I have on hand only 1,600 lbs. of musket powder.

I have quite a large amount of ammunition on hand. Lt. Dubose has not yet gotten here. I have it all put up and am expecting wagons daily to receive it, as he wrote you some days ago he would send for it.

I am now putting up about 10,000 rounds per day, and could

just as easily put up 20,000 rounds if I am supplied with powder, by increasing my force.

On this day, the papers were filled with varied items. A dispatch from Washington said that 18 or 20 Union warships were ready for sea, but were detained because of the lack of seamen.

From Virginia came news that the 2nd Virginia Union Regiment (colored) had been attacked and routed by a Confederate force near Suffolk, Va.

South Carolina reported that the Confederate ironclad steamer *Ashley* had been launched at Charleston.

Governor Joseph E. Brown, in his message to the State of Georgia Legislature, said the South should ever keep before the North the idea that she was ready to talk peace whenever the North was willing to recognize the rights of the States to govern themselves.

SATURDAY, MARCH 12, 1864

Hill to Capt. J. J. Dubose, Chief of Ordnance of Indian Territory, Dokesville, Choctaw Nation.

I herewith enclose you invoices and receipts for stores this day delivered to W. R. Slaughter, Asst. Wagon Master, for transportation to you. A duplicate of those receipts I sent you by mail.

Please sign and return receipts as soon as convenient.

President Lincoln issued an order relieving Major General Halleck from duty as commander-in-chief of the Union Armies, and assigned him to duty as Chief of Staff under the Secretary of War. General Grant was assigned to duty as commander-in-chief of the Union Armies. Major General McPherson was placed in command of the Army of the Tennessee and Major General Sherman in command of the Military Division of Mississippi, comprising the departments of Ohio, Cumberland, Tennessee and Arkansas.

Hill to Maj. Thos. G. Rhett, Chf. Ord. & Arty, TMD, Shreveport, La.

In 2 or 3 days I will send by wagon train, three or four hundred rounds of small arms ammunition and also four or five hundred cartridge boxes, cap boxes and belts complete. Please request Capt. S. C. Faulkner to send me by the return train ten or fifteen more boxes of tin.

From the Federal Fortress at Monroe, Va., came news that General Butler's Gatling guns were tested by the 3rd Penna. Artillery. Dr. Richard Gatling of North Carolina, the inventor of the gun bearing his name, made his first "revolving volley guns" at Indianapolis in 1862 and they were tested by Union Army officers but rejected. Eleven of the guns were sent to Baltimore and were seen there by General Butler, who bought them for $1,000 each. They were taken to Butler's command and were used for the first time in that general's fruitless campaign against Richmond.

Farther south it was reported that a Union force under General A. J. Smith, assisted by Admiral Porter's fleet of 20 vessels, had captured Fort De Russy on Red River, near Alexandria, La., which had been defended by 200 Confederates.

Hill to Maj. Thos. G. Rhett, Chf. Ord & Arty., DTM, Shreveport, La.

You will oblige me greatly by having cast for me about 4,000 lbs. of cast iron balls for 12 and 6-pounder canister, and send them to me by return wagon.

The value of Confederate currency was dropping in a most alarming manner. News from Montgomery, Ala., told of the high cost of living there. Butter was $5.00 a pound;

beef—$2.00; pork—$4.00; lard—$4.00 and eggs were $3.00 a dozen.

Hill to Maj. Thos. G. Rhett, Chf. Ord. & Arty., TMD, Shreveport, La.

I have just paid to McMurty & Atkinson, $10,294.50 for lead and cartridge paper, as approved by you, on account.

This amount was not expected and I will fall short of money if I am not supplied with more. Please send me the amount I just paid out to McMurty & Atkinson.

The Richmond *Examiner* published an article defending the conduct of General Pettigrew's Brigade at Gettysburg. It had been alleged that Pettigrew's troops had not supported Pickett's men in their famous charge.

Prisoners in the gaol attached to the provost marshal's office at Eutaw and Camden Sts., Baltimore, made a desperate attempt to escape. Having procured a saw, the prisoners cut through a three-foot wall on West Alley. Provost Marshal Hanyer had learned of the plans to escape and doubled the guard. The first man to emerge from the hole in the wall was F. A. Price, a Baltimorean accused of disloyalty, who was immediately shot down by one of the guards. The other prisoners returned to their rooms. Efforts to make Price confess as to whom his accomplices were, failed.

Hill to Maj. Thos. G. Rhett, Chf. Ord. & Arty., DMT, Shreveport, La.

I have just turned over to Capt. J. E. Kirby, Acting Quartermaster, for transportation to Capt. Leavenworth, 337,000 rounds of ammunition (Buck & Ball, Miss. Rifle, Musket Ball, Enfield Rifle, Rifle Musket, Percussion Musket, Musket Rifle, Percussion Pistol Ball, Sharps Carbine, Colt's Navy Pistol), 500 cartridge boxes, 500 cap ditto, 500 waist belts, all of which leave here tomorrow.

If you can in any way procure for me some brass tacks suitable for saddles, I will be glad if you would do so, and send them by first opportunity.

Richmond newspapers told of incendiary fires in that city, and the *Examiner* said: "Put none but Southrons on Guard Duty." Baker & Co. iron foundry, which made cannon shells, was destroyed as were a number of tenements. The fires were close to the Government buildings. An attempt was also made to fire President Davis' mansion.

The Georgia Legislature adopted resolutions to the effect that after each Southern victory the Confederate authorities should make a peace proposition to the North. The resolutions also expressed confidence in President Davis.

The Cincinnati *Gazette* published an interesting article from the pen of Whitelaw Reid, its Washington correspondent, over his nom de plume of "Agate," concerning the Emancipation Proclamation. Among other things, Reid said the concluding paragraph of the proclamation was written by Secretary Chase.

MONDAY, MARCH 21, 1864

Hill to Maj. Thos. G. Rhett, Chf. Ord. & Arty. TMD, Shreveport, La.

I enclose report of work done at Tyler Ordnance Works for the week ending March 19, 1864, from which you will see that the hands at the Armory have been employed principally upon fabricating parts of guns, preparatory to whole work as soon as stock timber is received.

The steamer *Clifton,* formerly a Union gunboat captured by the Confederates, tried to run the blockade at Sabine Pass, Texas, with 1,000 bales of cotton, but ran aground and was burned to prevent her falling into the hands of her former owners, the Federals.

Hill to Maj. Thos. G. Rhett, Chf. Ord. & Arty., Shreveport, D.T.M.

Despite an order for 2,000 hides, I have rec'd only one hide per day, and the last two weeks have not rec'd any. I would like as many hides as possible. I find it impossible to buy hides here with money, and if none are sent, I will be short of leather. I rec'd some from the Quartermaster Dept., but they were of miserable quality.

While Col. Hill was complaining of the shortage of leather, Richmond, Va., was reporting a heavy fall of snow which was stated to have fallen in some places to a depth of ten inches.

Hill to Capt. J. C. Kirby, Acting Quartermaster, Tyler, Texas.

I have just rec'd an urgent order from Gen'l Smith, ordering all the ammunition on hand to be sent to Marshall, Texas. I would like to know how soon a train of 6 to 8 wagons can be got together? If they are not procurable in any other way, as Commander of this Post, I will impress them as the ammunition must be sent immediately, as the safety of the country depends on its reaching there.

General E. Kirby Smith, C.S.A., was evidently fearful of the intelligence that General Steele's army (U.S.A.) had left Little Rock, Ark., in pursuit of General Price's command.

On the previous day, General Nathan Bedford Forrest, C.S.A., captured the Federal force at Union City, Ky., taking 150 prisoners, and today, followed up his success by attacking the Union force at Paducah, Ky., and drove the defenders to the shelter of their gunboats while he destroyed large quantities of their stores. His command then withdrew.

Hill to Maj. Thos. G. Rhett, Chf. Ord. & Arty., Shreveport, DTM. by courier.

I have shipped Capt. Dubose 174,000 rounds of ammunition on March 12th, Capt. Leavenworth 337,400 on the 19th, and on the 27th am sending about 50,000 rounds to Capt. Faulkner at Marshall.

I am now making 10,000 rounds per day, and with an increase in force, could produce 12 to 14,000.

I will continue to send ammunition to Marshall unless ordered otherwise, and will send them by train as soon as I get 100,000 on hand.

I have only enough lead to make 60,000 rounds more.

I shall continue to make daily reports as directed in your telegram and send them by courier.

Hill to Maj. Thos. G. Rhett, Chf. Ord. & Arty., Shreveport, DTM.

My new blacksmith shop is almost completed. My work in Armory is progressing finely. I shall turn out 7 guns today and after this from 8 to 10.

The balance of the month, Hill complains almost daily (27th, 28th, 29th, and 30th) to Major Rhett as to the lack of lead with which to make cartridges.

Meanwhile, the Wheeling, (W.Va.) *Intelligencer* related a strange story that a soldier in Company D, 8th West Virginia Regiment, U.S.A., had been found to be a girl. She said her name was Mary E. French of Hagerstown, Md., that every man in the company knew her to be a girl, and that she would rather fight than eat.

FRIDAY, APRIL 1, 1864

Hill to Maj. Thos. G. Rhett, Chf. Ord. & Arty., Shreveport, D.T.M.

I am still out of lead, and so am unable to make cartridges, but I do have on hand 80 or 90 newly made guns which I will send just as soon as I am able to procure a train.

From Waterbury, Conn., came the report that two

[55]

women were killed by an explosion of powder at the works of the American Flask & Cap Co.

The Union Steamer *Maple Leaf,* returning to Jacksonville, Fla., from Pilatka, was sunk by a Confederate floating torpedo.

MONDAY, APRIL 4, 1864

On this date, Lt. Col. Hill was able to write to Major Rhett that he had received on that date, 12,998 pounds of lead from Capt. S. C. Faulkner, Marshall, Texas. Cartridge making could resume at Tyler.

On this same Monday, the schooner *Mary Sorley,* while running out of Galveston, was captured by the Union gunboat *Scioto.* Also, Capt. Phelps of the Union Navy captured a Confederate mail carrier with 5,000 letters from Richmond, 60,000 percussion caps for General Price's army and a lot of greenbacks.

TUESDAY, APRIL 5, 1864

Col. Hill advised Major Rhett that 17 of his cartridge boys were out sick with measles.

An explosion at the powder mill at Raleigh, N. C., killed several persons, while in the north, four men were killed by an explosion at the Union Powder Works, New Durham, New Hampshire.

WEDNESDAY, APRIL 7, 1864

Nineteen of the cartridge boys at the Tyler Ordnance Works were now ill with measles, and in writing Major Rhett, Col. Hill expressed the opinion that a surgeon should be stationed at Tyler.

In another letter to Major Rhett on the same date, a report of work done at Tyler reflected 1,110 buck & ball cartridges had been made as well as 473 pounds of Enfield rifle balls, and 195½ pounds of musket balls and 5,000 cartridges boxed.

Not so far from Tyler, General Banks, USA, continued the retreat of his Red River Expedition, and on April 7th, Gen'l Wirt Adams' Confederate cavalry made a dash into the Union lines near Port Hudson, La., and captured a cannon and many prisoners.

FRIDAY, APRIL 8, 1864

General Banks' army was badly defeated by the forces of General Richard Taylor at Mansfield, La. The Union army numbered about 25,000 and the army of Taylor about 9,000. The Confederates captured 2,200 prisoners, 20 cannon, many flags, and 250 wagons. The battle practically ended Banks' Red River campaign. General Alfred Mouton of the Confederate army was killed.

TUESDAY, APRIL 12, 1864

Hill to Maj. Thos. G. Rhett, Chf. Ord. & Arty., Shreveport, D.T.M.

I learn that Capt. Pitts of Bonham has a full set of Army and Navy pistol moulds which I would like very much to get. I have none on hand, and it would take sometime to make them. I would be glad therefore if you would order Capt. Pitts to turn over what he has to me.

The day previous, General Nathan Bedford Forrest began his investment of Fort Pillow on the Tennessee River, which was defended by 550 white and colored troops under Major Booth. On the 12th, the Confederates captured the fort by assault. The union troops, mostly negroes, did not surrender, but instead, attempted to retreat to the protection of the Union gunboats. The Union vessels left them to their fate, and the retreating Federals fell into a trap and were shot down by scores. Nearly 300 were killed and wounded. The Confederates captured 7 officers and 219 men, 6 cannon and quantities of stores. The capture of the fort led to a Congressional investigation in the North, and it was reported that the negro troops had been massacred. Later testimony showed that the charges against the Confederates were unfounded.

WEDNESDAY, APRIL 13, 1864

Hill to Maj. Thos. G. Rhett, Chf. Ord. & Arty., Shreveport, D.T.M.

I am nearly out of band iron for bands for my guns. Can not you send me some? I want it 1½ inches by 2 inches wide and ½ inch thick. It will be almost impossible for me to do without it. Let me know if it can be had, and I will send for it.

FRIDAY, APRIL 15, 1864

Hill to Maj. Thos. G. Rhett, Chf. Ord. & Arty., Shreveport, D.T.M.

I am nearly out of thread to make cartridges, and I find it impossible to get in the surrounding country. Please send me some at once or I shall have to stop work. I am also nearly out of tin. I have not yet got the 15 boxes that you ordered from Marshall, and I have not the wagons to send for it.

I see a lot of tin in the stores sent to this place by Capt. Leavenworth which I will use some of if I can get it out. I also need gun shalack.

A report from Savannah, Ga., told of a bread riot in that city. Gaunt, ragged women paraded the streets crying for bread. Several provision stores were looted. Troops were called out and the ringleaders were arrested.

SATURDAY, APRIL 16, 1864

Hill to Maj. Thos. G. Rhett, Chf. Ord. & Arty., TMD, Shreveport, La.

I am now consuming 200 lbs of powder per day, making between 12 and 15,000 cartridges. At the present rate, all powder will be consumed in about 6 weeks. We will also soon be out of lead. Please try to supply us with same.

A dispatch from Wheeling, W. Va., said that General Sigel, USA, in command there, had issued an order confiscating all firearms in the hands of residents of the surrounding country, whether loyal or disloyal, except those belonging to the militia.

Hill to Thomas G. Rhett, Chf. Ord. & Arty., Shreveport, D.T.M.

For the last two weeks little work has been preformed in the Laboratory, the reason being that 21 of my men have been down with the measles. However I will send out a train as I now have on hand 160,000 rounds of small arm ammunition, 1,700 cartridge boxes, cap boxes and belts, and I will have ready by next Saturday, at least 160 small arms.

Shall I send direct to Jefferson or to Shreveport. I believe that by now the river must be down and I think it best to send to Shreveport direct.

General Steele's Union Army in Arkansas sustained a heavy blow when General Marmaduke's cavalry attacked a foraging party of nearly 200 wagons, guarded by 1,500 troops and 4 cannon, which Steele had sent out to get much needed supplies. The Union command was routed. The Confederates captured all the wagons, 1,000 mules, 4 cannon and several hundred prisoners. The engagement was known as the Battle of Poison Springs.

Hill to Maj. Thos. G. Rhett, Chf. Ord. & Arty., Shreveport, D.T.M.

Enclosed you will find a communication from the AQM at this place. He says that it will be impossible to get forage on the road. I therefore can not send the train. As commander of the Post, I have ordered him to send extra wagons to haul forage, but I think something should be done so that we can get forage on the road, and that Major Alexander should be supplied off the main public road. This Post is almost destitute of forage and it will be a great tax if we are compelled to haul all the forage for trains leaving for Marshall or Shreveport. Please have some orders issued in the case.

Hill attaches to this letter a statement of lead received from McMurty & Atkinson, "Contractors, Cotton Gin, Texas, showing that they had shipped him as follows:

March	11,	31 planches,	4,266	of lead	
"	15,	65 Pigs,	3,888	"	"
April	8,	33 planches,	3,401	"	"
"	12,	12 "	1,557	"	"
"	"	126 pigs,	7,606½	"	"
"	13,	42 planches,	5,165	"	"

FRIDAY, APRIL 22, 1864

Hill to Lt. T. A. Woods, in charge of Laboratory, Tyler Ord. Works.

You will proceed at once to the mill you spoke to me about this morning and see what arrangement can be made for being supplied with timber for gun-stocks.

Hill to Maj. Thos. G. Rhett, Chief Ord. & Arty., Shreveport, D.T.M.

I notice among the stores at this place for Shreveport, a large lot of white fool's cap paper, an article that I am very much in need of for making out my reports, that which I have on hand being so greasy that it is impossible to write neatly upon it.

Please give an order on Capt. Leavenworth to turn over a supply to me.

Hill to Lt. T. A. Woods, in charge of Laboratory, Tyler Ord. Works.

Your report to postpone your trip for a few days is granted. As soon as you feel able, you will proceed to carry out the order given you of this date.

Hill to Maj. Thos. G. Rhett, Chf. Ord. & Arty., Shreve-port, D.T.M.

Private Robert Ward, a conscript, Smith County, on re-examination has been recommended for duty in this Department on account of club-foot.
He is recommended as a good gunsmith, and you would oblige me by getting him detailed here.

Such little hints as the above give us an idea as to the state of affairs within the Confederacy. As of April 22, 1864, men with club feet were being drafted for active service! Gives those of us who remember World War II with memories of exemptions for ruptured eardrums, something to think about.

MONDAY, APRIL 25, 1864

Hill to Maj. Thos. G. Rhett, Chf. Ord. & Arty., Shreve-port, D.T.M.

I send Capt. Polleys down with a train of 10 wagons with ordnance and ordnance stores. The train will leave here tomorrow morning. An invoice of the stores will be sent to the commandant of the Shreveport Arsenal by the next mail.

Capt. Polleys, it will be remembered, was in charge of the "Works at Arkadelphia" prior to that establishment's removal to Tyler. At Tyler, Capt. Polleys was in charge of the Armory.

WEDNESDAY, APRIL 27, 1864

Hill to Maj. Thos. G. Rhett, Chf. Ord. & Arty., Shreve-port, D.T.M.

I sent a train of ox wagons yesterday in charge of Capt. Polleys for Shreveport. It contained:

   25,000 Miss. Rifle Cart.
   66,000 Enfield Rifle Cart.
   83,000 B & Ball Cart.
   ————————
   174,000 total cartriges.

40 Hills Rifle (long) cal. .54
40 Hills Rifle (short) cal. .54
80 Texas Rifle, cal. .57
60 bayonets.
_____

160 rifles, 60 bayonets.
1,100 cartridge boxes.
1,100 cap boxes.
1,100 belts.

Invoiced to Capt. Leavenworth, previous to your last letter directing them to be turned over to Capt. Charles W. Wailey.

Notice might be taken that included in this shipment are no cartridges for flintlock arms, nor will any be found in the "invoices" which follow. The reader can make of this what he will.

Outside of Tyler, newspapers were reporting that the defeat and capture of the supply trains (Federal) at Poison Spring and Mark Mills caused General Steele's Union army to evacuate Camden, Ark., and retreat to Little Rock.

It was also reported that the British Schooner *O.K.* was captured off the Florida coast by the Federal gunboat *Union.*

MONDAY, MAY 2, 1864

Over the weekend, General Steele's Union army retreating from Camden to Little Rock, Ark., was attacked while crossing the Saline river at Jenkins Ferry. The Confederates were repulsed.

The Richmond *Enquirer* said a company for the establishment of a volunteer navy had been organized in Richmond with a capital stock of $10,000,000 of which $1,500,-000 was paid in.

Hill to Maj. Thos. G. Rhett, Chf. Ord. & Arty., Shreveport, D.T.M.

Means of transportation is very bad at this Post because of the large train (commissary) required to supply the Federal prisoners. There is not a wagon to be gotten in the country. If the fuze paper is wanted for immediate use, and the boxes designated in your letter, I can send one of my ordnance wagons with them.

The "Federal prisoners" to which Col. Hill refers, were confined in Camp Ford, which was built in 1863 and named in honor of Capt. Rip Ford. It was located about 3½ miles northeast of Tyler, and consisted of a ten-acre tract of land enclosed by a stockade fence. Inside this stockade were all kinds of small log houses (called "she-bangs") and dugouts, each of the prisoners being permitted to provide his house to suit his own needs. These huts just about completely covered the inside of the enclosure except for a parade ground of one acre, no house being built closer than 30 feet from the stockade wall—this 30 feet being the deadline. By 1865, nearly 6,000 men were confined.

When first established, Camp Ford was commanded by Col. Allen, who was succeeded by Col. Jamison. In April 1864, it was placed under the charge of Col. Anderson. *(A History of Tyler & Smith Co., Texas;* pages 39-41).

Recently much has been written over alleged mistreatment of Federal prisoners of war by the South. May I suggest that those so incensed examine the records of Fort Delaware, a Union prison operated along lines which would have inspired the admiration of Hitler.

In any resentment against alleged starving of Union prisoners of war I also suggest that Col. Hill's letter of May 2nd, be digested, for here it is apparent that transportation of food for prisoners was placed before transportation needed to carry ammunition to troops in the field.

WEDNESDAY, MAY 4, 1864

Richmond newspapers carried a pathetic account of an affair at Charlston, S. C. While Miss Anna Pickens, daughter of the Governor, was being married to Lt. Andrew De Rochelle of the Fort Sumter garrison, a shell from the Union batteries entered the house and exploded, striking down nine of the wedding party and mortally wounding the bride. At the bride's request the minister continued with the ceremony, the bride being stretched upon a couch in her blood-stained wedding gown. She died a few minutes after the ceremony was concluded.

From Memphis came a dispatch which said that Gen. Wirt Adams' Confederate cavalry had captured and destroyed the Union gunboat *Petrel* mounting five guns, near Yazoo City, Miss.—who ever heard of cavalry capturing a naval vessel before?

Hill to Maj. Thos. G. Rhett, Chf. Ord. & Arty., Shreveport, D.T.M.

We have made about 1,000 tin magazines for cartridge boxes, but it will take some time to make the cartridge boxes. Rather than continue the making of magazines should I not put the tinner to work making canteens, or if there is any tinner's work you would like done, please advise. My tinners are splendid workmen.

Hill to Mrs. Jas. B. Rather (no address given).

Your contribution of thread in answer to my call from this Department has been received.

In this prompt response, you have shown that willingness which has ever characterized the ladies of the South to contribute all in their power for the defense of their country.

Accept Madame, my thanks for the thread and be assured it will be usefully expended.

Hill to Capt. W. A. Pitts, Chf. Ord. Officer, N.S.D., Bonham, Texas.

Enclosed, I send you an order from Major Rhett to turn over to me such army and navy pistol-ball moulds and rifle, carbine and musket ball moulds as you can spare.

I have now quite an extensive laboratory in operation and you will facilitate the manufacture of ammunition here very much by letting me have 1 set of each kind embraced in the order.

Blank invoices and receipts will be sent by Sergt. Ford to whom you will please deliver the moulds.

Hill to Maj. Thos. G. Rhett, Chf. Ord. & Arty., Shreveport, TDM.

My men all want to know what to do if they are paid their June pay in the present issue of Confederate notes. If paid in the present issue, they will have to lose 33 1/3 percent. Please write me word what they are to be paid in, and give me instructions what I am to do with what money I have on hand after the 1st of July?

In regards to the above: Feb. 17, 1864, an Act was passed by the Confederate Congress "To reduce the volume of currency; and to provide for a new issue of notes and bonds.—All non-interest bearing notes, not funded into four percent bonds, by April 1st, 1864, east of the Mississippi; and by July 1st, west of the Mississippi, shall cease to be received for public dues, and shall be taxed thirty-three and one-third percent until so funded. All interest-bearing notes shall be taxed in like manner; but with an additional ten of ten percent per month until so funded." This was an attempt on the part of the Confederacy to curb inflation and counterfeiting, both of which were rife.

May 7, 1864—General Sherman's army began its advance, the Confederates under General Johnston withdrawing from Tunnel Hill, Ga. Sherman had 98,000 men and 254 cannon. Johnston had 45,000 men and 112 cannon. Most of Johnston's men figured the two forces to be about evenly matched.

SUNDAY, MAY 8, 1864

A little band of Marylanders did a good service for the Confederacy this day. Sheridan with his 10,000 superbly mounted and equipped troopers on his first Richmond raid were sweeping towards the Confederate Capital like a cyclone when General Bradley T. Johnson, with the 1st Maryland Cavalry, about 150 men under Col. Ridgely Brown, flung themselves across the path of the raiders. So desperately did the Marylanders fight that Sheridan was delayed long enough to permit a larger force of southern cavalry to get between him and Richmond. The Maryland command again won well deserved praise for "saving Richmond."

Hill to Capt. C. W. Wailey, Comdg. Shreveport Arsenal.

I send private A. Q. Potrel with a box of flannel and a box of fuze paper for you and a box of stationary for Major Rhett which I was directed to send without delay. Please see that my team is supplied with forage.

Sunday dinner was a costly affair in Savannah today. Peas were $10 a half peck, strawberries $10 a quart, beef $2.50 a pound, pork $3.00 per pound, and butter $10.00 a pound.

MONDAY, MAY 9, 1864

Hill to Maj. Thos. G. Rhett, Chf. Ord. Arty., Shreveport, DTM.

I sent by express wagon this morning a box of stationary for you, and a box of flannel for Capt. C. W. Wailey. You in your communication said "send a box of flannel, say no. 36." I opened #36 and it contained leather, and as you said you wanted flannel I looked until I found a box of #7. I also sent Wailey a box of 75 lbs of fuze paper.

Wailey has stored here a large amount of good harness leather. Would you not let me have a roll or two of it? I am very poor in the leather line and have not a hide fit to make any kind of harness. He also has a lot of rivets for belting 16 bags. Please let me have one as I am very much in need of them.

THURSDAY, MAY 12, 1864

Hancock's corps of the Army of the Potomac delivered

a heavy blow to Lee's army in Virginia. There was an exposed salient of the Confederate line which was held by the division of Maj. Gen. Edward Johnson. By an early morning rush the Federals surprised the Confederate troops holding the salient, captured Gen. Johnson and Brig. Gen. George H. Steuart of Maryland and 2,500 men and broke Lee's line. Confederate troops were rushed to the danger point and there followed one of the most desperate struggles of the war, the men fighting with bayonet and clubbed musket. So heavy was the musket fire that several big trees were cut down by bullets, and the bodies of the slain were used as breastworks for the living. Generals Abner Perrin and Junius Daniel of the Confederate army were among the killed. It was during the desperate fighting of the Confederates to hold the gap that General Lee started to lead his men to the charge, when the soldiers shouted, "Lee to the rear," and refused to go forward until their commander had sought a safer place.

Lieutenant General James Ewell Brown Stuart, better known as "Jeb" Stuart, chief of cavalry of the Army of Northern Virginia and one of the knightliest figures of the war, died in Richmond of a wound sustained at the battle of Yellow Tavern the day before. His last words were: "God's will be done."

Hill to Capt. S. C. Faulkner, Comdg. Ord. Depot, Marshall, Texas.

The wagon train with stores from you has just arrived. As soon as invoices are received I shall send receipts.

I have received invoices from Capt. Wailey at Shreveport for 10 barrels, 1,000 lbs cannon powder which the wagon master says was put off at Marshall supposing it to be damaged. The powder is intended for this point. Please forward on as soon as practicable.

Hill to Capt. C. W. Wailey, Comdg. Shreveport Arsenal.

Your invoices for cannon powder dated May 4th has been received.

The cannon powder was stopped at Marshall by mistake. I have informed Capt. Faulkner of the error. As soon as it is received I will forward receipt.

Hill to Maj. Thos. G. Rhett, Chf. Ord. & Arty., Shreveport, DTM.

I started today a train of 10 wagons loaded with the most valuable of the Shreveport ordnance stores here under Mr. Bennett's care to Jefferson. The train will take nearly ½ the stores, and I will send the others on return of train unless otherwise ordered. Knowing you are in need of ammunition I had a great mind to load the train with that instead of sending the stores, but if you say so, I can load the train the next trip.

If it can be done, I think you had better get them to send from Jefferson a larger train for the ammunition. The train I have is an ox train and is nearly broken down and can only carry about ½ a load to a wagon. It will be impossible for us to get us another. Everything in the Dept. of Transportation is employed in hauling commissary stores for the Federal prisoners.

I now have on hand about 108,000 buck & ball cartridges, 4,800 Miss. Rifle ditto, and 81,000 Enfield rifle cartridges and by the end of this week I shall have about 50,000 more Enfield and about 50,000 more Buck & ball. I now have only about 1,800 lbs of lead on hand. I will continue to make Enfield cartridges. I will be able to make nothing after my lead goes, and I shall soon want powder and paper.

On this day occurred the famous battle of Newmarket, Va., in which the cadet corps of the Virginia Military Institute won undying fame. General Sigel, who was advancing up the Shenandoah Valley as a part of Grant's great Richmond campaign, found himself opposed at Newmarket by a force of 4,500 Confederates hastily gathered

by Gen. John C. Breckenridge. This force included re-
serves—old men—and the cadet corps of the Institute. Sigel
had about 6,500 men. In the battle, Sigel was badly defeated. The cadet corps., composed of 16-year-old boys, distinguished itself by capturing a six-gun battery. In the
charge the cadets lost 8 killed and 46 wounded out of 225
cadets. The total Confederate loss was 577, and that of the
Federals 831.

WEDNESDAY, MAY 18, 1864

*Hill to Maj. Thos. G. Rhett, Chf. Ord. & Arty., Shreve-
port DTM.*

There has been no mail here from Shreveport since last Thursday, May 12th. They have been trying to change the route so as
to come by Henderson. There seems to be some difficulty and
there is no saying when the mail will commence running again.

In consequence of this disturbance in mail facilities I have
received no communication from you since 12th inst. I write this
only to suggest would it not be better to send your mail for this
point by courier until it is ascertained that the mail is running
again?

Hill to Private W. J. Moore, Dixie Mills, Starrville, Texas.

Something must be done at once at your mill to supply me
with lumber that I have billed for. Capt. Kirby says that he has
furnished the mill with teams and negroes to get out the stocks
and that he is getting nothing. I am getting nothing. If something
is not done, and done at once towards supplying us, I shall relieve you from that duty and order you to this place, and make
other arrangements for supplying myself from elsewhere. Let me
know at once what the mill can do.

Grant's army made a final desperate unsuccessful effort
to break Lee's line at Spottsylvania Courthouse. The Second and Sixth Corps made the assaults, which were repulsed with heavy loss to the Federals.

Hill to Maj. Thos. G. Rhett, Chf. Ord. & Arty., Shreveport, DTM.

I understand that you have on hand a small planing machine. If it were given to me, it will save much labor and cut down the use of files by one half. It can be used for planing lock plates and different parts of mountings for guns. If you will send it, it will be the most useful machine in the Armory. I understand that Capt. Wailey has 2 or 3. I ask for one of the small ones.

Hill to Maj. Thos. G. Rhett, Chf. Ord. & Arty., Shreveport, TDM.

You will oblige me very much by having an order issued relieving Private C. P. Yarbrough, 1st Regt. Texas State Troops (Cav.) from duty in this Department. He has been on duty ever since Jan. 14th, and has done only 30 days work in said time. He gets off on one plea and another through the surgeon. He is not much of a workman, and is a man that will cause dissatisfaction where-ever he goes. I wish very much to get rid of him.

Hill to Maj. Thos. G. Rhett, Chf. Ord. & Arty., Shreveport, TDM.

I now have on hand ready to ship, over 300,000 rounds of ammunition. I received from McMurty & Atkinson yesterday 2,093 lbs iron and 1,887 lbs cartridge paper. Now all these stores, ammunition and whatever articles I have fabricated, I know are needed at Shreveport, but I have tried my best to get a train to forward them, but can not do so. I would therefore respectfully suggest that you get an order for a train of twenty or thirty wagons and send for the stores that you are needing.

I am out of lead entirely and no train that I can learn of is on the road from Cotton Gin with any. I have enough balls I think to keep my boys employed until the end of next week. I am now making 20,000 rounds per day.

I can spare a considerable lot of iron if you are in much need of it, but this country has not got the transportation in it either to impress or to hire, as the ACS and AQM have everything in the shape of wagons, mules, etc. hauling corn and provisions to supply the yankee prisoners.

SATURDAY, MAY 21, 1864

Hill to Maj. Thos. G. Rhett, Chf. Ord. & Arty., Shreveport, TDM.

Men in my Department often ask me for leave of absence for about a week to look after their wheat, and at their request, I have promised to write to you.

Please inform me whether I may grant to my men, leave of absence for about a week, for the purpose of harvesting their wheat. Many of them live near here, and it will be with difficulty that they will be able to gather their crop unless they are present to attend to the work.

Capt. Andrew Laypole of Washington County, Md., a Confederate soldier, was hanged at Fort McHenry, Baltimore, having been found guilty by a military commission of being a spy. Capt. Laypole had been imprisoned a year. The scaffold was erected on the drill ground of the fort, and the 7th Ohio Regiment guarded the condemned man. Before the execution Laypole made a speech in which he said he was not a felon, that he was proud to give his life for the South, and that he forgave his executioners. He then prayed and met death without flinching.

MONDAY, MAY 23, 1864

Hill to Capt. C. W. Wailey, Comdg. Shreveport Arsenal.
(Capt. Wailey has evidently replaced Capt. F. P. Leavenworth in command at the Arsenal.)

Enclosed please, find receipts for 500 lbs rifle powder, and 20 kegs. I have heard nothing further from the 1,000 lbs of cannon powder for which I have received invoices.

Hill to Capt. S. C. Faulkner, Comdg. Ord. Depot, Marshall, Texas.

Enclosed please find receipts for 113 lbs pig copper, 5 kegs nails, and 15 boxes containing 3,287 sheets tin.

[71]

Hill to Maj. Thos. G. Rhett, Chf. Ord. & Arty., Shreveport, TDM.

I am out of 2 inch screws for making ammunition boxes. No smaller screws will do so well. I believe that some are on hand at Marshall, and I would like 50 gross. 1¾ inch screws can be made to serve the purpose, but 2 inch is the proper size.

WEDNESDAY, MAY 25, 1864

Hill to C. H. Higgenbotham, Tyler, Texas.

In answer to your proposition to trade leather for hides, will say that I do have hides on hand, and I would be willing to trade at the usual rate—4 lbs of hides for 1 lb of leather. I want all the sole and harness leather you have on hand as I am very much in need of it.

On this same date, Col. Hill wrote an identical letter to "Mr. John Miller."

News from other parts of the South on this Wednesday was not too cheerful from a Confederate point of view. From Richmond came the information that every theater in the Confederate capital was closed—the actors had all shouldered guns.

Baltimore newspapers said that the captured blockade-runner *Greyhound* had arrived at Boston in charge of a prize crew. The *Greyhound,* one of the fastest of the blockade-runners, was captured on a voyage from Wilmington, N. C., to Nassau by the Union gunboat *Connecticut.* Among the prisoners was Miss Belle Boyd of Winchester, Va., who won fame as a Confederate spy, and who had spent a year in a Union prison. During the pursuit of the *Greyhound,* it was said, Miss Boyd seated herself on a bale of cotton, with the shells exploding around her, and seemed to enjoy the excitement.

SUNDAY, MAY 29, 1864

The close of May in the year 1863 saw Southern hopes

running high. Lee's army had successfully won Chancellorsville, and was preparing for its advance into Pennsylvania. Things were different in 1864. Grant wired Secretary of War Stanton that his army had crossed the Pamunkey River at a point which lay only 15 miles from Richmond. Farther South, Sherman wired Stanton that the Confederate army under Johnston was falling back.

WEDNESDAY, JUNE 1, 1864

The great battle of Cold Harbor, Va., began between the Army of the Potomac, 115,000 men under General Grant, and the Army of Northern Virginia, 68,000 men under General Lee.

The South had little fear of the outcome, having implicit trust in General Robert E. Lee. Faith in their currency was not so great as reflected in general prices in Richmond where flour sold for $400 to $500 per barrel, and bread was $1.25 a loaf.

FRIDAY, JUNE 3, 1864

The faith in General Lee was justified this day. The battle of Cold Harbor, 15 miles northeast of Richmond, ended in a bloody repulse of Grant's army which lost about 13,000 men.

MONDAY, JUNE 6, 1864

Hill to Maj. Thos. G. Rhett, Chf. Ord. & Arty., Shreveport, DTM.

By the day after tomorrow I will be entirely out of powder and will be compelled to stop work in the Laboratory.

I plan to send an 8 ox wagon train to Jefferson with ammunition in a few days, and want powder by the return train. I also want the planing machine to be sent to Marshall so that my wagons can pick it up on their return.

I am also almost out of files.

Hill to Capt. C. W. Wailey, Comdg. Shreveport Arsenal.

I enclose receipts for 165,000 rounds of Enfield cartridges, 38,000 Miss. cartridges, which this day were turned over for shipment to you.

Hill to Maj. J. M. Taylor, Enrollment Officer, 5th District.

The following named men now on duty in my Department as citizens, I wish enrolled and their detail made to this Department: #1, Daniel Jones, tinner, #2, Gotlieb Brack, asst. foreman, #3, G. Grimland, blacksmith, #4, J. M. McIntosh, blacksmith, #5, W. S. N. Biscoe, gunsmith, #6, Joseph Griffiths, gunsmith, #7, J. W. Battle, armorer.

All these men have been in my Department for sometime. Their services are absolutely necessary to carry on my Works, and I hope that as soon as they are enrolled that this communication will be forwarded to General Greer, and that he will make the detail.

W.S.N. Biscoe, listed above as #5 is undoubtedly the same person who was previously connected with Short in the firm of Short, Biscoe & Co.

Hill to Capt. E. M. Bacon, Post Quarter Master, "Tax in Kind," Marshall, Texas.

I would like the privilege of collecting the tithe-in-kind in this district for forage. Oats are now coming in and I want as much as I can get for my teams which are now suffering very much. When corn comes in I want to collect on that as well. This year I have depended upon the Quartermaster Dept. for forage and as a result I am nearly starved out. The Quartermaster has as much as they can do to get their own forage.

Hill to Maj. Thos. G. Rhett, Chf. Ord. & Arty., Shreveport, TMD.

J. J. Alexander of Co. B, 17th Texas Cavalry, now on detail as a guard at these Works, wants to rejoin his regiment because all his relations are in the same command. He being a good soldier, I am loth to give him up, but do not wish to throw any obstruction in the way of putting a good soldier in the field. I therefore ask that he be relieved in this Department and ordered to report to his command.

General Morgan, C.S.A., captured Mt. Sterling, Ky., and took 400 Union prisoners.

A Federal raiding force organized by General Butler attempted to surprise and capture Petersburg, Va.; the defenses of which had been stripped almost bare to re-enforce General Lee. General R. E. Colston hastily organized a force of home guards and citizens—old men and boys—and repulsed the attack. The militia lost 62 men out of a total force of 125, but Petersburg was saved—for the time being.

FRIDAY, JUNE 10, 1864

General Morgan, C.S.A., continued his successful raid by capturing Lexington, Ky., with great quantities of stores.

General Nathan Bedford Forrest, C.S.A., won one of his most brilliant victories of his career. With about 3,500 men, he attacked and routed a picked Union force of nearly 10,000 men with 16 guns at Brice's Cross Roads, Miss. Forrest captured 14 cannon, 250 wagons and 1,600 prisoners. The Confederate loss was less than 500. The Federals lost 600 killed and wounded in addition to the captured.

A popular sport of the Federals in the border towns of Maryland and Virginia was to stretch a Union flag across the street, and compel the "Secesh" to walk under it. On this day, a Miss Clara Gunby of Salisbury, Md., was arrested at her home and sent to Baltimore to be tried for treason. Miss Gunby boldly refused to walk under a flag stretched across the sidewalk at Salisbury. For her "disloyalty" the Union authorities had a flag hung over the front door of her home, whereupon Miss Gunby entered

[75]

and left her house by climbing in and out of a window until the authorities placed her under arrest. Miss Gunby was tried by a military commission and ordered deported. Later she was sent South and became a Confederate Army nurse.

General Morgan, C.S.A., captured Cynthiana, Ky.

The Confederate cruiser *Alabama,* Commanded by Capt. Raphael Semmes, entered Cherbourg Harbor, France.

Baltimore newspapers published a dispatch from the Charleston, W. Va., correspondent of the *New York Times,* telling of the death at Dublin, W. Va., of General Albert G. Jenkins of the Confederate army. He was wounded and fell into the hands of the enemy. The General's wife and three children were permitted to visit the dying General under flag of truce. Before the war, General Jenkins was a very wealthy man, and the correspondent commented upon the fact that his wife was in rags and his children without shoes or stockings, showing the straits to which the Southern people were reduced.

General Sheridan with 10,000 Yankee troopers started on his second Richmond raid. But it was brought to an abrupt end on June 11, (4 days later) at Trevilian Station by the Confederate cavalry of Generals Hampton and Fitz Lee with about 6,000 men. Although badly outclassed as to horses and equipment, the Southern cavalry was still superior to that of the North. In the battle, Sheridan lost about 1,000 and the Confederates 800.

TUESDAY, JUNE 14, 1864

Hill to Maj. Thos. G. Rhett, Chf. Ord. & Arty., Shreveport DTM.

I am now entirely out of transportation. The mules that we had for the last few months have been taken by their owners.

It is necessary that I have 6 mules. It is impossible to get along without them. I respectfully request an order allowing me to impress mules, for they can not be gotten in any other way in this country.

Lieut. Gen. Leonidas Polk, bishop of the Episcopal Church, was killed by a cannon ball at Pine Mountain, Ga. With Generals Johnston and Hardee he had ridden out to examine the enemy's lines, when three cannon shots were fired from a Union battery a mile away. One of the balls struck General Polk in the chest.

The Union steamer *Kearsarge,* Captain Winslow, arrived at Cherbourg, France, in search of the Confederate cruiser *Alabama,* which was in the harbor.

Details of the capture of the Union gunboat *Water Witch,* in Ossabaw Sound, Ga., were received in the North. The vessel was captured by volunteers from the Confederate Navy under Lieut. E. P. Pelot. Pelot and four men were killed and twelve wounded in capturing the *Water Witch.* One of the men killed with the Confederates was a negro pilot.

WEDNESDAY, JUNE 15, 1864

Hill to Maj. Thos. G. Rhett, Chf. Ord. & Arty., Shreveport DTM.

With all I can work, I have only about 30 days work on hand. I have tried all the Iron Works around, and can not get a supply of gun scalps, and I have no iron on hand fit to make them. It is my understanding that Major Alexander has on hand a large quantity of old rifle barrels. If I could get 3,000 of them, it would give me enough material to carry on for sometime. I have already worked over all the old rifle barrels on hand that are worth anything, and am now using them, but the percentage that will not stand the test is very great. I respectfully request an order from Maj. Alexander for his old rifle barrels.

The Maj. Alexander to whom Col. Hill refers, is Major George D. Alexander, who prior to the evacuation of

Arkansas was in charge of the Post at Camden. With the evacuation to Texas of C. S. Ordnance, Major Alexander was placed in charge of the C. S. Arsenal, Marshall, Texas, this being a different establishment from the C. S. Depot at the same place. Col. Hill's letters do not indicate any great affection or admiration for the major.

The Army of the Potomac, under General Grant, late at night began to join the Army of the James under Butler before Petersburg, Va. This was the beginning of the Siege of Petersburg which was to end when Lee's lines were broken April 2, 1865. Today, Beauregard was holding the defenses with 2,200 men while in his front were 18,000 Union troops.

FRIDAY, JUNE 17, 1864

The day previous, General Early's command reached Charlottesville, Va., having marched more than 80 miles in four days. General Early had been ordered to the Shenandoah Valley to halt the activities of the Union general Hunter. The 1st encounter between the two armies occurred today near Lynchburg, Va. Early lost 200 men while the Union loss was 700. The action caused Hunter to retreat.

Large bodies of troops from Grant's army joined the army of Butler south of the James River and attacked the Petersburg defenses held by Gen. Beauregard with a few thousand men. The fighting was desperate, and part of Hancock's corps effected a lodgment on the Confederate line. Beauregard wired frantically for reinforcements, but Lee was slow to respond. It was one of the few instances of the war when Lee apparently was deceived as to the enemy's movements. In the attempts to take the Confederate trenches, the Federals lost 8,000 men. The Confederate loss was about 1,000.

On this day 22 young women were killed and many

more were injured by an explosion in the arsenal at Washington, D. C., where they were engaged in making cartridges.

A dispatch from Washington said that sick and wounded soldiers in the hospitals there were dying at the rate of 50 per day! From Richmond came the news that the grave diggers at Hollywood Cemetery could not bury the dead as fast as the bodies were received.

The famous "Duel to the Death" between the Confederate cruiser *Alabama,* Capt. Raphael Semmes, and the Union frigate *Kearsarge,* Capt. John A. Winslow, took place off Cherbourg, France, and was witnessed by thousands of excited Frenchmen and tourists. Special trains were run to carry spectators to see the fight. The ships were well matched as to size. The *Alabama* had a crew of 149, the *Kearsarge* 163. The *Alabama* carried one more gun than the *Kearsarge,* but the latter's battery was heavier. The *Kearsarge* was faster and was partially protected by an ingenious armor of iron cable. The action lasted one hour and the *Alabama* was sunk. Capt. Semmes and 40 of his officers and men were saved by the English yacht *Deerhound.* The *Kearsarge* lost 1 killed and 2 wounded; the *Alabama,* 9 killed, 21 wounded, and 10 drowned.

Hill to Maj. Thos. G. Rhett, Chf. Ord. & Arty., Shreveport DTM.

I have a chance to buy 200 pounds of good rifle powder. It is much needed here. Please advise if I can buy it, and what price I should pay for it?

Hill to Maj. Thos. G. Rhett, Chf. Ord. & Arty., Shreveport DTM.

I have your requisition for Capt. W. H. Lewis, and am sorry

to say that it can only be partially filled. I have on hand only buck & ball, Miss. and a few Navy and Army pistol cartridges. I have no powder nor have I had any this month, and have been forced to suspend operations on account of it. I have very few musket or sporting caps.

I can only supply 15,000 buck & balls, 40,000 Miss. and about 50,000 musket caps. His requisition calls for 50,000 Enfield Rifle, 25,000 Texas Rifle, 10,000 Belgium and 10,000 rifle musket cartridges and 200,000 musket caps.

If supplied with powder I can give Capt. Lewis everything he needs very soon. Please send me some as soon as possible as my cartridge boys are doing nothing.

THURSDAY, JUNE 23, 1864

Hill to Lt. B. Atkinson, Dept. Ord. Officer, Fort Washita, Choctaw Nation.

I am sending you by wagon train 45,000 buck & ball cartridges and 50,000 musket caps.

The powder sent by you is received in bad condition and will have to be completely overhauled to ascertain the condition.

FRIDAY, JUNE 24, 1864

Hill to Maj. Thos. G. Rhett, Chf. Ord. & Arty., Shreveport, D.T.M.

Your requisition to Lt. B. Atkinson of 50,000 musket caps leaves me without any. When you send the powder, please send some musket caps.

General Shelby's cavalry captured the Union gunboat Queen City on White River.

SATURDAY, JUNE 25, 1864

Hill to Lt. B. F. Atkinson, Ord. Off. Fort Washita, C.N.

I herewith enclose your receipts for condemned powder received from you a few days ago as follows:
6,884 ¾ lbs rifle powder, 26 lbs rifle powder, 29 powder casks, and 8 packing boxes.

The work of digging the mine under the Confederate

lines at Petersburg was begun under the direction of Lt. Col. Henry Pleasants of the 48th Penna. Regt., a former mining engineer.

Hill to Lt. Philip B. Kay, Shreveport, La.

Yours of the 20th inst. handed me by Capt. King. I will take your three mule carts and give you for them $6.00 per day and would like for you to send them up at once, and I will continue to pay you at whatever rates are established by the commissioner for this State. There are no established rates for three mule carts, but six mule wagons, drivers etc are rated at $10.00 per day, and I will give you $6.00 for your cart and think it will be a fair rate.

This day Sherman's army made a number of desperate assaults upon the Confederate line on Kennesaw Mountain, Ga. The attacks were repulsed with a loss of 3,000 Federals to about 600 Confederates. The Union army could better afford the loss of the 3,000 than the Confederates could their 600.

President Lincoln accepted the renomination for the Presidency.

Hill to Capt. C. W. Wailey, Comdg. Arsenal, Shreveport, La.

Enclosed you will find receipts for 1 hand planing machine, 3 lead kettels, 2 packing boxes, also 1,000 lbs cannon powder, 116 lbs cotten rope and 10 powder barrels.

Hill to Maj. Thos. G. Rhett, Chf. Ord. & Arty., Shreveport DTM.

I am greatly in need of something in the way of stationary. The quarter is now about closed and I must make my return, and it will be impossible for me to do so with my present stock of stationary. I have 20 steel pens, not a gill of ink, no lead pencils that I can use, and not a sheet of cap paper. Sometime ago there was some ink in this place to sell but I could never succeed in getting more than ½ gal. of it from the seller. Please send me as soon as possible, 2 gro. steel pens, a lot of ink powder or ink, 2 doz. good lead pencils, and 3 reams of fool's cap paper.

WEDNESDAY, JUNE 29, 1864

Hill to Maj. Thos G. Rhett, Chf. Ord. & Arty., Shreveport DTM.

Under instruction of circular of June 10, 1864, from your office given in accordance with communication #3153, Dept. Hd. Qtrs, I have assigned to duty as AQM and ACS, Thos. A. Woods, 1st Lt. Ord. & Arty. CSPA, who will enter on his duties on the 1st July, 1864.

Hill to Maj. Thos. G. Rhett, Chf. Ord. & Arty., Shreveport DTM.

I am nearly out of material for making gun barrels. I have on hand only 150, and I think that 30% of those will be condemned. I understand that Major G. D. Alexander has a large supply of old sporting rifle barrels on hand, and I would like to have them. In the meantime while waiting for something to do, I will stock double barreled guns.

I will soon be out of spring steel. Since I have been here I have been using for this purpose old circular saws, having purchased 2 or 3 old ones last winter, but I am now nearly out. I know where there are 6 or 8 more not fit for sawing, but the people will not sell them. I would like permission to impress them, as unless I get steel very soon I will be entirely out. I am now using scraps.

SATURDAY, JULY 2, 1864

The milling shop at the Springfield (Mass.) Armory was burned.

SUNDAY, JULY 3, 1864

To relieve the pressure upon the Confederate army at Petersburg and Richmond, General Jubal A. Early, CSA, was sent up the Shenandoah Valley with a sizable force to threaten Washington, D. C. It was hoped that by so doing Lincoln would recall some of the Federal forces in front of Richmond to protect the Northern Capital. Today, General Sigel's Union army evacuated Martinsburg before the advance of Early.

WEDNESDAY, JULY 6, 1864

General Bradley T. Johnson's brigade of Confederate cavalry entered Hagerstown, Md.

THURSDAY, JULY 7, 1864

Hill to Major C. Hill, Chf. of Trans. Bur. QMD.

I have just received a communication from the Chief of Ordnance informing me that you have been ordered to turn over to me four, six-mule teams and wagons, and I would like to know how long it will be before I can get them. I am very much in need of them, and if you will send them to me at once, it will very much facilitate my works.

Hill to Capt. W. H. Lewis, Chf. of Ord. District Indian Territory.

On the 29th June, 1864, I forwarded to you a letter addressed by you to Major Rhett in relation to ammunition now being prepared for you at these works, with an endorsement as follows; "The ammunition for the Indian Dept. will be ready the 15th July 1864. The calibre of the Texas rifles made here is the same as the Enfield .57."

Hill to Major G. D. Alexander, Comdg. Arsenal Marshall, Texas.

I received a letter last night from Major Rhett enclosing a copy of an order on you for 1,000 sporting rifle barrels and 400 Enfield rifle barrels.

If you can possibly send them direct to this place, please do so.

Hill to Maj. Thos. G. Rhett, Chf. Ord. & Arty., Shreveport DTM.

During the last quarter (April 1st thru June 31, 1864) the Armory fabricated 360 Texas Rifles, 81 Hill Rifles, using for barrels the old sporting rifle barrels brought from Little Rock and the percent that will not stand the test is very great. We have had finished 673 gun barrels of which 197 have bursted in the 1st testing, and 35 in the second. This is caused by the iron in the sporting barrels being very inferior, and much of our other work on guns is lost in the same way. Of the main springs, we lose over half because of the indifferent quality of the steel. All the guns that we have completed have been thoroughly tested and well finished and have an effective range of about 400 to 500 yards. The Texas Rifles are of two kinds, both calibre .57. One is fitted with bayonets for infantry, the other without bayonets for cavalry. The Hill Rifle, calibre .54 is a splendid gun, made from the old Hall's carbine barrels, and is intended for cavalry service—all of them being patent breech guns. We have had much trouble in procuring stock timber. I am now using birch and holly, and they make a very good stock.

I have also stocked and repaired 10 double-barreled shot guns, and altered to percussion 16 old flint muskets. Much other work has been done in the Armory in the way of making and mending tools for all the shops connected with it. This kind of work is about ½ of the work that is done in the Armory. Besides, we have completed and moved into a large and fine blacksmith's shop, running 6 forges.

I have on hand enough barrels to last until the end of this month. I am in need of steel and files, and also need 6 good gunsmiths.

In the Laboratory we fabricated during the quarter 754,222 cartridges of all kinds, and have lost much time because of the lack of lead or powder. I am working negro boys 12 to 15 years old and they do a good job of making cartridges. If I am supplied with powder and lead, I can turn out from 20 to 25,000 per day.

In the Tin Shop we fabricated 3,100 infantry magazines, 568 cavalry magazines and 1,818 canteens. Much other work was done on belt hooks, canteen hooks etc.

In the Carpenter Shop it is impossible to enumerate all they have done, fabricated etc., but we have built and partially completed a building for quarters 75 x 25 in one way and 40 x 25 the other, with two stories, the house in the form of a 'T.' In addition, the carpenters have got out of the woods for gun stocks, 8,000 ft of timber.

In Harness Shop we have had much to contend with having never been able to complete until very lately any arrangements for leather. I have been compelled to use a lot of leather purchased from the Quartermaster Department of a very inferior quality on which there was much wastage. However we fabricated 2,225 infantry cartridge boxes, 267 cavalry boxes, 1,336 percussion cap boxes, 1,778 waist belts, 3 McClellan saddles, and have done a good deal of work for officers passing; mended and kept in repair all the harness used in the Department.

I am in need of more carpenters, and also need more men for guard duty, but am happy to say that I think my Works are now in a flourishing condition, and that next quarter will show some improvement.

The quarterly report from Tyler, is quite enlightening. Let us recapitulate, and from it, a few conclusions may be reached.

First of all we learn that from April 1 through June 31, 1863, 360 "Texas" rifles were completed. All of .57 caliber, they were nevertheless of "two kinds." One kind was provided with bayonet (for infantry), and the other without bayonet (for cavalry). The barrels for this lot of 360 rifles were made "from old sporting rifles" brought from Little Rock to Tyler.

From the statement that they were of "two kinds" makes it obvious that one was distinguishable from the other, and suggests that there was a provision on the infantry arm for the attaching of a bayonet, such as a lug for a sabre bayonet. Had they been equipped with a triangular bayonet, each would have been identical. It is also possible that the cavalry rifles were provided with swivel ram rods.

Besides the "Texas" rifles, 81 "Hill," cal. .54, are noted to have been completed during the quarter in question. These were designed for cavalry and were made from the barrels of old Hall's carbines to which had been added patented breeches. As the Hall rifles were originally breech loaders, this was a deliberate alteration from breech—back to muzzle loading, certainly setting the clock back.

The Hill rifles were both "long" and "short." This description probably applied to barrel length as no other difference is noted.

In addition to the Texas and Hill rifles, 10 double-barreled shotguns were restocked and repaired, and 16 flintlock muskets were altered to percussion. Due to difficulty in obtaining suitable timber, Hill resorted to the use of holly and birch for gun stockings, a fact that might be remembered by the reader for purposes of identification.

Besides firearms, the Ordnance Works fabricated in this three-month period about 1,000,000 cartridges of various calibers, 3,000 leather cartridge boxes complete with tin filler, 1,500 percussion-cap boxes, waist belts and tin canteens, along with quantities of various and unfinished components.

Truly, Col. Hill had had a busy three months.

FRIDAY, JULY 8, 1864

Potatoes sold for $20 a dozen in Richmond.

Dispatches from Harrisburg and Chambersburg said the Confederate army under General J. A. Early was concentrating near Frederick, Md. All the available Union troops were being mobilized under General Lew Wallace, the Federal commander at Baltimore.

SATURDAY, JULY 9, 1864

Hill to Maj. Thos. G. Rhett, Chf. Ord. & Arty., Shreveport DTM.

Your telegram of the 1st, via Jefferson and through Capt. Leavenworth has just been received. It will be impossible for me to send the remainder of his stores just now for want of transportation. The ox team that the Quartermaster has generally been sending for me has been taken and put to hauling corn for the Federal prisoners in place of mule teams used here-to-fore, which have gone to Shreveport with Federal prisoners. The four six-mule teams ordered turned over to me have not yet been received.

On the banks of the Monocacy River, near Frederick, Md., a Union force under General Lew Wallace was defeated by the invading force of Confederates under General Jubal A. Early. Wallace, who had hastily gathered a force of 6,000 men, lost 692 killed and wounded and 1,188 captured. Early, who had a superior force engaged in the battle, lost about 700 men.

MONDAY, JULY 11, 1864

Hill to Major George D. Alexander, Comdg. Arsenal, Marshall, Texas.

If your wagons leave Marshall before mine arrive there, please send the barrels. They can be piled snuggly on the wagon without being boxed, under the inspection and in the care of the wagon master, and holding him responsible for the loss of any.

Hill to Capt. S. C. Faulkner, Comdg. Ord. Depot, Marshall, Texas.

I send by wagon for Capt. C. W. Wailey at Shreveport, one box containing 113 lbs fuze paper and one desk for General Huger.
Please forward the fuze paper to Capt. Wailey as soon as possible as he is greatly in need of it, and deliver the desk to Gen. Huger.
Please send by return wagon the nitric acid left with you for me by Major Alexander.

The militia of the District of Columbia was called out to defend the Capital. Baltimore was in a panic because of the approach of the Confederate invading force under General Early. The City Council met in extraordinary session and passed an ordinance conscripting all able-bodied males of 16 years and over for the defense of the city. All able-bodied negroes were gathered up by the police and soldiers and put to work on the defenses of the city. The entire militia force of the city was under arms and companies of volunteers were armed and drilled. Confederate cavalry under orders of General Bradley T. Johnson, burned the home of Governor Bradford on Charles St. Ave., about four miles north of the city, in retaliation for the burning by General Hunter of the home of Governor Letcher of Virginia.

Mosby's Rangers crossed the Potomac River at Conrad's Ferry and marched to Poolesville, Md.

TUESDAY, JULY 12, 1864

Hill to Capt. G. S. Polleys, In Charge of Armory, Tyler, Texas.

You will repair at once for Capt. Richardson's company, 37 Texas rifles, and 1 Miss. rifle, not stopping the line of workmen on new guns, but stopping all other work to do the repairs.

Mosby's Rangers burned the camp of the 8th Illinois Cavalry, near Seneca Mills, Md.

After a severe skirmish in front of Fort Stevens, Washington, D. C., Early's army began its retreat from in front of the defenses of the Union Capital. A heavy force of Union troops followed.

THURSDAY, JULY 14, 1864

Hill to Maj. G. D. Thomas, Comdg. QMDA, Gilman, Texas.

I send you 4 McClellan saddles, the only ones completed. The others will be done by the 1st or middle of next week. I also send 1 bridle without the bit.

Early's army recrossed the Potomac River into Virginia near Leesburg, carrying a large quantity of captured stores and prisoners, and thus ended the Confederate's last real threat to the Union capital.

[88]

General John B. Hood, relieved General Joseph E. Johnston in command of the Confederate Army of the West. Johnston had skillfully retreated before Sherman to the defenses of Atlanta, but the Confederate Administration was dissatisfied with the conduct of the campaign.

SATURDAY, JULY 30, 1864

Hill to Maj. Thos. G. Rhett, Chf. Ord. & Arty., Shreveport, DTM.

I send Capt. King down with my fund to be deposited, and beg you to send me some more funds to pay my hands who are very much in need of it, having not yet received last months pay.

I also gave Capt. King a list of the things that I am needing and hope you will let him have them. I am entirely out of files. I am out of powder, and doing no work in the Laboratory.

I have all the ammunition ready for the Indian Nation and have now, Col. Good's arms, equipment and everything ready for him. I send to Marshall 2 wagon loads of canteens and straps, and shall invoice them to Capt. Faulkner.

The mine under the Confederate works in front of Petersburg, Va., was exploded at daybreak. The roar shook the ground for miles around and a mighty mass of earth, cannon and men was hurled high into the air. The explosion left a hole or "crater" in the earth 170 feet long, 60 feet wide and 30 feet deep. Following the explosion a strong force of white and negro troops charged to break through Lee's lines at the "crater." Quickly rallying, the Confederates drove the Federals into the "crater" where they died by the hundreds. In this affair, the Federals lost 2,385 men killed and wounded and 1,413 captured. The Confederate loss was about 1,100 men.

Chambersburg, Pa., was burned by a raiding party of Confederate cavalry under General John McCausland. General McCausland presented an order from General

Early directing the town to pay $500,000 for the reimbursement of Virginia residents whose homes had been burned by the Federals. The order directed that if the money was not paid, the town should be burned. The citizens refused to pay the ransom, and McCausland ordered Col. Harry Gilmor of the 2nd Maryland Cavalry to carry out the order. The firing of the town was performed in an orderly manner by the Marylanders, few of whom had any liking for the work.

MONDAY, AUG. 1, 1864

Hill to Capt. C. W. Wailey, Comdg. Shreveport Arsenal.

Enclosed, please find invoice and receipt for one cavalry bugle, sent to you today by Capt. King.
Please sign receipt and return.

Hill to Capt. S. C. Faulkner, Comdg. Ord. Depot, Marshall, Texas.

Enclosed, please find invoices and receipt for 400 infantry cartridge boxes, 400 cap boxes, 400 waist belts, 1026 canteens and 1026 canteen straps, forwarded to you by wagon today.
Please sign receipt and return.

Hill to Capt. W. H. Lewis, Chf. Ord. Off., Dist. Ind. Territory, Doaksville, Choctaw Nation.

Enclosed, please find invoices and receipt for 30,000 buck & ball cartridges, 73,000 Enfield rifle cartridges, 40,000 Miss. rifle cartridges, 10,000 Belgium cartridges, 10,000 rifle musket cartridges, 200,000 musket percussion caps, and 50,000 sporting caps, forwarded to you today by wagon train—G. Shawner, wagonmaster.
Please sign receipt and return.

WEDNESDAY, AUG. 3, 1864

Hill to Col. Scott Anderson, Comdg. Camp Ford, Tyler, Texas

I understand that the detachment you sent out after deserters has returned, and if so, I would be very much obliged if you would return the arms that I loaned to you to arm said detachment. The arms are all infantry guns and a part of a lot that I have set aside for my own men. I would like to get them as they are the only guns that I have for the protection of my works. When you got them it was with the understanding that they were to be returned as soon as the detachment returned.

FRIDAY, AUG. 5, 1864

Hill to Maj. Thos. G. Rhett, Chf. Ord. & Arty., Shreveport DTM.

I received yesterday from Major Alexander, 600 sporting rifle barrels. They are too small. There are a very few one inch in diameter, while still fewer are the smallest fraction larger. I do not believe that I shall be able to select 50 from the whole 600 large enough to answer for making the guns I am making here; the Texas rifle finished being 1⅛ inch, and the Hill rifle 1 inch. The barrels then are too small to say nothing of the allowance for turning. Please order to be turned over to me all that will measure at least 1⅛ inch.

Rodes' and Ramseur's division of Early's army crossed the Potomac from Virginia at Williamsport, Md. Vaughn's cavalry occupied Hagerstown, and Breckenridge's division occupied Sharpsburg, Md. Governor Curtin of Pennsylvania issued a proclamation calling for 30,000 volunteers to repell the threatened invasion.

The great battle of Mobile Bay took place between the Union fleet of four ironclads and 10 frigates and gunboats under Admiral Farragut, and the Confederate forts and fleet under Admiral Franklin Buchanan, who commanded the Confederate ram *Virginia* (*Merrimac*) in the battle of Hampton Rhoads. Buchanan's fleet consisted of the ironclad *Tennessee* and three small gunboats. One of the gunboats was captured, a second driven ashore and burned and the third escaped leaving the *Tennessee* to battle the whole Union fleet. The Union monitor *Tecumseh* struck a Confederate torpedo and sank with most of its crew of 114 men, and the gunboat *Philippi* was also sunk. After a fight at close quarters, the *Tennessee* was disabled and surrendered. Buchanan was wounded. During a part of the fight Farragut was lashed to the rigging of his flagship the *Hartford*. The Union loss was 52 killed, 93 drowned and 170 wounded. The Confederates lost 12 killed and 20 wounded.

SATURDAY, AUG. 6, 1864

The Union fleet at Mobile Bay began the bombardment of Fort Gaines, Ala., commanded by Col. Charles D. Anderson.

General Early's army recrossed the Potomac River at Williamsport, Md., into Virginia.

Officers went to arrest William Adams of Baltimore, employed on board the Steamer *Chester,* who had been drafted and failed to appear for enrollment, and Adams seized a hatchet and chopped off the fore and index fingers of his left hand to incapacitate himself for military service. He was locked up.

SUNDAY, AUG. 7, 1864

Fort Gaines, one of the forts defending Mobile Bay, surrendered to the Union Fleet under Farragut.

Francis Key, son of Francis Scott Key, arrested and imprisoned in Fort McHenry for disloyalty, was released on parole.

MONDAY, AUG. 8, 1864

Hill to Major George D. Alexander, Comdg. Arsenal Marshall, Texas.

Enclosed, please find receipt for 992 sporting rifle barrels and 250 Enfield rifle barrels received from you. The sporting rifle barrels are worthless and I will not be able to use more than 75 from the lot.

TUESDAY, AUG. 9, 1864

Seventy men were killed and 130 injured by an explosion of a large quantity of ammunition belonging to Grant's army at City Point, Va.

Hill to Maj. Thos. C. Rhett, Chf. Ord. & Arty., Shreveport DTM.

Enclosed you will find the proceedings of a Board of Survey on some guns that I loaned to Col. Scott Anderson on the 29th of last month to go in pursuit of some deserters—100 of his regiment having deserted the night previous. I loaned him 46 Texas rifles in splendid order, and a few days ago I told him that the guns having been only loaned to him to apprehend the deserters and the men having returned, I wished my guns brought back, and on yesterday 36 of them were sent in—all that could be found. The guns have been in the hands of his men only 19 days and I never in my life saw guns so much abused and I surely think something should be done with the company officers for allowing such destruction of Government property.

You sent me an order to repair for Col. Anderson 115 arms and I never in my life saw arms so much abused and it is all mere carelessness for his regiment has not had the arms more than 3 months. If arms are to be abused in this way, it is perfectly useless to issue them, and I assert from what I have seen of arms at the Prison Camp that there could not be found in the whole camp 20 guns that are in shooting order.

Sheridan's army of 45,000 men began its march up the Shenandoah Valley.

Hill to Col. N. W. Townes, C.S.P.A.

Yours of this date has come duly to hand and in answer, I am sorry to say that you can not have the articles you wish without paying for them in $5.00 bills of the new issue.

I have according to orders received, deposited with the Depositor at Shreveport all the Confederate money I had on hand of the denomination over $5.00 bills and if I was to take now, your bills over that amount, they would be useless to the Ordnance Dept. as I could not use them, and they would have to be deposited and the Ordnance Dept. would not receive any credit for same, or be supplied with current money in its place.

My accounts in the old issue are closed and if I were to receive bills from you of the denomination you offer, I would have to open them again.

Hill to Lt. T. A. Woods, In Charge Laboratory & Shops, Tyler, Texas.

You will stop operations in the Lead Shop until further orders after this evening. Put your force now employed in the Lead Shop on guard duty on tomorrow morning.

SATURDAY, AUG. 13, 1864

Hill to Maj. Thos. G. Rhett, Chf. Ord & Arty., Shreveport DTM.

On the evening of the 11th inst. a man by the name of Spivey, a shoe maker in this place, told 2 of the little negroes working in the Laboratory, that if they would get him some caps and powder, he would pay them any price, and hold them harmless— that he would take all the blame, and see that they were not punished. One of the negroes upon this representation, stole several bundles of cartridges 'Colt's Pistol' and the other immediately informed the foreman, Mr. T. J. Wiley, of the whole circumstance.

When apprised of the facts of the case, Lt. Woods, then in charge of the Laboratory, caused the negroes to be searched, found the cartridges, and caused the boy who had informed to take the cartridges to Spivey and endeavor to sell them. Post Surgeon McGregor, and Lt. Wood, saw Spivey pay the negro when Lt. Wood immediately entered his shop with a file of men, and secured the cartridges hidden in scraps of leather and shoe pegs on his bench.

Spivey does not bear a very enviable reputation for honesty, and has been before suspected of this practice.

I would like to have him prosecuted. Will you authorize me to employ counsel for that purpose? I think he may be convicted and severely punished.

Please answer this as soon as practicable.

Hill to Maj. Thos. G. Rhett, Chf. Ord & Arty., Shreveport DTM.

Enclosed, please find statement of iron, lead and cartridge paper received from Messrs. McMurty & Atkinson, since the 23rd of April 1864 of which no account has been previously rendered.

The accoutrements will be sent as directed to care of Capt. Leavenworth at Jefferson, the last of this week.

MONDAY, AUG. 15, 1864

Hill to Capt. C. W. Wailey, Comdg. Shreveport Arsenal.

Enclosed, please find receipts for 49 assorted files, 2 gross buckles, 5 qrs. sandpaper etc., etc., received here yesterday.

WEDNESDAY, AUG. 17, 1864

Hill to Maj. George D. Alexander, Comdg. Arsenal Marshall, Texas.

Yours dated Aug. 4th was duly received. I delayed answering in order to determine on the matter. I have no gunsmiths whom I could transfer to you in exchange, but I have an excellent blacksmith whom I would be willing to let you have. If you are willing to make the exchange, send in your man and I will at once order an excellent blacksmith to report to you.

FRIDAY, AUG. 19, 1864

Hill to Brig. Gen. Grier, Comdg. Bureau Conscription, TMD, Marshall, Texas.

I have three tanners in my Department, and they can scarcely supply me with sufficient leather. I am putting up constantly—cartridge boxes, cap boxes, waist belts etc. & etc., and it is important that I be supplied with leather.

I am assured by reliable persons that I know, that Julius Pobst, whose name and description is contained on the within enclosed, is a good tanner, has a tan yard and could benefit the country more by supplying leather than in any other way.

I would be glad if you would order him detailed, and to report to me, so that I could put him to work furnishing leather to my Department.

SATURDAY, AUG. 20, 1864

Hill to Capt. S. C. Faulkner, Comdg. Ord. Depot, Marshall, Texas.

Enclosed, please find receipt for 500 harness needles, 32 lbs. cast steel, 530 lbs. rifle powder etc. etc., received from you.

News was received in Baltimore of a desperate cavalry skirmish at Bunker Hill, Va., near Winchester, in which the 1st and 2nd Maryland Cavalry bore the brunt of the fighting on the Confederate side. Col. Harry Gilmor of the 2nd Maryland was seriously wounded, and Lts. Henry C. Blackiston and John William Albaugh of the 1st Maryland were killed.

MONDAY, AUG. 22, 1864

Hill to Col. G. Good, Comdg. Bt. Cvly, Bonham, Texas.

Enclosed, please find wagon masters receipts for stores sent to you. I hope they will arrive safely and prove satisfactory.

Hill to Maj. Thos. G. Rhett, Chf. of Ord. DTM, Shreveport, La.

I sent off by wagon train on Saturday the 20th inst. to Col. Good, Bonham, Texas, the ordnance stores called for by his requisitions and approved by you.

I shall send off in the morning all the accoutrements on hand ready for shipment to Capt. C. W. Wailey, care of Capt. F. P. Leavenworth, Ord. Officer, Jefferson, Texas.

Hill to Maj. Thos. G. Rhett, Chf. of Ord. DTM, Shreveport, La.

I stand very much in need of a crib in which to put my corn for the public animals belonging to these Works, and it is necessary that I should have one built.

There is a wealthy man named William Weaver, near Tyler, having some land about 3 miles from this place upon which there are a plenty of pine poles, and there are none other anywhere near here.

He says he will not sell them or let the Government have them in anyway, and that he intends to protect his land by force of arms. He is wealthy and might furnish the poles without inconvenience to himself.

I respectfully ask that I be permitted to impress a sufficient number to build a crib for the purpose mentioned above.

Marshal Murray at New York, seized 32 cases, each containing 80 Savage Arms Co. revolvers. It was alleged that the weapons were to be shipped to the Sons of Liberty, in Indiana. The Sons of Liberty were said to be a "treasonable organization of Indiana Democrats."

Hill to Col. Good, Bonham, Texas.

Please find enclosed invoices and receipts for 255 Texas rifles, 120 Hill rifles, 375 cavalry cartridge boxes, etc. etc., sent you by wagon train in charge of T. M. Hayse, Wagon master on last Saturday, 20th inst. Please sign and return receipts as soon as the stores are received.

Hill to Capt. C. W. Wailey, Comdg. Shreveport Arsenal.

Enclosed, please find invoices and receipts for 1000 inftry crtge boxes, 650 cvly crtge boxes, 1550 cap boxes, etc. etc., this day shipped to you through Capt. F. P. Leavenworth, Jefferson, Texas, via wagon train. Please sign and return receipts as soon as the goods are received.

Hill to Maj. G. D. Alexander, Comdg. Arsenal, Marshall, Texas.

A train of wagons will arrive at Marshall from Jefferson in a few days bound for this place. The wagon master will call on Capt. Faulkner for any stores at Marshall intended for this place.

Please have sent the remaining 500 lbs. powder called for in the order obtained by Capt. King from Major Rhett.

Hill to Maj. Thos. G. Rhett, Chf. of Ord., DTM, Shreveport, La.

I send this morning to Capt. Leavenworth at Jefferson for Capt. Wailey, 1100 inf. cart. boxes, 650 cav. ditto, 1550 cap pouches, 1750 waist belts and 648 tin canteens and straps, all that I had boxed and ready for shipment.

I now have on hand, 2608 tin canteens but have no straps for them, and here-to-fore I have marked none without straps. Shall I send these forward without them?

I have also on hand 1,534 inf. crtg. boxes and 168 cav. do. but I have no belts or cap pouches to pack with them and I have always here-to-fore packed one of each in packing so that they would be ready for issue to the troops. Shall I continue to do so, or shall I send them forward incomplete?

It will be impossible for me to put up a canteen strap with every canteen as I can not get the leather, so I shall have them packed and send them forward as soon as the Quartermaster can furnish transportation. Shall I send them to Jefferson?

From the above it is evident that troops in the Dept. of the Trans-Miss. were supplied with a waist belt, a cartridge box and a cap pouch—all at the same issue. It is also apparent that the canteens issued from Tyler, Texas, had leather straps. Many Confederate canteens carried a cotton web strap.

Fort Morgan, Mobile Bay, was surrendered to the Union Army and Navy which had been operating against it for nearly a month. The fort was commanded by Gen. Richard L. Page, who had about 400 men. General Page had the distinction of being also a commander in the Confederate States Navy.

WEDNESDAY, AUG. 24, 1864

Hill to Capt. J. C. Kirby, AQM, Tyler, Texas.

I am very much in need of the four six-mule teams and wagons ordered turned over to me, and would like very much for you to supply me in some way, as I will have to stop my Works unless I am supplied. The two teams that you turned over to me of Mr. Bryant's, have been taken by their owner on the ground that they had never been properly impressed, and that according to the law, you could not impress them, and I had to give them up.

I would like to know if you can furnish the teams or if you could let me have any wagons for temporary use, until you can fill the order in full?

The Blacksmith Shop. Tyler, Texas, 1865.

No. 2 of the rifles surviving from Tyler, Texas.

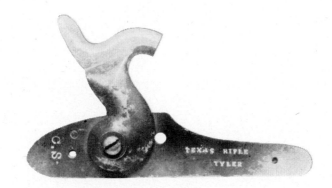

Closeup of the lock plate of No. 2.

No. 3 of the rifles surviving from Tyler, Texas.

Closeup view of the breech and lock plate of No. 3.

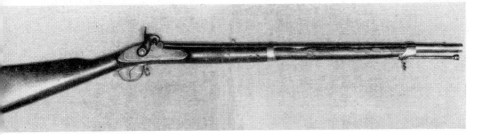

No. 4 of the rifles surviving from Tyler, Texas.

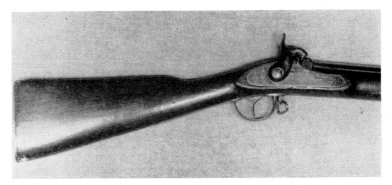

Closeup of breech, lock, and butt of No. 4.

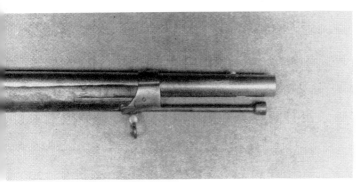

Fore-end of No. 4.

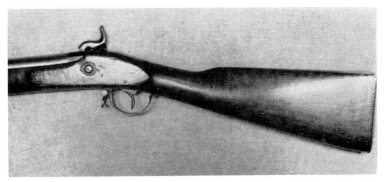

Left side of No. 4, showing how lock is attached to the stock with one screw.
Confederate tin canteen of the type probably made at Tyler, Texas.

A "militarized" shotgun with shortened barrel. Fore-sight added. Note swivel in butt f«
carrying straps. Thousands of such "carbines" were supplied the Confederate cavalry.

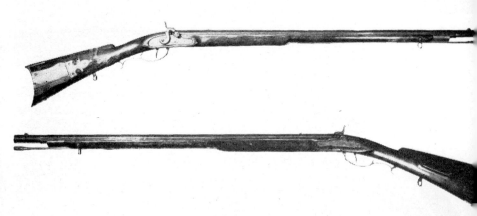

Two views of a "militarized" Kentucky rifle. Note how the fore-end has been turned on
lath so that it might be fitted with a bayonet.

Confederate cavalry belt, holster, cartridge box, and percussion-cap box.

A Texas revolver made by George Todd in Austin, Texas, shortly before the war.

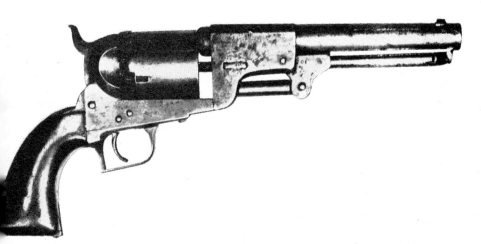

A Texas revolver of the Civil War period. Made by Tucker Sherrod & Co.

Texas revolver made by Dance Bros. during the Civil War. These revolvers were made hout recoil shields.

Confederate wood canteens. Because of the scarcity of metal, the Confederates were forced to rely upon many substitutes.

Confederate belt plates and buckles from Texas and Louisiana.

Confederate infantry percussion-cap box. This has "C.S." stamped on the cover. Most were devoid of marking.

Typical Confederate general's uniform. Worn by Brig. General Marcus J. Wright, C.S.A.

Confederate accoutrement: 1. Iron bridle bit with brass rosette on which is a large "C." 2. Brass stirrup. 3. Brass spur.

Confederate coastal battery. This picture was taken at Pensacola, Florida. It is typical of those batteries which defended the long coastline of Texas.

Hill to Maj. Thos. G. Rhett, Chf. of Ord. DTM, Shreveport, La.

Please send Capt. Faulkner an order to supply me with as many buckles for waist belts as you can spare. My wagons will call for them on their return from Jefferson. (Sent by telegraph from Henderson, Texas.)

THURSDAY, AUG. 25, 1864

General A. P. Hill's corps of Lee's Army inflicted a crushing blow upon the Second and Eleventh Corps of the Union Army at Reams Station, outside of Petersburg, Va. The Confederate loss was 720 killed and wounded while the Federals lost 669 killed and wounded and 2,073 captured.

SATURDAY, AUG. 27, 1864

Hill to Capt. C. C. Green, Asst. to Chf. of Ord. DTM in chg. Shreveport, La.

The ammunition for the Indian Territory was sent on the 1st inst. in full of the requisition. I was under the impression that you had been notified of the shipment until the receipt of your letter.

On the 23rd June, I sent: 45,000 buck and ball crtges
                             50,000 musket per. caps

On the 1st Aug., I sent: 30,000 buck & ball crtges
                             73,000 Enfield crtges
                             40,000 Miss. ctrges
                             10,000 Belg. crtges
                             10,000 Rifle musket crtges
                            200,000 musket perc. caps
                             50,000 sporting perc. caps

The remainder called for in the requisition.

SUNDAY, AUG. 28, 1864

A Dispatch from the Army of the Potomac tonight said; "Not a gun was fired from daylight to dark tonight in front of Petersburg."

Hill to Capt. C. C. Green, Asst. to Chf. of Ord. DTM in Charge, Shreveport, La.

My men are very much in need of some money and I would like to be able to pay them some as soon as possible.

C. G. Clark left yesterday for Shreveport to appear before the Board for the examination for ordnance officers. He will start on his return about next Friday. Please send by him any funds you have for my department.

Confederate Ordnance Regulations provided that all officers assigned to ordnance duty with troops in the field should report directly to the head of the Bureau. In the event an ordnance officer was not assigned by the Bureau, corps, division and brigade commanders were to designate their own ordnance officers, to be known as Chiefs of Ordnance, Division and Brigade Ordnance Officers respectively. In order that only capable men might be detailed to the Corps, the Adjutant-General wisely announced certain educational requirements necessary, and in addition created an examining board. The Board was composed of Col. T. S. Rhett, Col. W. LeRoy Broun, Maj. S. Stansbury and Capt. Benj. Sloan. These officers visited the various armies in the field and examined candidates who had made application for appointment in the ordnance service. Notice of examinations was required to be published in the Richmond *Enquirer*. It was provided that no candidate could be commissioned to the rank of captaincy unless proficient in the subjects of algebra, trigonometry, mechanics and chemistry. Brig.-Gen. Benj. Huger, formerly of the U. S. Ordnance Corps, had been appointed Inspector General of Artillery and Ordnance, and enforcing regulations of the service came under his purview. A waiting list or register was provided of those who passed the examinations but for whom no vacancy existed, the successful candidates to be given rank according to merit when finally appointed. Examination for promotion was also prescribed. In short, in matters of personnel, the Bureau was so proficient that today's United States Civil Service Commission is a direct outgrowth of this service.

TUESDAY, SEPT. 6, 1864

Hill to Capt. C. C. Green, Asst. to Chief of Ord., D.T.M. in Charge.

I enclose to you a copy of an order detailing private C. M. Bivens, Adam's Co., 12th Brigade, Texas State Troops. As the organization of State Troops has been abolished, and under an order of General Green all belonging to the same, that have been detailed, are required to be conscripted and re-detailed if necessary. Priv. Bivens has been enrolled, and I fear I shall lose him unless I can get him detailed again. He is one of my tanners, and the best one I have. He furnishes more leather and better than any other. Please have him detailed as a conscript from Smith County, and ordered to report to me for duty as a tanner.

WEDNESDAY, SEPT. 7, 1864

Hill to Capt. W. A. Pitts, Chf. Ord. Off., N.S.D., Bonham, Texas.

Your requisition dated July 25th, for: 1,500 canteens, the same number of straps, 20,000 buckshot cartridges, 20,000 Colt navy cartridges and 4,040 Sharps ditto, are received.

The canteens and straps and Colt's navy cartridges are now ready and I can give them to you at any time when you send for them. The buckshot and Sharps carbine cartridges I shall have to make, and I have no powder on hand at present suitable to make them of. As soon as I can get some powder, which I shall try to do as soon as possible, I will make them, and inform you when to send for them.

When you send your wagons, invoice and send along your damaged ammunition and unserviceable guns, and I will receipt to you for same.

Hill to Capt. C. C. Green, Asst. to Chf. of Ord., D.T.M., in Charge.

I have just received request for 1,500 canteens, 1,500 straps, 20,000 b-shot cartridges, 20,000 Colt navy ditto, and 4,040 Sharps carbine ditto, for Capt. W. A. Pitts, Chief Ordnance Officer, NSD Texas.

The canteens and Navy Pistol cartridges are ready, but I have no powder on hand fit to make the Buckshot and Sharps carbine cartridges. It requires good rifle powder and I wish therefore you would take the necessary steps to supply me. Please furnish the powder as soon as possible.

About the time that Col. Hill was writing the above, Northern newspapers were featuring President Lincoln's "thanks of the nation" to General Sherman for the capture of Atlanta, and to Admiral Farragut and General Canby for the victory at Mobile. Such news, while shocking to the South, was nevertheless not entirely unexpected. More shocking was the news that Major General John H. Morgan of Kentucky, "Morgan the Terrible Raider," was killed at Greenville in east Tennessee by soldiers of General Gillem's Union cavalry. Morgan, with a handful of men, had retreated to Greenville and the Union troops swooped down upon the town. After the fight, Morgan's body was found in the front yard of a house, shot through the heart. No other Confederate soldier was with him when he was killed, and conflicting stories of his death were told afterwards. It was said that the Union cavalry was notified by a woman of Morgan's presence in the town. At any rate, the South lost a gallant and splendid soldier, and at a time when all such were needed.

FRIDAY, SEPT. 9, 1864

Hill to M. Williams, Capt. & AQM, Tyler, Texas.

I have ready to forward 15 boxes. 12 contg. canteens (207 lbs each—2,484 lbs), 2 contg. cav. cart. boxes (310 lbs each—620 lbs), and 1 contg. Inf. cart. boxes—250 lbs. Total weight 3,354 lbs.

Making 3,354 lbs in the aggregate. The boxes are large and it is not so much the weight as the inconvenience of packing. It will require 2 wagons. They are to be sent to Marshall, to be forwarded from that place to Shreveport.

Please inform me when you can furnish transportation for same?

Hill to Capt. C. C. Green, Asst. to Chf. of Ord., DTM., in Charge.

I herewith enclose receipts for $20,000 as requested in your letter of Sept. 8, 1864.

Please return receipts given by Mr. Charles J. Clark for $18,000.

Hill to Maj. Thos. G. Rhett, Chf. Ord & Arty., Shreveport DTM.

As you directed when here, I now apprise you of my many wants, that you may have them filled if possible. I am very much in need of powder and caps, and would like very much to get another invoice of the Enfield Rifle barrels—if any more are to be had, as I have stocked nearly all that have been sent me. Of the 500 ordered, I have only received 250. I would like also to get about a doz. of the fine calf skins which were sent from Mexico. If possible, let me have some nails, 6 & 8, for I am entirely out. Please also send me some of the linen, and have made for me the griddle for cooking cakes.

I will send a train to Shreveport or Marshall either, for the things as soon as I am notified I can get them.

Baltimore newspapers were filled with the story of a duel between Col. John S. Mosby, the famous ranger and Col E. V. White of the Loudoun Rangers. Col. Mosby was said to have been killed. Fortunately for the Confederacy, the entire story was a canard. The same paper carried an account of two women wearing the uniforms of Union cavalrymen who were sent to Baltimore by the provost marshal at Harpers Ferry, and committed to jail. They gave their names as: Kate Johnson of Parkersburg and Emma Frances of Martinsburg (both West Virginia), and said they were regularly enlisted members of the 11th West Virginia Cavalry.

Hill to Brig. Gen. H. E. McCulloch, Comdg., N. S. Dist., Bonham, Texas.

Yours of the 9th received. The arms, etc. for Col. Duff will be ready by the 10th day of Oct.

If it can be arranged so that the wagons can arrive here about that time, it will be well, as the stores can be sent then without any delay.

Hill to Maj. Thos. G. Rhett, Chf. Ord & Arty., Shreveport DTM.

There is only one surgeon at this Post, and he has more than he can do to attend to all the sick belonging to all the Departments at this Post. I have now 240 in my Department and necessarily at all times there are some of them sick, and it is impossible for the Post Surgeon to give them the necessary attention owing to the burden of business on his hands. I would like, in order that the sick in my Department might be properly attended to, to have a Surgeon assigned to duty for the Ordnance Works in my charge. Until such is the case, my men while sick will necessarily suffer for want of proper medical attention, which has already been the case. My men are good hands, and labour steadily and cheerfully in the performance of their duty while well, and I desire to see them properly attended to when sick.

They have already complained to me for want of attention. I do not intend to charge the Post Surgeon with anything like neglect of duty, for he is at all times diligent in the performance of same, but he has now, and has had here-to-fore, more to do than any one Surgeon can perform.

Hoping that this request may be granted.

The siege of Petersburg, Va., was now on in full force. The Richmond *Examiner* said the Union forces had been shelling that city with great fury for several days past.

"Night or day, there was no cessation of the deluge of shot and shell." Scores of houses were wrecked.

Hill to Col. Ben. Allston, Ins. Gen., DTM.

In obedience to your request, I have the honour to present to you the following report of commissioned officers, detailed men, and employees in the Ordnance Works at Tyler, Texas.

1—Lt. Col., Comdg. Works, 2 captains—one in charge of armory and one of laboratory and shops, 1 1st Lieut., ACS & AQM for ord. works, 1 acting MSK, overage and exempt, 1 Asst. A.M.S.K., overage and exempt, 1 clerk—surgeon certificate, 3 clerks—citizen employees, 2 being discharged soldiers, 1 Master Armorer, 2 foremen, 1 draftsman, 1 machinist, 50 armorers, 21 blacksmiths, 13 carpenters, 26 harnessmakers, 1 butcher, 4 tanners, 3 in leadshop (all on surgeons cert.), 2 labortorians, 2 tinners, 1 coal burner, 10 guards (1 overage, 2 surgeons cert.),—total 148. There are employed at these works, 85 negroes (48 cartridge makers—small boys), 25 laborers (burning coal, strikers at Armory etc.) 6 teamsters, 6 women (spinning and cooking).

The above gives us a pretty clear picture of the personnel which comprised the Ordnance Works, Tyler, Texas, Lt. Col. G. H. Hill, Comdg.

Hill to Capt. J. Q. St. Clair, AQM, Tyler, Texas.

Yours of this date just rec'd, and I have ordered one of my men to report to you that can repair the Mill, but I must decline in future doing any more work of that kind as it is the Quartermaster's duty to do such work, and not mine. I would have declined furnishing a man at this time, but I know how hard pressed your Department is for Meal, Flour, etc, that I have done it as a favor.

Hill to Maj. George D. Alexander, Comg. Arsenal, Marshall, Texas.

On the 23rd of June 1864, I rec'd from Lt. B. F. Atkinson, Ord. Officer, Fort Washita, C. N., 6,884 ¾ lbs Rifle powder, 26 lbs cannon ditto, which was damaged.

I sent you a part of it today. The remainder I will send by the 1st opportunity when I will send also invoices and receipts for same.

I will send your Barrels to you when I send the rest of the damaged powder.

A train to which was attached a special car carrying General Grant and some of his staff returning from Philadelphia to Washington, collided with a string of freight cars near Havre de Grace, Md. The cars were wrecked and passengers on the train badly shaken up. The General was said to have narrowly escaped injury. Doubtlessly there were many in the South who were disappointed by this latter fact. One cannot help speculating upon the vastness of results had Grant been killed or even injured.

FRIDAY, SEPT. 16, 1864

Hill to Capt. C. C. Green, Asst. to Chf. Ord. Off. DTM.

The 4,000 lbs of powder is rec'd from Capt. Faulkner.

I had no ammunition on hand of any consequence outside of that necessary to fill orders already on file with which to load the wagons on their return.

I have been out of powder for sometime heretofore, and have not therefore made much ammunition, and what has been made was necessary to file requisitions for the Indian Country etc.

I loaded the wagons with damaged powder rec'd from Indian Country, to Major Alexander.

Hill to Maj. Gen. B. Huger, In Chg. Ord. Bur., Marshall, Texas.

Since I have been on duty in charge of these works, I have never rec'd a general order nor a copy of one, either emanating from the War Dept. or Dept. Headquarters. I am sometimes referred to several orders and can never find the order referred to.

If it is possible, you will greatly oblige me by arranging it in someway that I may receive copies of the several orders, that I may keep posted and know how to regulate my works.

Only one who works for the Government can know how frustrating, how exasperating it can be to be referred to (and told to comply with), an order which has never been received.

Hill to Maj. Issac Read, Chf. of Nitre & Mining Corps, DTM, San Antonio, Texas.

I rec'd from W. L. Abbott today the last lead sent by you. It was rec'd by me as follows:

Aug. 17th—31 slabs— 4,884 lbs—Swink
Aug. 29th—20 slabs— 3,501 lbs—Mitchell
Sept. 3rd—38 slabs— 6,249 lbs—Abbott & Hamilton
Sept. 16th—83 slabs—13,722 lbs—W. L. Abbott

———— ————
  172   28,356

You see it falls short 349 pds which I must think is caused by the difference in weights, as the pieces were whole and bore no evidence of any part having been taken from them, and the whole number of pieces were rec'd (except 1 piece brought by W. L. Abbott which he says he cut on the way and took off 23 lbs.)

I have corrected your invoices and send you recpts for the amount rec'd by me. I have paid the freight on the 2 last shipments, that by Abbott & Hamilton, and that by W. L. Abbott at $3.00 per hundred, per hundred miles.

SATURDAY, SEPT. 17, 1864

Hill to Capt. S. C. Faulkner, Comg. Ord. Depot, Marshall, Texas.

Enclosed please find receipts for 4,017 lbs of Rifle Powder and 23 gross of buckles rec'd from you a few days ago.

Quite obviously, Marshall, Texas, must have been the site of considerable ordnance activity. Here, according to addresses on Col. Hill's letters already examined, was an Arsenal, an Ordnance Depot (in charge of funneling supplies stored at the Arsenal), and here also was located Maj. General Ben. Huger, "In Charge, Ordnance Bureau."

Hill to Maj. Thos. G. Rhett, Chf. Ord & Arty., Shreveport DTM.

On the 29th June, 1864, I addressed to you a communication stating that I would soon be out of spring steel; that I had been using old circular saws, that there were a good many more in the county, useless to the persons who owned them, but who would not sell them, and asking you to obtain an order from the Comg. Gen'l permitting me to impress them.

I again call your attention to the matter and request that an order may be obtained, otherwise I shall soon have to discontinue finishing guns entirely for want of spring steel.

Think of an operation as large and as essential as the Ordnance Works, Tyler, Texas, main source of supply of arms and ammunition for the Confederate Armies of the Trans-Mississippi Dept., being forced to cease operations for the lack of a few old circular saws, to be used for making the various springs essential in the manufacture of rifles. Reading such letters, and considering carefully their import, the amazing fact is, not that the South was defeated, but that she managed to hold out for four long years!

TUESDAY, SEPT. 20, 1864

Hill to Maj. Gen. Ben Huger, Chf. of Ord. Bur., Marshall, Texas.

I have been trying in every way since I have been here to get a surgeon ordered into duty with my works. I have endeavored to get one through Major Rhett and have also tried through Surgeon Haden but have failed, and I now apply to you as the Chief of the Ordnance Department, DTM, hoping that you will use your influence and get ordered to report to me if possible a surgeon or assistant surgeon. It is absolutely necessary that we should have one as my men are now shamefully neglected and I have no way at all to have them properly attended to. I have 300 men in my Dept. which are allowed medical attention. I have a great many men now sick and they are scattered all about for want of Hospital room. If I had a surgeon of my own, I would very soon have me a hospital in which I could take care of my men, but now my sick are absolutely suffering for want of medical attention and I do earnestly beg of you to give this your earliest attention as my Dept. is very much crippled for want of a proper medical officer.

THURSDAY, SEPT. 22, 1864

Hill to Capt. C. C. Green, Asst. to Chf. of Ord., DTM, Shreveport.

Enclosed you will find receipts for $20,000 sent to me by you for my signature, as the first sent by me were informal.

I have rec'd from Capt. Wailey the 3,000 lbs of Leather (sole). I was glad to receive it and would be glad to receive more, as it is with the utmost difficulty that I can keep my harness shop in operation for want of leather.

On the 13th inst., I rec'd from Capt. Faulkner, 4,017 lbs Rifle Powder which will be entirely consumed by the 6th or 7th of Oct. I would like to receive more from some quarter by that time.

Hill to Maj. Geo. D. Alexander, Comg. Arsenal, Marshall, Texas.

Yours of Sept. 16th is rec'd. I am glad to hear that you will be able to furnish me with powder, and particularly so as it is a good article.

I rec'd on the 15th inst. 4,017 of Rifle Powder from Marshall which will be expended by the 6th or 7th of Oct., by which time I would like to be furnished with more.

At least one less Texan was alive on this date, he being, George W. McDonald, alias M. M. Dunning, who was shot to death by a firing squad at Fort McHenry, Baltimore, Md., for desertion. He made a speech declaring that he deserved his fate and that death had no terror for him. According to the records, McDonald was a deserter from both sides. He was a member of a Confederate Texas Regiment, was taken prisoner at Antietam in 1862, and sent to Fort Delaware Prison. When the 3rd Maryland Cavalry

[109]

was organized largely of Confederate deserters, McDonald joined it. He soon deserted and escaped from Baltimore. Being pursued, he took refuge in a farmhouse in Montgomery county where he held a company of soldiers at bay until the house was fired. He was 35 years old.

SATURDAY, SEPT. 24, 1864

Hill to Maj. Thos. G. Rhett, Chf. Ord. & Arty., Shreveport, DTM.

I am nearly out of tin. Have only enough to keep my tinners at work 10 days. Please have me supplied.

Hill to Maj. Thos. G. Rhett, Chf. Ord & Arty., Shreveport DTM.

Capt. Polleys who was in Marshall on leave of absence a few days ago, informs me that while there, he saw Maj. Gen. Huger turn over to Maj. Alexander "or to his clerk Mr. Neely," $60,000 to pay the expenses of his Dept. and that he heard Gen. Huger remark at the time that he had plenty of money.

My men have only rec'd a small portion of their pay that is due them and stand very much in need of more money. There are bills outstanding against my Dept. and those to whom I am indebted are very anxious to get the money.

If such a thing is possible, I would like to have enough money to pay off everything against the Dept. I write this as much as a suggestion as anything else. I am not disposed to be troublesome on the subject, but am very desirous to be furnished with money if possible.

Hill to Maj. Thos. G. Rhett, Chf. Ord. & Arty., Shreveport DTM.

Yours of Sept. 19th is at hand. I have rec'd the 4,000 lbs Powder from Marshall and will expend the same by the 6th or 7th Oct., at which time, I would like to be supplied with more.

I wish you could send me some sporting caps for putting up pistol cartridges.

I will send next week, if I can obtain transportation from the AQM, (and I think I can), 1,572 Canteens, 8,400 Navy cartridges, 21,000 Army pistol crtgs, 8,000 Buck & Ball crtgs., 110,000 Miss. cartg. and 43,000 Enfield Rifle ditto.

MONDAY, SEPT. 26, 1864

Hill to Capt. J. M. Williams, AQM, Tyler, Texas.

Col. Allston, Insp. Gen., TMD ordered me to turn over to you 483 sporting rifle moulds weighing 96 lbs, as that much old iron, they being entirely unfit for any purpose in the Ord. Dept., to be expended by you in making horseshoe nails.

Very little seemed to be wasted in the Trans-Mississippi Dept. of the Confederacy. When an article ceased to be useful it was converted into something else.

On this day the Trans-Mississippi Dept. had some small cause for rejoicing. Gen. Sterling Price with 12,000 men, of whom only 8,000 were armed, began what is known as the Missouri Raid on Sept. 1, 1864. The Yankee army retreated steadily before him, and by the 25th, General Shelby's cavalry had occupied Frederickstown, Mo. On the 27th, General Price began his attack on Pilot Knob, Mo., defended by General Ewing, who evacuated the place the next day and retreated to Lexington. Although victories for the South, they were small, and had little bearing on the overall result. Nevertheless, at this point, any victory, regardless of size, was welcomed in the Confederacy. Speaking of size, fashion notes observed that "hoop skirts would not be worn so large." Regardless of war or peace, victory or defeat, women must obey the dictates of fashion.

Hill to Capt. C. W. Wailey, Comg. Shreveport Arsenal, La.

Enclosed, please find invoices and receipts for 1,296 tin canteens. Please sign and return receipts as soon as rec'd.

Hill to Maj. Thos. G. Rhett, Chf. Ord. & Arty., Shreveport DTM.

I am nearly out of gun barrels. If Maj. Alexander or Capt. Wailey have any on hand, please order a lot to be sent to me. I have used all the old sporting barrels that will make a gun and have on hand now only about 100 old Enfield Rifle barrels.

I wrote you last week that I expected to be able to send you a train of ammunition, but the AQM says that he cannot furnish me with the necessary transportation. If the ammunition is much needed, if you will have an order issued for the Quartermaster to forward at once, I think he will then send it forward.

The above is conclusive proof that at least a portion of the rifles and arms made at the Tyler Ordnance Works were made by turning down old sporting rifle barrels and those from old or damaged Enfields.

Hill to Maj. Thos. G. Rhett, Chf. Ord. & Arty., Shreveport DTM.

In obedience to your circular of date Sept. 24, 1864, I herewith have the honor to furnish the enclosed certified statement of funds of old issue deposited by me up to this date. I shall have on hand on 1 Oct., about $350 or $500 of five dollar bills of old issue for deposit.

A Certified Statement of Funds deposited by Lt. Col. G. H. Hill, Comdg., Ord. Works, Tyler, Texas, Aug. 6, 1864.

Amount deposited at C. S. Depository at Shreveport, La. Old Treasury notes for receipts. $23,780.00.

> Ord. Office, Tyler, Texas,
> Sept. 30, 1864.

I certify on honor that the above's a correct statement of all funds of the old issue deposited by me with the C. S. Depository to the credit of the Confederate States Treasury.

Thinking in terms of money, according to the *Savannah Republican,* the bombardment of Atlanta by Sherman had caused damage estimated at $5,000,000. Forty-seven buildings were wrecked. Four hundred and ninety-seven persons were killed and six hundred and ninety-one were wounded.

SATURDAY, OCT. 1, 1864

Hill to Capt. Polleys, In Charge of Armory, Tyler, Texas

You will make all your arrangements at once for burning 500,000 brick for making additions to the Armory. When agreed upon, Mr. Goff, now on duty with Lt. Woods, will report to you with 5 hands, and you can put him in charge of the brick yard. You will do everything in your power to facilitate the contemplated addition to the Armory. Hire as many negroes as possible and in fact do everything in your power to hasten the work.

You can make a drawing of the ground floor and side view of the addition to be added, and send it to this office as soon as possible.

MONDAY, OCT. 3, 1864

Hill to Capt. J. L. StClair, AQM, Tyler, Texas.

Enclosed you will find your letter of Sept. 20, 1864 to Maj. Thomas with Endorsements, and also an order on Capt. G. S. Polleys, Comdg. C. S. Armory, to repair for you a corn sheller.

If you will send your corn sheller out to the Armory with the order, it will be repaired, if possible.

Please return the enclosed letter, as the endorsements are necessary to me to show my authority for having the work done.

Hill to Capt. G. S. Polleys, In Charge, C. S. Armory, Tyler Texas.

I shall leave in the morning on a leave of absence for ten days, and I may be absent longer if I can succeed in getting my leave extended.

You will be in command of the works during my absence and before leaving, I will give you my idea of how I should like to have things conducted during my absence, and as I shall be absent only a short time, I would be very glad if you will try to carry out my plans as nearly as possible.

In the 1st place, we should do everything we can to burn the

[113]

500,000 bricks for building the contemplated addition to our Armory. To do this, you will have to hire as many negroes as required, to cut wood and make shingles and get stone for the foundation. I think that 30 negro fellows will be enough. The shingles I would order Mr. Turnbow to get, giving him the hands for that purpose. I would hire as many as 15 or 20 more 6 mule teams and wagons if possible, and order Lt. Woods to get as much corn and fodder possible, and have it stacked and stored.

In making brick, I would use the little negroes in the Laboratory. You must at once try to make arrangements for what lumber you immediately need and I will make arrangements for the work permanently as soon as I return.

The magazine must be built at once as it is very much needed and use for that purpose the brick we have on hand. The harness makers, let them go on with their usual work. Try and send to Shreveport or Marshall all ammunition and equipment as soon as fabricated.

It would appear that Capt. Polleys would be something more than busy during the following ten days if he carried out all of his commanding officer's wishes.

TUESDAY, OCT. 4, 1864

Hill to Capt. S. C. Faulkner, Comg. Ord. Depot, Marshall, Texas.

I send to you today by wagon, 75 boxes containing 75,000 Enfield Rifle Crtges, marked to Capt. C. W. Wailey, Shreveport Arsenal, and 1 barrel sugar and 2 sacks flour marked to Maj. Thos. G. Rhett, Shreveport, La., all of which you will please forward as soon as possible to Shreveport.

I have rec'd the powder, but no invoices.

Hill to Maj. Thos. G. Rhett, Chf. Ord. & Arty., Shreveport DTM.

I send today by wagon, 75,000 Enfield Rifle Crtges marked to Capt. C. W. Wailey, to Capt. S. C. Faulkner at Marshall, to be forwarded as soon as possible to Capt. Wailey. I could not send any more for want of transportation.

I have both accoutrements and ammunition on hand, packed

and ready to send, and will forward as rapidly as I can get wagons
to haul.

*Hill to Maj. Thos. G. Rhett, Chf. Ord. & Arty., Shreveport
DTM.*

It is impossible to hire negroes and teams at scheduled prices
unless I am allowed to give more. I cannot proceed with the building operations. The least at which negroes can be hired here is
$2.50 per day. The machinery and hands from Marshall and
Anderson could be usefully employed here before the improve-
ments are completed, which will be by the 1st of Jan. if I can
get permission to employ at such prices as the necessary forces
can be obtained.

There is ready to forward: 10,400 Navy Pistol Cart., 21,000
Army ditto, 114,000 Miss. Rifle ditto, 13,000 Belgium Rifle ditto,
29,000 Enfield Rifle ditto, 48,000 Rifles Musket ditto, 92,000 B &
Ball ditto.

Besides, a lot of accoutrements ready and more ready to pack.

The AQM can not furnish transportation without an order
authorizing him to impress.

*Capt. G. S. Polleys, Comdg. Ord. Works, Tyler, Texas, to
Issac Reed, Maj. & Chief, Nitre & Mining Corps, D.T.M.*

Yours of Sept. 28th was rec'd this morning and in answer to
your requests, will briefly state that the lots of lead spoken of,
was correctly and carefully weighed, and can not be reweighed
as part of the same has been expended.

You were receipted for the exact amount of lead rec'd and it
is not customary to acknowledge the receipt of more of an article
than is rec'd.

Freight was paid only on the amount received here, and not on
the whole amount stated by you to have been sent.

This is the first letter written by Capt. Polleys during
Col. Hill's absence on leave. Judging from this letter, and
bearing in mind that it was written to an officer superior
in rank, it would seem safe to assume that here was one

man who was not going to be shoved around. The letter of course is a follow-up of Col. Hill's to Maj. Reed dated Sept. 16th. Evidently Maj. Reed had insisted that Tyler Ord. Works receipt for 28,705 pounds of lead instead of the 28,356 pounds which were actually received.

Polleys to Capt. John I. Wood, Enl. Officer, Anderson County, Texas.

Yours of Oct. 7th enclosing special requisitions for ammunition is rec'd. You do not say what kind of ammunition you want. You say '600 rounds of fixed ammunition.' I can not tell what you want.

If you will state what kind of ammunition you want, I will send it. Please state whether you want Buck & Ball, or Buckshot, or Mississippi Rifle, or what kind of cartridges, if any, you want.

On this same date, there were two items of interest appearing in Richmond papers. The *Whig* denied the reported death of Gen. Adam Johnson in Kentucky. General Johnson had both eyes shot out, but afterward returned to duty and reorganized his command. He was unique as the only blind general in modern history.

The *Enquirer* confirmed the death of Mrs. Rose O'Neal Greenhow, Confederate spy and dispatch bearer. Mrs. Greenhow was trying to run the blockade into Wilmington, N. C., with dispatches for President Davis. The blockade runner was chased ashore by Union gunboats. Mrs. Greenhow attempted to escape in a small boat which overturned, and she was drowned.

WEDNESDAY, OCT. 12, 1864

Col. Hill evidently returned sooner than expected for the "Day Book" continues with letters signed by him.

Hill to Capt. S. C. Faulkner, Comg. Ord. Depot, Marshall, Texas.

Enclosed please find receipts for 5,011 lbs of Rifle Powder, 120 yds striped linen, 100 powder kegs, rec'd from you a few days ago.

*Hill to Maj. Thos. G. Rhett, Chf. Ord. & Arty., Shreveport
DTM.*

It will be impossible for me to do anything in the way of
building until I can get transportation. My officers by my order
have been all over the county trying to hire, and they report
that it is impossible to hire wagons and transportation with
Confederate money, that the people say that they do not want
Confederate money, but if we pay special which they can get
from the contractors for hauling cotton, that we can get their
teams, but without special, we can't have them.

I have my lumber to haul 18 miles, and require now about
20 or 25 wagons and teams.

I respectfully request that you procure me an order from the
Comdg. Gen'l, allowing me to impress such transportation as I
require. I am hard at work making bricks and by 1st of Nov. will
have them ready to go to work putting up my buildings. All I
now require is transportation and negroes. The latter I can get,
but the former I shall have to impress.

THURSDAY, OCT. 13, 1864

*Hill to Maj. Thos. G. Rhett, Chf. Ord. & Arty., Shreveport
DTM.*

I have the honor to submit the following as my report of operations during the last quarter at the Tyler Ordnance Works.

We have *FABRICATED* at the Armory during the quarter:
140 long Hill rifles, 70 short Hill rifles, 7 long Texas rifles, 13
rifled muskets, 181 Enfield rifles; in all, amounting to 411 guns.

REPAIRED: 43 Texas rifles, 48 Mississippi rifles, 39 muskets,
31 musketoons, 5 double-barrel shotguns—in all, 160 guns.

Also much work done in repairing and making tools for the
other departments.

We have on hand only 100 barrels in all left, and unless we
receive more, we will be forced into just making spare parts and
not guns. The men at the Armory are in good discipline and are
well managed. Capt. Polleys is in immediate charge at the
Armory, and does a good job.

The *CARPENTER SHOP*

FABRICATED: 305 ammunition boxes, 24 chests, 39 packing boxes, 3 coffins, 6 tables, 3 tool chests, 13 boxes of different sizes, 2 benches, 1 shotmachine, 1 tallow press, 8 single trees, 12 window shutters, 1 platform for weighing heavy weights, 6 mallets, 1 wagon bed, 30 cartridge and cap box formers, 6 binding blocks. The shop also finished quarters for the men, the office and coal shed, also spring house. Nails and lumber are urgently needed. All lumber has to be hauled 18 miles.

The *TIN SHOP*

FABRICATED: 3,531 canteens, 1,250 cavalry and 11 infantry magazines for cartridge boxes, 4,500 burrs, 500 canteen straphooks, 625 gunsling hooks, 20 tin cups, 35 tin plates, 28 tin pans and any quantity of other little things. My tinners are both excellent men. I am entirely out of tin.

LABORATORY, out of material, and worked only a short portion of time.

FABRICATED: 173,240 Enfield Rifle Cgtrs., 59,720 rifle musket ditto, 26,140 Buck & Ball ditto, 51,130 Mississippi Rifle ditto, 22,960 Belgium Rifle ditto, 20,180 Buck-shot ditto, 7,000 Sharps carbine ditto, 5,190 Navy pistol ditto, 15,746 Army pistol ditto, 500 blank test ditto. We have moulded: balls for the Enfield, Rifle musket, Musket, Mississippi Rifle, Belgium, Army pistol, and Buckshot. Besides this work I have made 59½ gal. neats foot oil, 3,364½# tallow and 41½# thread.

The *HARNESS SHOP*

FABRICATED: 1,707 cavalry crtg. boxes, 230 infantry crtg. boxes, 2,674 cap boxes, 2,128 waist belts, 47 sabre belts, 10 saddles, 23 saddle trees, 32 pair of stirrups, 2,583 canteen straps, 925 gun slings, 1 set of cart harness, 3 breast straps and 3 halter bridles.

Considering the circumstances under which he labored, Col. Hill's quarterly report is most commendable.

FRIDAY, OCT. 14, 1864

Hill to Maj. Thos. G. Rhett, Chf. Ord. & Arty., Shreveport DTM.

I have a number of men from the Reserve Corps turned over to me as guards.

I have only 3 men to the post, and these 3 men are on duty all the time—2 hours on post and 4 hours off. The duty is much harder than the duty in the field in a regiment or company, and I wish to know whether or not they are entitled to extra duty pay. I should think that they were, and all my mechanics would rather do any kind of work than to stand guard for a week, as it is the hardest duty we have in the Dept.

Please let me know as soon as possible whether or not I am to give them extra duty pay?

No doubt that standing guard is unpleasant duty, but whether "the duty is much harder than the duty in the field in a regiment or company," is something else. Possibly some of the men from Lee's Army of Northern Virginia fresh from the trenches in front of Richmond or Petersburg might question such a statement and Col. Hill's letter requesting extra duty pay for same.

Hill to Maj. Thos. G. Rhett, Chf. Ord. & Arty., Shreveport DTM.

I am entirely out of nails. What am I to do for them in building my new Armory and Shops? I understood that you had some at Navasota or some other place between this and San Antonio. If you have any on the way here, and could give me an order for some of them, I think I might hurry them up by sending an agent down for them. It will be impossible for me to do much without nails.

Hill to Lt. Col. Soule, Commandant, Slave Labor Bureau, Trans Miss. Dept., Shreveport, La.

I have the honor to respectfully apply for 50 negro fellows for duty in my Dept. I am now very much in need of them, as I am adding to and enlarging my works.

MONDAY, OCT. 17, 1864

Hill to Capt. S. C. Faulkner, Comg. Ord. Depot, Marshall, Texas.

I enclose you invoices and receipts for 300 cavalry cartridge boxes, 900 infantry ditto, 1,200 cap boxes and 1,200 waist belts. Please sign and return receipts as same are received.

I sent in the same wagon, 4 barrels flour for Mrs. N. A. Gains which you will please deliver, also, 1 box containing 8 lbs glue for Maj. Alexander, and 1 keg of vinegar for yourself.

The stores rec'd from you are all right except the files. There were rec'd from you 24½ doz. files altogether. The mill files are wanting. I enclose you the invoices and receipts which you will please correct and return and I will sign the receipts and return them to you.

P.S.—The boxes are all right, and I suppose the files were left out in packing.

TUESDAY, OCT. 18, 1864

Hill to Capt. John J. Word, Enl. Officer, Anderson, Texas.

I send to you by stage in 2 ammunition packing boxes, 750 sporting percussion caps, 6 lbs Rifle powder, 20 lbs buck-shot.

I enclose to you special requisition with recpts. Please sign the certificate to the requisition and the recpts and return by mail.

Hill to Capt. T. A. Fluellen, En. R.Off. Smith Co.

Yours of this date just rec'd, and as I do not recognize your authority to give me orders in relation to my men or anything else in my Dept., I return your communication and shall totally disregard its contents.

Col. Hill plainly was not lacking in the ability to straighten out a junior officer.

WEDNESDAY, OCT. 19, 1864

Hill to Capt. W. A. Pitts, Chf. Ord. Off., NSD, Bonham, Texas.

Enclosed please find invoices and receipts for 19,800 Navy Pistol Crtgs., 20,000 Buckshot ditto, 40,000 Sharps carbine ditto, 1,512 tin canteens, and 1,512 canteen straps, sent by wagon to you a few days ago. I sent them by the same train of ordnance stores for Col. Duff. Please sign and return receipts as soon as the stores are rec'd.

Please get the glass from Capt. Allen and send it as soon as possible.

Newspapers carried an account of 23 armed Confederates who made a raid from Canada upon St. Albans, Vt., and carried off a large amount of gold from the local banks. Depending upon whose ox was being gored, they were "bank robbers" or "dashing heroes."

THURSDAY, OCT. 20, 1864

Hill to Maj. Thos. G. Rhett, Chf. Ord. & Arty., Shreveport TMD.

On the 15th I forwarded to Capt. Faulkner, Comg. Ord. Depot Marshall, 1,200 cartridge boxes, 1,200 cap boxes and 1,200 waist belts.

On the 17th, I forwarded to Capt. W. A. Pitts, Chf. Ord. Off., NSD, Bonham, Tex., 19,800 Navy cartridges, 20,000 Buckshot ditto, 4,000 Sharps carbine ditto, 1512 canteens and straps, and on the same day to Col. Duff (Comdg. Regt. Tex. Cav., Bonham, Tex.), 160 Enfield rifles, 300 cavalry cartridge boxes, 410 cap boxes, 374 waist belts, 519 gun slings and 20 sabre belts. I will send to Capt. Wailey the iron and artillery axles as soon as I can possibly get transportation.

There is evidently some strong appeal for uniforms to the ladies of West Virginia. On this date, one Maggie Simpson was brought from Harpers Ferry to Baltimore and there placed in durance vile. She was arrested wearing the uniform of a Union soldier.

TUESDAY, OCT. 25, 1864

Hill to James T. McCowan, AQM, Huntsville, Texas.

Yours of the 20th is just rec'd. I am sorry to inform you that I have no money on hand with which to settle for the cloth furnished to my Dept. by yours. It is being issued to the men and deducted from their pay. As soon as I can get the money, I will send it by messenger to you. I regret very much my inability to do so now.

General Price's Missouri Raid had ended after a defeat at Westport, Mo., by a strong Union force under Generals Pleasanton and Curtis, and a dispatch from Kansas City said that Price's army was in full retreat. At Mine Creek, Mo., he was again defeated and the Confederate Generals Marmaduke and Cabbell were among those captured.

FRIDAY, OCT. 28, 1864

Hill to Maj. Thos. G. Rhett, Chf. Ord. & Arty., Shreveport DTM.

I forwarded yesterday to Capt. C. W. Wailey, 62,000 Enfield Rifle cartridges and 31,000 B & B ditto, and will continue to send forward as rapidly as I can obtain transportation.

The Confederate ram *Albemarle* was sunk at Plymouth, N. C., by a torpedo exploded by Lieut. W. B. Cushing of the Union Navy. Cushing with 14 men, set out in a launch equipped with a spar torpedo which they exploded at night under the ram. Cushing and one man escaped. Two were drowned and 11 captured. Both North and South hailed this venture as one of the most gallant feats of the war.

SATURDAY, OCT. 29, 1864

Hill to Capt. W. H. Lewis, Chief Ord. Off. D. Indian Territory, Fort Towson, C. N.

Enclosed, please find invoices and receipts for 10,105 lbs of lead sent to you today by wagon train.

Hill to Maj. Thos. G. Rhett, Chf. Ord. & Arty., Shreveport DTM.

I have just rec'd from Major Alexander 40 men which he has sent me as armorers. I have never rec'd a copy of any order ordering him to send them to me. If he has been ordered to send them, please let me have a copy of his orders, for he has not sent a tool for them to work with, and it is with great difficulty that I can find them employment until he sends me tools. I understand that he has kept the best gunsmiths and has picked out all of the best tools and intends keeping them. I would respectfully

[122]

ask that these men be sent me and all the gunsmith tools be sent with them, for what men I have are only workmen and to do good work, I must have some fine workmen.

I shall very soon run out of work for lack of material. If possible, send me more files, iron and gun barrels. If there are any Enfield barrels on hand, please send them to me as soon as possible. I would not remove the men from Anderson yet for I have not the room to put them to work and too many sent me here now will only be in each other's way.

Please order me some more lathes and iron placing (planing?) machines.

Maj. Alexander has 2 wood plaining machines. Please order me one of them for it will be impossible for me to do without it.

I have put the Marshall men to work. By the middle of the week will be able to turn out 10 guns per day instead of 5 as heretofore, and will be able to keep this up and put up my buildings at the same time if I am kept in material.

As soon as I get up my other building and get my machinery, I expect I shall be able to do double that amount of work. It is going to be a slow job building for I have not negroes enough to do the work such as cutting wood for burning brick, digging out foundations etc., and another thing, all my lumber has to be hauled 17 miles, but I shall push such things to their uttermost and do the work as fast as possible.

If there is any band iron 1/16 x 2, or 2½ or 3 inches, please send it to me for I am now forging all my bands and steel plates out of old condemned sporting barrels, and it is a very slow process.

Major, I have not a doubt from what I can understand that Maj. Alexander is not going to send me anything that it is possible for him to get around not sending, for the men inform me that all the tools of any value have been picked out and the ones he intends sending me are almost worthless, and that the lathes he intends sending me are almost worn out. I wish my work to pay and want to do a good work and I therefore hope that you will give me the tools and machinery to work with, and therefore respectfully ask that you be very particular and explicit in giving Maj. Alexander orders what to send me for he hates to part with anything. He has more than any man I ever saw, and will not send me a single thing worth having that he can avoid.

Mendelhall, his best workman he keeps. Please let me have him, for as I have the Armory of the Trans Miss., I would like to get the credit of such work as he will be kept at and I ask it as a favor that he be sent me. He can do his pistol work just as well here as at Marshall and then we will get the benefit of his tools which he will keep with him.

This is a long letter and shows many things: a decided friction between Col. Hill and Maj. Alexander; that the Armory at Tyler is producing five guns a day, and hope to raise this total to ten or even higher after the new armory is completed. It shows that barrel bands, butt plates, etc. are being hand forged out of old sporting-rifle barrels. The colonel says that this latter is a slow process, which is believeable. Perhaps the most important facet of this letter is the mention of a "Mendelhall," the best workman at Marshall, who is engaged in some capacity with pistol making. Although it is possible that this referred to some type of single-shot pistol, this seems hardly likely, for by the fall of 1864 energies along this particular line were expended on multi-shot pistols or revolvers. It seems safe to assume that Mr. Mendelhall was engaged in some form of revolver making. However, to date, none of his products have appeared.

TUESDAY, NOV. 1, 1864

Hill to Capt. R. W. Temple, Sups., Gov. Iron Works, Marshall, Texas.

Enclosed you will find accts of 8 yds of Jersey sent you today by wagon master. The cloth is in a bundle and directed to care of Gen'l Huger, and will be left with Capt. Faulkner. You will please sign the papers and remit the money for same as soon as convenient. I sent by the wagon master for the 6 large pots which you sent me order for, I will receipt for same as soon as I get the invoices of the vessels.

Hill to Maj. Thos. G. Rhett, Chf. Ord. & Arty., Shreveport DTM.

Sometime ago, I rec'd a communication stating that an Asst. Surgeon had been ordered to me for duty in my Dept. He has not yet reported and I have a good many of my hands sick, and they are not properly taken care of. I respectfully ask that he or some other be sent me at once that my men may be properly cared for.

It is absolutely necessary that I should have a medical officer. My works are out of town and a man comes and reports himself sick and I have no surgeon to see him, and can not tell whether the man is sick or not. The Post Surgeon has always done what he can, but it very often occurs that it is impossible for him to visit my men or give them proper medical attention.

About this time, six Confederate soldiers were executed at St. Louis in retaliation for the alleged murder of a Major Wilson and six Federal soldiers. The victims were: James W. Gates and George T. Bunch, 3rd Mo. Cav.; Harry H. Blackburn and Charles W. Minniken, Ark. Cav.; John Nichols and Asa R. Ladd, Mo. Cav. They faced the firing squad without a tremor. Minniken made a speech in which he said he had been a good soldier, had never violated the rules of civilized warfare and that he forgave his executioners. Unlike the men at Tyler, Texas, these six were no longer in need of a surgeon's services.

WEDNESDAY, NOV. 2, 1864

Hill to Capt. S. C. Faulkner, Comg. Ord. Depot, Marshall, Texas.

I sent by wagons yesterday, 11 bars—796 lbs iron, 6½ pair iron axles to be forwarded to Capt. Wailey at Shreveport, I sent also, 8 yards Jersey for Capt. Temple, Supt., Gov. Iron Works.

FRIDAY, NOV. 4, 1864

Endorsement

In relation to spare parts of guns and stock timber on hand at Marshall.

[125]

Respectfully forwarded to Maj. Thomas G. Rhett, asking that the locks and all spare parts of guns and stock timber be forwarded as soon as possible as they are very much needed. Please also order all the gunsmiths' tools sent forward as my men all this week have been engaged in making tools for the men sent me from Marshall to work with.

Hill to M. J. Hall, C. S. Depositor, Marshall, Texas.

I Left with your clerk sometime ago, $295.00 in five dollar bills and as you were not in, I asked Capt. B. Huger to call for the certification of deposit, but he informed me that you would not give him the certification without some statement from me as to why I did not deposit it before the 1st of October.

I therefore send you the following certification, and ask that you will send me receipts for same. I certify on honor that the $295 in five dollar bills is money which I had on hand before the 1st of Oct. belonging to the Ordnance Dept. and for which I was accountable to the C. S. Treasury, and that my reason for not having deposited it before was that there was no depository at this place, and I could not leave my business conveniently to go to Marshall to deposit the same before that time.

WEDNESDAY, NOV. 9, 1864

Hill to Major G. Alexander, Comdg., Arsenal, Marshall, Texas.

The following is a complete list of stores rec'd from you on the 18th and 19th: 307 double-barrels, 247 sporting rifle ditto and 480 assorted ditto (rec'd on the 18th). Rec'd on the 19th: 886 sporting barrels, 32 assorted ditto, 498 musket ditto, 119 Enfield ditto, making in all: 307 double barrels, 498 musket barrels, 1,133 sporting ditto, 119 Enfield ditto and 512 assorted ditto.

I rec'd on the 18th, 2,120 bayonets and 1 lot of old gun mountings, and on the 19th: 114 Halls carbines, 9 short flint muskets, 7 old Tower flint muskets, 3 flint muskets (making 19 flint musets), 10 carbines, 23 short percussion muskets, 12 Arkadelphia rifles and 12 Halls rifles—all unservicable.

Here is proof positive that rifles were actually made at

Arkadelphia, and that in some way they were recognizable as having been made there. As already stated, none are known to exist.

Hill to Maj. Thos. G. Rhett, Chf. Ord. & Arty., Shreveport DTM.

Enclosed you will please find a requisition for clothing for my men if you can get it approved in anyway. Please have the clothing ordered turned over to us and it will be a Godsend to the men. If they will not allow us the cloth and other things, please try to get us the shoes for the men are very much in need of them.

Hill to Capt. C. W. Wailey, Comg., Arsenal, Shreveport.

Enclosed, please find invoices and receipts for 500 infantry cartridge boxes, 450 cavalry ditto, 950 cap boxes etc. sent you to-day. Please sign and return receipts as soon as the stores are received. I send also by the same train, one small box for Major Rhett which you will oblige me by delivering to him.

Hill to Maj. Thos. G. Rhett, Chf. Ord. & Arty., Shreveport DTM.

I sent today by train to Capt. Wailey, 500 infantry cartridge boxes, 450 cavalry ditto, 1,056 canteens, 1,056 canteen straps, 950 cap boxes, 950 waist belts, 91,000 B & B cartridges.

I sent also by the same train, 1 box containing 2 lbs of beeswax and 3 bridle bits. I enclose invoices and receipts for same. It is all the beeswax I could send you at this time.

Hill to Capt. Thos. Buchanan, Ord. Dept. Marshall, Texas.

Enclosed please find vouchers for 1 bridle bit sent to you today by wagon train. Please sign and return the same with the money. I hope the bit will please you.

Hill to J. M. Hold, Govt. Iron Wks., Marion County, Texas.

Enclosed, please find receipt for 6 kettles rec'd from you a few days ago.

Hill to Capt. C. W. Wailey, Comg. Arsenal, Shreveport, La.

Enclosed, please find receipts for 45 lbs English Harness leather and 20 lbs of alum.

TUESDAY, NOV. 15, 1864

Hill to Major George Alexander, Comg., Marshall, Texas.

Yours of the 10th in relation to Private James Bennyson was rec'd last night. The man got here yesterday morning under guard. If I had rec'd your letter with the prisoner I should have sent him back to you under guard, but as the guard has left, I have none to send with him. I have ordered the man to report to you without delay. I would like to have the man and would put him to work, but as you were not authorized to send your machinists to me, but gunsmiths, I do not feel authorized to receive him, and I therefore send him back, and ask as justice to me and the service that you keep your machinists and send me gunsmiths which you have kept to put in your machine shop. The three Ramseys and your carpenter, men that classed with your best gunsmiths, you have kept and you send me Mr. Bennyson, one of your best machinists. This is so plain a case of injustice to me that I can not let it pass, and therefore send your Mr. Bennyson back and will not receive him.

FRIDAY, NOV. 18, 1864

Hill to Maj. Thos. G. Rhett, Chf. Ord. & Arty., Shreveport TMD.

I have just rec'd a requisition of Col. Bourlands for 475 cavalry guns with same number of cartridge and cap boxes which is approved by you. I am ordered to make the guns and issue them. I have the guns on hand ready to issue if permitted to issue Enfields. Respectfully ask for instructions whether to issue the Enfields, or to make the Texas and Hill Rifles and issue them?

Baltimore newspapers published the report of the special committee appointed by the court to estimate the damage done by Sheridan's cavalry in Rockingham County, Va. The report showed: 30 houses, 450 barns, 3 factories and 31 mills burned; 100,000 bushels of wheat and 50,000

[128]

bushels of corn carried off or destroyed, 1,750 horses, 6,233 head of cattle, 4,200 sheep and 3,350 hogs killed or carried off. Rockingham county was one of the richest in the State and the committee estimated that its loss by fire and confiscation aggregated $25,000,000.00. The reader might remember that these losses were suffered by individual private citizens and not by the military, or the Confederate government. Bearing this in mind, it is not hard to understand why the South is so vividly aware of "The War" even though almost 100 years have passed.

SATURDAY, NOV. 19, 1864

Hill to Maj. George Alexander, Comdg. Arsenal, Marshall, Texas.

Yours of Nov. 14th is rec'd, saying you have a man in your wheelwright shop whose business is that of making wooden stirrups. I have 1 man who is a good man at that, as well as a saddle tree maker, and I do not want any more.

Hill to Maj. Thos. G. Rhett, Chf. Ord. & Arty., Shreveport DTM.

I am very much in need of soldering irons, and must in some way have them. I got some pig copper from you last summer and it is utterly worthless. If there is any in the Store Room at Marshall, please order Capt. Faulkner to turn me some over. I can make the irons if I have the copper. The ones I have are entirely worn out, and my tinners can hardly get along at all. When I spoke to them today about the small quantity of work they did this week, they replied that it was the want of proper soldering irons.

My wagon will go to Marshall next week, and if possible, please send me some 3 or 4 irons, or copper to make them with.

MONDAY, NOV. 21, 1864

Hill to Major W. Warren Johnson, Comdg., Labor Bureau, Washington, Ark.

In accord with your circular of date Oct. 12, 1864, I enclose to you a certified muster roll of all negroes employed at Tyler Ord. Works and over whom I have control, belonging to citizens of Arkansas.

Apparently West Virginia girls were not the only ones fascinated into wearing a uniform. One Mary S. Turner, wearing the uniform of a Union cavalryman, was brought to Baltimore from Harpers Ferry under guard and locked up. She had enlisted in the 88th Pennsylvania Cavalry.

FRIDAY, NOV. 25, 1864

Hill to Capt. J. M. Williams, AQM, Tyler, Texas.

I have ready for forwarding to Capt. C. W. Wailey, 10,000 lbs. of lead. I would be glad if you would furnish transportation for same. Please let me know if you can do so, and at what time?

Thanksgiving Day, 1864, had not been a particularly happy one in the Confederacy. Aside from military reverses everywhere, note the following prices for necessities (quoted in Richmond), which would hardly make anyone happy: flour—$350 a barrel, cornmeal—$55 a bushel, bacon—$11 a pound, coffee—$15 a pound, sugar,—$10 a pound, chickens—$8, and turkeys—$25!

Hill to Capt. C. W. Wailey, Comg., Arsenal, Shreveport, La.

Enclosed, please find invoices and receipts for 528 canteens, 528 canteen straps, 14,000 Enfield Rifle cartridges & etc. etc., this day turned over to Capt. J. C. Scivly for transportation to you. Please sign and return receipts as soon as stores are rec'd.

Hill to Capt. C. W. Wailey, Comg., Arsenal, Shreveport, La.

In obedience to Major Rhett's order, I have ready to send to you, 10,000 lbs lead, but the difficulty is want of transportation.

I called Capt. Williams the AQM at this post for the necessary transportation and I enclose you his reply.

I have not wagons to do the necessary hauling for the Post. I will send it as soon as I can get transportation.

Hill to Surgeon C. A. Custman, In Charge, Ord. Laboratory, Marshall, Texas.

Please find enclosed, invoices and receipts for 132,725 damaged musket percussion caps this day shipped to Capt. S. C. Faulkner, Comg., Ord. Depot, Marshall, Texas, for you. Please **sign** and return receipts as soon as stores are received.

SATURDAY, NOV. 26, 1864

Hill to Capt. Thos. G. Buchanan, Ord. & Arty, Marshall, Texas.

I rec'd your vouchers and money for 1 bridle bit, and I am glad you were pleased with it.

I have to ask as a favor that you telegraph in my name to Major Rhett for an order on Capt. Faulkner for 50 lbs block tin. I am out, and am compelled to have some.

If Capt. Faulkner has not rec'd the order for the Pig Copper, please mention them in the telegram. Send bill for telegram to me, and I will pay for it.

Hill to Capt. S. C. Faulkner, In Charge of Ord. Depot, Marshall, Texas.

I send Private A. J. Porter with ambulance to Marshall for 500,-000 musket percussion caps, and 20 doz. assorted files lately ordered to be turned over to me. I wrote Maj. Rhett a few days ago an order on you for Pig Copper or 3 or 4 soldering irons. If you have rec'd the order, please send me the copper or irons, as the case may be.

Hill to Maj. George Alexander, Comdg., Arsenal, Marshall, Texas.

I send by Private A. J. Porter, one saddle for Lt. Belknap which you will please deliver to him.

The Richmond *Whig* in an editorial said that while there was not the remotest chance of Grant capturing Richmond, yet even if he did, and the Capital fell, it would have no effect on the war. Four months later Richmond fell to the Yankees. Readers today may bear this in mind when reading editorials in their own favorite newspaper. Editorial writers of today are just as apt to be wrong as they were 100 years ago.

Unaddressed letter from Hill.

Capt. Your request for 1,500 tin magazines for cavalry cartridge boxes and 500 tin ditto infantry is rec'd, and the magazines are being made as rapidly as possible. I will let you know when they are ready, in time for you to send for them without causing any delay.

Hill to Major A. J. Lindsay, Chief of Ord. Dist., Anderson, Texas.

I rec'd your letter, enclosing requisition for arms, etc. etc. for Col. Bourland. I have the arms nearly ready and am making the accoutrements as rapidly as possible.

I will let you know when they will be ready in time for arrangements to be made for transportation without causing delay. I think they will be ready Christmas, or by the 1st of Jan. 1865.

Hill to Lt. T. A. Woods, in Charge of Laboratory Work, Shops, etc., Tyler, Texas.

I find on inspection that your lead shop is in a filthy and wretched condition, all owing to neglect. I also find little or no discipline there. You will in the morning before commencing work, have the shop put in thorough order, and you will order all the little white boys to the Laboratory and put the negroes in their place.

Also order Mr. Wiley to take his little boys in the morning and have the yard at the Magazine put in thorough order for it is in such condition that I am afraid it will breed a pest.

Hill to Dr. Geo. S. Wein, in Charge, Ordnance Hospital.

The house known as the 'Taylor House' has been placed at my disposal for a hospital for this Dept.

You will at once proceed to have it fitted up for a hospital and put in such condition to receive the sick belonging to these works, procurring the bunks which were turned over to Dr. McGregor and making such other arrangements as well conducive to the comfort and welfare of the sick of this Dept.

At last it seems that Col. Hill had a surgeon and was now going ahead with his plans for a hospital.

MONDAY, DEC. 5, 1864

Hill to Maj. Thos. G. Rhett, Chf. of Ord., TMD, Shreve-port.

I wish, if it is possible for you to do so, that you would let me have some money, or so arrange that I may get some. My men are very much in need of money. I have not paid them for Sept. or Oct., and it is almost impossible for them to get along without money, and I need some in order to meet the ordinary expenditures of this works.

Please let me know what are the prospects for me to get some, so that I may be able to base my calculations? My building operations etc. cause me to be constantly in need of funds.

Here it is Dec. 5th, and Col. Hill writes that as yet he has not paid his workmen for Sept. or Oct.! A review of the records of other Confederate ordnance establishments makes it plainly evident that the problem of finances was not peculiar to Tyler, Texas, alone—it was so all through the South. Once again wonderment comes to mind at the devotion of a people to a cause which made them labor without much hope of pay. Faced with such an emergency as these people were, could we, or would we do the same today?

TUESDAY, DEC. 6, 1864

Hill to Capt. R. R. Jones, Act. Ord. Off., Fourney's Di-vision, Brindon, La.

Yours of date Nov. 24th is rec'd.
I have no belts or accouterments of any kind on hand except

[133]

those to fill requisitions approved by Major Rhett, Chief of Ord., T.M.D.

This is purely a manufacturing establishment, and as fast as stores are fabricated they are forwarded to Shreveport and Marshall for issue. Nothing is issued here except on order or requisition by Major Rhett.

As Commander of an Armory, Lt. Col. Hill had no authority to issue arms or stores directly, and could so issue only upon authority from an Arsenal, where arms and accoutrement were normally stored. The reader might remember that an Armory was where arms were made, an Arsenal was where they were stored and issued after having been received from the Armory.

WEDNESDAY, DEC. 7, 1864

Hill to Maj. Thos. G. Rhett, Chf. of Ord., TMD, Shreveport, La.

I rec'd an order from you dated Oct. 11, 1864 for 20,000 lbs lead for Capt. Faulkner, and one dated Nov. 17, 1864 for 10,000 lbs for Capt. Wailey, making in all 30,000 lbs. I now have on hand (or had on the 1st Dec.), 35,977 lbs, and if I fill those orders I shall have scarcely any on hand and consequently my negro cartridge boys will be left idle as my Laboratory must stop soon for want of it.

I have as yet no means of sending it, otherwise I should have done so, but I now write this for your information and that you may do that which you may think best in the matter.

Hill to Capt. R. W. Temple, Supt., Government Iron Works, Marion County, Texas.

I send by wagon train today, 1 box containing 20 lbs of glue, and 5½ lbs small wire, marked care of Maj. Gen'l Huger. The wagon master was ordered by me to deliver it to Capt. S. C. Faulkner for you. As soon as it arrives you will find it in Store at Capt. Faulkner's. I will send invoices and receipts by next mail.

Can you possibly furnish me with 10 ovens and lids for baking bread, and a 10 gal. pot and 6, 5 gal. pots for cooking purposes?

My hospital is very much in need of these articles and so are my men for messing. Please let me know, and if possible, oblige me in this matter.

Hill to Capt. S. C. Wailey, Cmg., Arsenal, Shreveport, La.

Enclosed, please find invoice and receipts for 69,000 Enfield Rifle cartridges, 18,000 Buck & Ball ditto, 3,000 Miss. Rifle B & B cartridges, sent you yesterday. Please sign and return receipts as soon as stores are rec'd.

Hill to Maj. Thos. G. Rhett, Chf. of Ord., TMD, Shreveport, La.

In compliance with your circular, I have the honor of reporting that I have now under my controle 5, six-mule wagons and teams—four turned over by Capt. J. G. Kirby AQM and receipted for by my AAQM, one hired of Mrs. Carson, a citizen of this county, 2 four-mule wagons and teams, one belonging to the Ord. Dept. brought from Little Rock, and one hired from Mr. Jesse S. Thomas, a citizen of this county. Four four-yoke ox team hired from Mrs. Jas. Johnson, is in very bad condition, the oxen being nearly broken down, 1 light spring wagon and 2 horses belonging to the Quartermaster Dept. My mule teams are kept very busy hauling coal, lumber, brick and forage. My coal is hauled 7 miles, my lumber—18, and forage from 12 to 20 miles, and to do all this work, I should have at least 8 or 10 more wagons. Lt. Dupre is now out trying to hire them. My ox teams are now hauling stock timber to the mill to be sawed, and will be so employed for a month, as I have to haul said timber from 3 to 6 miles. These ox team I will have to discharge as soon as they get through with the work that they are now doing, for it will not pay to forage them this winter in the condition in which they now are, for they can not do more than ½ the work that a 6 mule team can. I am in hopes that Lt. Dupre will hire me some wagons before he gets back. I have promise of 3 more six mule teams which I expect to get in a few days.

*Hill to Major Gen. Ben Huger, Chief, Ord. Bureau, TMD,
Marshall, Texas.*

I have the honor of enclosing a plan of the building which I
am about to erect. It is to be an addition to my present Armory
and is absolutely necessary as my present one is entirely too small.
I have the foundation dug, and one piling (?) is in. The men are
in the woods getting the shingles. The lumber is being sawed.
The brick are made and ready to be burned, and I shall continue
my operations until I receive other instructions.

The following is an estimation of material and cost therefore
—viz:

No. of brick—456,180 made by our own hands.
No. of ft. of lumber—100,000 at $75. per thousand, $7,500.00.
No. of shingles—70,000, to be gotten by our own hands.
No. of nails—1,000. Have no idea of cost.
No. of boxes of glass—32 @ $75 per box—$2,400.00.
No. of bushels of lime—2,000 @ $3 per bushel—$6,000.

This building and one other I contemplate building next summer will enable me to get my works together, which is very de-
sirable. At present, ½ my works are in town, and the other a mile
from, which is very inconvenient.

The reader will remember that Col. Hill's Laboratory
was located right in the town proper, in a three-storied
brick buiding belonging to a Col. George Yarbrough. His
Armory and various shops were situated about a mile out
of town in the building constructed by Short & Biscoe as
their original armory in which they planned to make 5,000
Mississippi-type rifles for the State of Texas.

One sentence seems to stand out in Col. Hill's letter to
the Chief of the Ordnance Bureau, Trans-Mississippi Dept.,
and that is; "This building and one other I contemplate
building next summer. . . ."

What kind of a man was Lt. Col. Hill? From his letters
we feel that he was the kind of officer who took care of his
men. Apparently he was mild tempered, but when aroused

could write a pretty biting letter. He evidently was far-sighted and one who looked to the future. Certainly there is no indication of stupidity, and yet here is a man who in late 1864 could write about a building he intended to construct for the Confederacy in the summer of 1865! Was this blind faith, or was it the sublime courage of one who could never concede defeat, even to himself? Whichever it was, Confederate Ordnance Bureau seemed to be well stocked with such officers who had exactly the same viewpoint. Come to think of it, the entire United States of that time seemed to be full of such people.

MONDAY, DEC. 12, 1864

Hill to Maj. Thos. G. Rhett, Chf. of Ord., TMD, Shreveport, La.

A great many of my men who have families here have begged of me to give them a week at Christmas to kill their hogs and to attend to other necessaries for their families, and I now respectfully ask that I may be permitted to do so, for I know that it is necessary that they should have some time to do these things, and unless they do get it, their families will suffer, and a little time given them, will enable them to make themselves comfortable and thereby make them more contented, and in that way I can get more work out of them. You know not how hard it is for them to get even the necessaries of life at this place, and by giving them a little time, they can go off and get what it would be impossible for them to get here. I do most respectfully request that you approve this for it will make my men more contented, and in that way I think it will be a benefit to the service rather than a drawback.

Clearly, Col. Hill was a man years ahead of his times, at least in matters concerning personnel, and evidently believed that loyalty worked both down the ladder as well as up—a fact that seems to be ignored by many in command.

Hill to Maj. Thos. G. Rhett, Chf. of Ord., TMD, Shreveport, La.

I am entirely out of block tin, and I have not more than enough solder on hand to last my tinners this week. If I do not get some very soon, my Tin Shop will be doing nothing. Please arrange in some way so that I can be supplied with this important material.

Hill to Lt. T. A. Woods, AQM, Tyler Ord. Works, Texas.

You have charge of 11 six mules, and 2 four mule teams and wagons. You will keep them employed as follows:
Keep 2 four mule teams hauling wood.
Keep 2 six mule teams hauling brick.
Keep 1 six mule team hauling coal.
Keep 4 six mule teams hauling lumber and corn.
This plan must not be deviated from in any way without orders from me. Your ox teams will haul the shingles from Mr. Cotharp's mill and then be put to hauling rock. In every case, the evening before starting your teams to the mill, report to Capt. Polleys so he may send for the kind of lumber needed.

This is not the kind of letter a superior officer writes a junior *if* he has confidence in his ability.

Hill to Maj. Thos. G. Rhett, Chf. of Ord., TMD, Shreveport, La.

I got from Marshall a short time ago a lot of mettle said to be copper. I want it to make soldering iron of, things that my tinners are perfectly destitute of almost, and I can not use it, it will not work. Capt. Polleys informs me that it is a composition of tin, lead and copper and is not maleable at all. You will oblige me very much if you will give me an order for some good copper. I am also entirely out of block tin. My tinners are now cutting out, but can finish nothing for want of it. Please send me an order for 50 or 100 lbs of that.

This is the sort of letter that would make a grammar teacher throw up her hands in horror. Every rule in the book has been disregarded or violated, and yet, it is perfectly understandable. Col. Hill needs good copper, and an order of block tin.

Hill to Maj. Thos. G. Rhett, Chf. of Ord., TMD, Shreveport, La.

Yours in relation to the lead ordered to Marshall has been rec'd, and I have in every case tried to be prompt in obedience to orders from your office without question or comment, and I would have sent in this case the lead, but it was impossible for me to get the transportation. I used every exertion in my power to obtain the same without success, and I wrote to Cap. Wailey as soon as I got the order, ordering 10,000 lbs to him, that it would be impossible for me to send the lead as I had no transportation and I could not get it. Capt. Rivbez (?), AQM, had 3 wagons going to Shreveport since I got the order, and as they could carry only a small part of the lead ordered, I concluded to send on the wagons ammunition. I therefore loaded the wagons with that instead of the lead. Lt. Dupre is now out with one man trying to hire mules and wagons. He has been out sometime, and how he will succeed is impossible to tell. Capt. Williams, and Capt. Kirby both have had me all over the county for 100 miles around this place, and they have failed to hire teams. Williams has been trying to get a train for the lead and I have been trying ever since I got the order and have failed. The country around here is almost entirely destitute of wagons and mules and in nearly every case when wagons have been impressed, Gen'l Smith has given orders to the owners to have them released.

I am satisfied of one thing, and that is that I have done my duty and tried in every way to carry out your orders to send the lead, but if the transportation is not in the county, there is one thing certain, I cannot get it.

I now have on hand only 19,000 llbs lead, and am using it up at the rate of about 1,000 lbs per day.

*Hill to Maj. Thos. G. Rhett, Chf. Ord., TMD, Shreve-
port, La.*

Lt. Dupre has just returned off of a ten day trip in search of
wagons and mules, which I sent him out to try and hire. I enclose
you his report.

The transportation is not in the county. The farmers have been
very much reduced by impressments of the Trans. Dept. I have
hardly enough wagons now to do the hauling that I require immediately around the works. I have to haul coal and lumber so
far, and all the corn I get to feed my animals on, I have to haul
from 15 to 20 miles. If you can do anything for me in this line,
I shall be very glad to get at least 10 more six-mule teams.

*Hill to Maj. Thos. G. Rhett, Chf. Ord., TMD, Shreve-
port, La.*

I am at this time using about 40 lbs cartridge paper per day,
and have only 160 lbs on hand.

I shall therefore be entirely out in a few days. You will please
therefore manage it so that I can have a new supply as early as
practicable.

The Laboratory is now doing good work, and I would regret
very much to see it stopped for want of anything.

*Hill to Lt. T. A. Woods, in Charge of Workshops, Labora-
tory, etc., Tyler, Texas.*

You will at once report to this office all the trace chains, Halter
chains and harness that you have rec'd from the Ord. Dept. You
will have any work done in the Harness Shop for Lt. Dupre on
the harness of the Quartermaster Dept. that he may apply for.
I want all the harness now in use put in thorough repair.

SATURDAY, DEC. 24, 1864

Hill to Capt. S. C. Wailey, Comdg., Arsenal, Shreveport, La.

The mistake in the kind of crtges may be easily accounted for and no doubt occurred, but if there was a box containing 830 Enfield cartridges, it must certainly have been opened on the route as I am perfectly convinced there never was a box of crtges sent from this works containing less than the proper number.

Hill to Capt. G. H. King, Comdg., Ord. Works, Henderson, Texas

Enclosed, please find invoices and receipts for 90 lbs candles sent to you a few days ago by Lt. Watson. Please sign receipts and return the same as soon as the stores are rec'd.

FRIDAY, DEC. 30, 1864

Hill to Maj. George Alexander, Comdg., Arsenal, Marshall, Texas.

Enclosed, please find receipts for 73 muskets unserviceable etc. etc., gun barrels, machinery, tools, etc. rec'd from you.

Your invoices and blank receipts for walnut lumber and block tin rec'd. The walnut lumber has been rec'd, but the block tin has not. As soon as it comes to hand, I will sign receipts and return them.

Hill to Capt. C. W. Wailey, Comdg., Arsenal, Shreveport, La.

On the 25th of Nov. 1864, I issued and forwarded to you 528 canteens, 528 canteen straps, 1,400 Enfield Rifle cartridges, 35,000 B & Ball ditto, 49 ammunition packing boxes, and 3 corn packing boxes, and at the same time forwarded to you by mail invoices and receipts for same.

I have not rec'd as yet receipts from you for same, they were turned over to Capt. J. C. Kirby, AQM for transportation to you and I have his receipt.

If you have rec'd these, please send me receipts for them as it is the end of the Quarter, and if you have not rec'd them, please inform me of that fact.

[141]

The year closed with a dispatch from the Union General Sheridan to General Emory: "I have no news today except the death of Mosby. He died from his wounds at Charlottesville." This was wishful thinking on Sheridan's part. Mosby was wounded and in hiding, but was far from being dead, as Sheridan and other Federal commanders soon learned.

SUNDAY, JAN. 1, 1865

Hill to Col. W. R. Bradfute, Comdg., Post, Tyler, Texas.

I understand that during my absence you have occupied a portion of the land belonging to the Tyler Ordnance Dept., and had material etc. carried there for the purpose of building a general hospital. You will please inform me by whose authority you are acting under in occupying land belonging to these Works and why I have not been consulted about the matter? As commander of the Works, and having controle over the land I think you should have at least consulted me before commensing your hospital. I object to the hospital being placed upon the land and therefore desire that you remove your material and find some other suitable place. The land was bought for ordnance purposes and from instructions from the Chief of Ordnance, Dept. of the Trans Miss. I can not permit the land to be used for other purposes and your hospital being situated where you contemplate putting it, would very materially interfere with my future plans.

MONDAY, JAN. 2, 1865

Hill to Capt. C. W. Wailey, Comdg., Arsenal, Shreveport, La.

The receipts for 528 canteens and straps etc of which I wrote to you on the 30th Dec. 1864, came to hand yesterday evening.

It seems they have been delayed in the dead letter office at Marshall. I write this so that you may not trouble yourself further on the subject.

The Augusta (Ga.) *Sentinel* said that it was reported in that city that the Confederate Vice-President Alexander H. Stephens had gone North on a peace mission. The report was false. Stephens was in Richmond.

[142]

THURSDAY, JAN. 5, 1865

Hill to Maj. Thos. G. Rhett, Chf. of Ord., TMD, Shreveport, La.

The mill that I am now getting my lumber from is about to give out and for the life of me I do not know what I shall do, for there is only one other mill near here and that the Quartermaster Dept. has control over.

The mill that I now have at work can not begin to supply me with lumber and I would like very much to get an engine saw etc and put up a mill of my own. I can not possibly get along without one.

I understand that Major Alexander has 2 very good mills and saws, and as I have no doubt but that he has nearly all his buildings finished, I think he might spare one. Please if possible, give me an order for one, and I can then do my building, but without it, I can not do anything.

Hill to Capt. C. W. Wailey, Comg. Arsenal, Shreveport, La.

Enclosed, please find receipts for 530 lbs bridle leather, 144 lbs upper ditto, and 1,201 lbs sole ditto from Helm & Harris.

General U. S. Grant telegraphed from City Point, Va., to Washington that the Richmond papers reported the death of the Confederate General Stirling Price. The report was false.

FRIDAY, JAN. 6, 1865

Hill to Maj. Thos. G. Rhett, Chf. of Ord., TMD, Shreveport, La.

In accordance with your orders, we have stopped all new work and I have put all hands to repairing guns in the hopes that all guns worth repairing will be got out. We have 600 guns of different kinds.

SATURDAY, JAN. 7, 1865

Hill to Maj. George D. Alexander, Comdg. Arsenal, Marshall, Texas.

Enclosed, please find invoices and receipts for 6,884 ¾ lbs Rifle

[143]

Powder and 26 lbs cannon powder—all unserviceable. I sent you a part of this lot of powder on the 15th day of September. 1864, and the rest yesterday.

With this lot I sent also some damaged powder left here sometime ago to be forwarded to Marshall, without any papers or anything to show where it was from, and the person in charge of the wagons knew nothing more about it.

Please sign enclosed receipts and return them as early as convenient.

It was reported in Augusta, Ga., that Generals Hood and Forrest had been killed. Fortunately for the South, these reports were false.

MONDAY, JAN. 9, 1865

Hill to Maj. Geo. D. Alexander, Comdg. Arsenal, Marshall, Texas.

Enclosed, please find receipts for 760 feet walnut lumber and 25 lbs block tin.

Hill to Lt. T. A. Woods, in Charge of Work Shops, Laboratory etc., Tyler, Texas.

You will have made for use of office, 100 letter envelopes immediately.

Hill to Capt. C. W. Wailey, Comdg. Arsenal, Shreveport, La.

Enclosed, please find invoices and receipts for 37,000 Enfield Rifle cartridges, 50,000 Buck & Ball ditto, and 3,000 Miss. Rifle ditto, sent to you on the 7th Dec., 1864.

Hill to Brig. Gen. B. McCulloch, Comdg. N.S.D., Bonham, Texas.

Yours of 27th Dec. is rec'd. I send by courier, 15,000 sporting percussion caps and enclose invoices and receipts for Capt. M. A. Harvey as you desire. These are all I can spare at present as I am ordered to put up the remainder with Colt's Pistol ammunition.

Col. Bourland's stores are ready. There are 28 boxes weighing in the aggregate 6,662 lbs. Four wagons ought to haul them.

*Hill to Maj. Thos. G. Rhett, Chf. of Ord., TMD, Shreve-
port, La.*

Today was a very busy day in the office and in making the
report of work done for the week ending the 7th Jan., the
amount of Powder, Caps and lead on hand was accidently omitted.

The following was the amount of each on hand as of Jan. 7,
1865;

Cannon Powder—1,546 lbs,
Musket Powder—100 lbs,
Rifle Powder—1,820 lbs,
Musket caps—501,140,
Sporting caps—243,315,
Lead—1,705 lbs.

TUESDAY, JAN. 10, 1865

*Hill to Lt. T. A. Woods, in Charge of Work Shops, Labora-
tory etc., Tyler, Texas.*

You will have made without delay, 2,000 cavalry cartridge boxes,
2,000 cap boxes and 2,000 waist belts to fill requisition for Indian
Country.

*Hill to Maj. Thos. G. Rhett, Chf. of Ord., TMD, Shreve-
port, La.*

I am very much in need of a good officer to put in charge of
my Laboratory, harness shops etc. Lt. Woods who I now have in
charge, I don't like at all and I am very anxious to get rid of him
anyway.

Capt. Bacon, now on duty with Maj. Alexander at Marshall as
AQM, is very anxious to come with me and I am very desirous
of having him and Gen. Huger told me that he would order him
to report to me if I applied for him to you, and you had no objections to the change. Maj. Alexander has 3 captains besides
the lieutenants he has. I have only one captain and am very
anxious to get another, and I hope that you will approve of the
transfer and let me have Capt. Bacon, and give Woods to Alexander, if he wants him.

The Richmond *Enquirer* and *Whig* published strong
editorials replying to the *Examiners* suggestion that Gen-

eral Robert E. Lee be made commander-in-chief. Both expressed fear that it was a step toward a military dictatorship. Thus it is evident that the fear of dictatorship is not common alone to the twentieth century.

WEDNESDAY, JAN. 11, 1865

Hill to Capt. C. W. Wailey, Comdg. Arsenal, Shreveport, La.

Enclosed, please find receipts for the 200 lbs cast steel etc. rec'd from you a few days ago.

Hill to Maj. Thos. G. Rhett, Chf. of Ord., TMD, Shreveport, La.

I have the honor to submit the following as my report of the operations at this Works during the 4th Quarter 1864, and resources for the present quarter.

We have fabricated during the quarter in the Armory: 133 Enfield rifles, the barrels for which were furnished us, but the locks, and all mountings and stocks were made here, 180 Texas rifles, 56 Hill rifles and 2 sporting rifles. In all, 371 new guns furnished.

We have repaired during the quarter, 173 guns of different kinds, and 43 Colts pistols, a large portion of these guns requiring new stocks and some of them new locks. In addition to this, we have made a great many tools now being used by the hands sent from Marshall, as those sent were useless and very few were sent.

During the quarter, we have had much to contend with for want of proper stock timber. Last summer I got out a good many stocks and sent them to a mill that was then doing my sawing and expected to have that timber ready to go to work on by this time, but owing to forfeiture of contract I have had to make other arrangements, and even now have not my timber so seasoned that I can go on with my fabrication of arms as rapidly as I would like to. A mill is very much needed in the Dept. and if possible it should be supplied as the one I now have a contract with is almost entirely worn out and it may at any time stop.

In the Carpenter Shop we have fabricated, 300 ammunition packing boxes, 21 canteen packing boxes, 16 window sashes, 4 arm's chests, 48,000 shingles, 6 wheel barrows, 36 axe helves. Besides this we have made and burned 300,000 bricks, finished one brick building for magazine 20 x 50 feet, and one brick building 30 x 17 feet for dwelling house. We have also erected and finished two double log houses for negro quarters and erected one furnace for making oil and glue. We have also dug the foundation for the contemplated addition to the Armory, and have hauled and ready to put in a large lot of rock, but owing to the scarcity of transportation and laborers to do the work, we have gotten along very slowly and will continue to do so with the force we have. I have tried every means to hire slaves, but it is impossible to do so.

We have on hand for the Armory and Carpenter Shop a sufficient quantity of material of all kinds (with the exception of cast steel nails and lumber) to keep the operatives profitably employed for the next 3 months.

We have fabricated in the Harness Shop 1,489 infantry cartridge boxes, 737 cavalry cartridge boxes, 2,234 cap pouches, 2,669 waist belts, 2,610 canteen straps, 25 saddletrees, 8 saddles, 14 saddletrees covered, 3 pair stirrups, 10 SS wheel harness, 20 SS lead harness, 13 blind bridles, 9 halter bridles, 3 halters, 1 pair breast straps, 96 feet leather belting, 2 sabre belts etc.

This shop is doing well and we have enough to keep us going for the next 3 months except buckles for waist belts. This should be supplied at once.

All orders in upon us are now filled with the exception of the 2,000 cavalry cartridge boxes and belts for the Indian Nation which we are now hard at work on.

In the Laboratory we have fabricated: Enfield rifle cartridges—358,480, Miss. rifle ditto—58,080, Buck & ball calibre .59—153,400, rifle musket cal. .58—250, Belgium Rifle—800, Sharps Carbine—900, Colts pistol (army)—2,394, Colts pistol (navy size)—228, Blank cartridges—800, Musket ball ditto—640, besides, 27,372½ lbs Enfield Rifle balls, 10,352 lbs musket balls, 3,277½ lbs Miss. Rifle balls, 3,905 lbs buckshot, 300 cartridge box buttons, 2,770 cap box buttons, 43½ lbs thread spun, 34⅛ gal neats foot oil made. Besides this work, my hands have made all the bricks that have been made.

I am having to stop operations in the Laboratory while that work was going on. I now have on hand only enough lead to run a few days, and I have on hand: 2,220 lbs of rifle and musket powder. I am hard at work on Colts Pistol Army and Navy cartridges and shall make as many as 50,000 rounds or more of each.

The last lot of paper rec'd from Marshall is of such inferior quality that it can't be used to make cartridges, but use it for wrappers entirely. We are very much in need of paper, lead and I will soon want more powder.

In my Tin Shop I have been for a long time in need of block tin and have not a great deal fabricated, as it is not reported until finished, but I have a good deal of work in progress. All the tin magazines for Capt. Pitts are made but want soldering. We have made during the quarter: 2,000 belt hooks, 1,350 cavalry cartridge box magazines, 500 infantry ditto, 1,002 canteens, 83 tin cups for men's mess, also 68 tin plates, 3,600 burrs, 10 dishes for mess and 3, 30 gal, cans for spirits of turpentine.

I have on hand enough tin I think to run us for the next quarter, but want very much some block tin, as I am now nearly out. The tin we get is of a very inferior quality and works to very poor advantage and it is almost impossible to make good canteens of it. If thick tin could be furnished and 2 more good tinners, I could very soon supply the army with canteens.

My officers and men are all orderly and attentive to their duties and work with a good will. Lt. Woods is dissatisfied and I would like very much to have him relieved, and another officer sent in his place.

The above quarterly report of work performed at the Ordnance Works, Tyler, Texas, gives us a remarkably clear picture of just what was made there during the last three months in 1864, and considering the difficulties to be surmounted, Col. Hill once again has every right to be proud of his accomplishments.

THURSDAY, JAN. 12, 1865

Hill to Col. W. R. Bradfute, Comg. Post, Tyler, Texas.

Yours of this date enclosing order from Maj. Gen. Walker, and requesting me to relieve Lt. Woods of this Dept. from duty, as you have placed him under arrest, has been rec'd.

I have ordered Lt. Wood not to obey the order of yours placing him in arrest, as I do not consider myself or any of my officers in any way under your command, and therefore consider that you have no authority whatever to arrest him or give him orders of any kind.

If you have any charges of any kind to prefer against him and will send me a copy of them, I will then do as I deem proper and arrest him myself, if I consider it necessary, but as to my complying with your request, or allowing him to comply with your order and remain in arrest, I respectfully decline so doing.

You as commander of this Post have nothing to do with my Dept., officers or men, as they do not in any way belong to the Post, and all orders issued by you to any of my officers or men will be totally disregarded. I have explicit instructions on the point from the Chf. of Ord., D.T.M. Lt. Woods will therefore, by my orders, totally disregard your order placing him in arrest, and I will take no steps whatever to have him relieved from duty until proper charges and specifications are preferred against him, and a copy of same furnished me.

Col. Hill might not have liked or been satisfied with Lt. T. A. Woods, who was in charge of his Laboratory, but most certainly he was not the type to permit any injustice done to his men or officers.

FRIDAY, JAN. 13, 1865

Hill to Col. W. R. Bradfute, Comg. Post, Tyler, Texas.

Yours of this date asking me to withdraw my letter of yesterday has been rec'd. I am very much surprised that you should ask of me any such thing. If Lt. Woods is guilty of any act which requires his being arrested, I, as his commander should arrest him upon charges properly preferred by a commissioned officer. If you have any charges to prefer, make them and send me a copy of same, and I will then as his commander (if his services can be spared and I think it necessary) will have him arrested, but I do not think you have the right to order him under arrest, and shall insist upon his totally disregarding any order coming from you. Any order sent to my officers should at any rate be sent through me as their commander.

God bless the good colonel and all others like him, who are not afraid to stand up for those things they believe right!

Hill to Capt. G. S. Polleys, In Charge, C.S. Armory, Tyler, Texas.

Have packed and sent in to the Store room without delay, all the new and repaired arms at the Armory. This is intended to embrace all guns in a condition fit to issue.

Hill to Col. W. R. Bradfute, Comg. Post, Tyler, Texas.

Yours of this date rec'd, and I am very glad to hear that you have forwarded my correspondence to Maj. Gen. Walker, for I know he will forward it to Dept. Hdqtrs, and it will be the cause of an explanation defining your connection as Post Commander with regard to my Dept. As to your informing Gen. Walker that you intended to prefer other charges again Lt. Woods for not complying with your order placing him under arrest, I have nothing to do with, as you can prefer what charges against him or anyone else you choose.

Hill to Surgeon J. M. Haden, Chief of Med. Bureau, TMD, Marshall, Texas.

Yours of Jan. 9th enclosing requisition for spades, shovels, copper wire, etc. is rec'd. It is impossible for me to furnish the articles called for in the requisition. Otherwise I would do so. I herewith return the requisition.

Up to this point, there had been one port in the South still open to receive goods from blockade runners. This was Wilmington, N. C. Other ports had been slowly strangled off by the increasingly efficient Federal blockade. Through Wilmington was received all the arms, supplies, etc., from Europe, each of which was urgently needed by the literally starving South. An attempt had been made by the North to close Wilmington but it was unsuccessful. On Jan. 12, 1865, the second expedition for the reduction of Fort

Fisher, guarding the harbor of Wilmington, arrived off the Fort. The fleet consisted of 60 ironclads and other warships under Admiral Porter and 8,500 troops on transports, and was the most formidable from the standpoint of power ever assembled up to this time. Fort Fisher mounted 44 guns and was defended by 2,000 men under Col. William Lamb.

On Jan. 15, Fort Fisher was captured by one of the first amphibious operations; a combined army and navy force after a desperate assault. An interesting feature of the assault was a daring charge of 1,600 sailors armed with pistols and cutlasses which was repulsed with heavy loss. About 1,800 Confederates, many of whom were wounded, were captured. Col. Lamb, the commander, was among the wounded. The Union loss was 955, all except 22 being killed or wounded.

The following day, the powder magazine at Fort Fisher exploded accidently killing more than 100 men, some of them Confederate prisoners. It was believed the magazine was exploded by a drunken sailor.

The loss of Fort Fisher was a terrible blow to the South as it meant that the port of Wilmington was henceforth closed.

MONDAY, JAN. 16, 1865

Hill to Messrs. Higginbotham Billips & Co., Mound Prairie, Texas.

If either of you will come up to see me, I will enter into a contract for furnishing gun scalps as I have just rec'd authority to do so from Gen. Huger, Chief of Ordnance Bureau. I would like very much if you would bring with you, if possible, a sample of the scalps that you intend furnishing, that I may judge of the quality of the iron.

A dispatch said that the meeting between President Jefferson Davis and Francis P. Blair, Peace Commissioner from the North, was cordial. Mr. Davis expressed a willingness to name a peace commission to meet a similar one from the North but made it quite clear that anything like submission to the North would be impossible.

Hill to Maj. Thos. G. Rhett, Chf. of Ord., TMD, Shreveport, La.

I am now doing nothing in my Laboratory for want of paper and lead. The paper send me from Marshall last, will not make cartridges it is so rotten, and I shall keep it for wrapping. I have enough fine paper to make about 100,000 pistol cartridges but as I had no caps to put up with them, I concluded I would wait until caps were sent me. I have on hand about 50,000 rounds of pistol cartridges and have enough balls made to put up 200,000 more. Please send me caps at once, or if I must put up the cartridges without caps, please send me an order.

Must I send you the arms I am repairing, if I can get transportation, as soon as I get a lot on hand? I now have everything repairing.

I have on hand about 240,000 sporting caps, but they are damaged, and although nearly all of them will fire, yet they are not fit to issue to troops in the field.

Hill to Maj. Thos. G. Rhett, Chf. of Ord., TMD, Shreveport, La.

I have no nails on hand, and I can not even put up a box for want of them. Please if possible, let me have a few for making boxes. I am now using screws for putting my ammunition boxes together, using 12 screws to the box. I also need very badly— buckles for waist belts, and I can not finish the order for 2,000 for the Indian Nation until buckles are supplied me.

The 25 lbs of copper you ordered Capt. Wailey to send me has not yet arrived. All the other things came, but no copper, and I am very much in need of it for soldering irons.

[152]

Hill to Maj. Thos. G. Rhett, Chf. of Ord, TMD, Shreveport, La.

Enclosed, you will please find an order for some cotton drilling. Please send it to me by bearer. Please pick me out some of the best and largest pieces you have on hand. I want them for my own use, and the other for sale to my officers. I sent to you by Capt. Temple, 3 bits. Please have them delivered with the enclosed vouchers for their signature and return them with the money, and I shall be very much obliged.

Hill to Surgeon C. O. Curtman, In Charge, Ord. Laboratory, Marshall, Texas.

I send one jug by the bearer. I have no bottles, otherwise I would have sent them. It is impossible for me to get bottles and therefore must rely in part upon you. Please send me the acid as I stand very much in need of it.

Hill to Capt. S. C. Faulkner, Comdg. Ord. Depot, Marshall, Texas.

I send by the bearer a jug. Please direct him how to call on Surgeon Charles O. Curtman for some nitric acid which he has ready for me.

I send also 1 gal. of oil for Maj. Thomas G. Rhett, please forward to him by earliest opportunity.

Hill to Col. S. S. Anderson, Asst. Ajt. Gen'l, TMD, Shreveport, La.

Pri. J. A. Kirk of Co. "C", McLane's Battalion, now on duty in this Dept. as a 2nd class mechanic, has no Discriptive List—none was furnished him by his captain when he left the regiment. Please order one furnished him as it will be impossible for the man to draw his line pay without it.

Letters similar to the above were written for the following names, to wit:

Pri. A. L. Harrison of Co. "D", 28th Texas Cav.
Pri. J. D. Allen, Co. "H", Col. Pleasant's Old Ark. Regt.
Pri. Ed. Woldert, Co. "C", Col. Cook's Heavy Arty.

Pri. Henry J. McBride, Co. "D", 15th Texas Regt. Inf.
Pri. M. B. Beheller, Co. "C", 22nd Texas Inf.
Pri. W. L. Campbell, Co. "E", 17th Texas Consolidated.
Pri. W. J. Gaisher, Co. "H", Col. Pleasant's Old Ark. Regt.
Pri. G. W. Lisenbey, Co. "A", 19th Texas Inf.
Pri. A. J. Small, Co. "G", 32nd Texas Cav.
Pri. O. J. Lawrence, Co. "C", McLane's Battalion.
Pri. T. S. Leasherman, Co. "A", Dawson's Regt. (19th Ark.)
Pri. J. C. McCoy, Co. "F", Col. Terrel's Regt.
Pri. G. R. Fisher, Co. "H", 7th Texas Inf.
Pri. J. C. Cobb, Co. "K", 31st Texas Cav. Dismounted.
Pri. Samuel Jenkins, of Capt. Carter's Co., 22nd Texas Inf.
Pri. W. J. Howell, Co. "C", McLane's Battalion.
Pri. John Rape, Co. "C", McLane's Battalion.

FRIDAY, JAN. 20, 1865

Hill to Maj. Thos. G. Rhett, Chf. of Ord., TMD, Shreveport, La.

Enclosed you will find applications for Pri. A. J. Small and 17 other descriptive lists. You will very much oblige me by forwarding them to Col. S. S. Anderson as I am desirous of opening regular company books with my men as they are now allowed to draw clothing.

SATURDAY, JAN. 21, 1865

Hill to Maj. W. H. Haynes, Chief of C. Bureau, TMD, Shreveport, La.

I rec'd yours date Jan 16th this morning stating that the clothing for my Dept. was ready.

Please turn it over to Capt. Wolf, the Transportation Quartermaster to be taken to Marshall to Capt. S. C. Faulkner to be by him forwarded to me by my wagons when I send for it.

MONDAY, JAN. 23, 1865

Hill to Surgeon J. F. Matchett, In Charge, Gen. Hospt., Crockett, Texas.

Yours of Jan 17th is rec'd, and I am under obligation to you. G. W. Hager was in my Dept. at Little Rock, but has been dropped as a deserter since Oct. 1863. I wish you would hold on to him and if the enrolling officer can possibly send him to me under guard, I would be glad if he would do it. I would send for him myself, but I am so badly pushed for want of men that I can not spare the necessary guard.

Please write in answer to this, and let me know whether the En. Officer can send him to me?

WEDNESDAY, JAN. 25, 1865

Hill to Capt. M. A. Harvey, Actg. Chief Ord. Officer, N.S.D., Bonham, Texas.

Yours of Jan. 18th inquiring if magazines for cartridge boxes to fill Capt. Pitts' requisition are ready is rec'd.

They are all ready, and you can send for them at once if it suits you to do so. I also informed Gen. McCulloch that Col. Bourland's stores were ready. Perhaps it would be well to send for both at the same time.

On this day it was rumored in Richmond that a 90-day armistice had been declared. The rumor was untrue. It was probably founded in the fact that Pres. Davis had named Vice President Stephens, R. M. T. Hunter, and James A. Campbell as Peace Commissioners. These gentlemen left Richmond the following Monday to confer with a similar Union commission to which it was supposed, Pres. Lincoln would name.

FRIDAY, JAN. 27, 1865

Hill to Col. W. O'Bannon, Chief of Quartermaster Bur., TMD.

Enclosed you will find a copy of an order issued from this office, ordering Lt. Dupre to relieve Lt. T. A. Woods as a AQM of this Dept. which I send for information in your office.

Hill to Maj. W. B. Blair, Chief of Com. Bur., TMD, Marshall, Texas.

Enclosed you will find a copy of an order issued from this

[155]

office ordering Lt. Dupre to relieve Lt. T. A. Woods as a ACS of these works, which I send you for information in your office.

Hill to G. S. Weir, AA Surgeon, Tyler Ord. Works.

On inspection of your hospital this morning, I find the negro ward in a miserable condition, no bunks etc., and the house in which they are, as dirty as a pig sty.

You must at once remedy this and make them comfortable. If anything is wanted to do this, you will at once report what it is, so that I may if possible supply you with it. The negroes must be made as comfortable as the white men.

Your matron reports that you are very much in need of vessels for dishing up meals in. Your steward also reports that you are much in need of spitoons etc. All these things can be and should be supplied by Dr. Johnston, but if it is impossible for you to get them from him, let me know what you require and I will supply you with what you can not get elsewhere.

The sick—both negroes and whites of this Dept. must and shall be well cared for, and if anything is needed, it will be supplied or found if it is in the Trans Miss. Dept., and I shall expect you to provide for the men, and give them whatever attention they require.

To those Yankees who had so fondly accepted "Uncle Tom's Cabin" as the standard treatment afforded to all Negroes by all Southerners, Col. Hill's letter would seem incredible. The idea of equal treatment of white and colored has never been novel in the South.

MONDAY, JAN. 30, 1865

Hill to Maj. Gen. Ben Huger, Chief of Ord. Bur., Marshall, Texas.

Accompanying, please find in 3 packages, the papers due this office for the 4th quarter of 1864, viz:

#1—Property return.

#2—Abstract of stores received from officers with vouchers 1 to 16.
  Abstract of Articles purchased.
  Abstract of Articles Purchased but not paid for.

Abstract of Articles Fabricated.
Abstract of Articles Repaired and Transferred.
Abstract of Stores issued to Officers with vouchers 1 to 29.
Abstract of Articles sold to Officers with vouchers 1 to 59.
Abstract of Articles issued and sold employees.
Abstract of Articles expended and consumed.

#3—Account Current
Abstract of Disbursements with vouchers 1 to 40.
Abstract of Repairs.

Hill to Maj. Gen. Ben Huger, Chief of Ord. Bur., TMD, Marshall, Texas.

Enclosed, please find corrected "Statement of Recpts and Expenditure of Monies' for the month of Dec. 1864.

The $20,000 rec'd from Maj. Rhett was not taken up because it was in check and was not in the office at the time the papers were made out. Please return the one sent.

The returns of detailed Hired men and slaves for Oct., Nov., and Dec., I will send by the next mail, and I hope hereafter to be able to transmit promptly all papers from this office.

Hill to Brig. Gen. H. E. McCulloch, Comg., NSD, Bonham, Texas.

Yours of Jan. 19th is rec'd. I am glad you rec'd the caps.

I will send you with Col. Bourland's stores, 20,000 Enfield Rifle cartridges which are the same calibre as Texas Rifle, and the tin magazines for cartridge boxes called for by Capt. Pitts requisition.

All these stores are ready for transportation.

WEDNESDAY, FEB. 1, 1865

Hill to I. M. Cobbe, Disb. Off., Govt. Iron Works, Marion county, Texas.

Enclosed, please find receipts for 900 lbs castings rec'd from you yesterday.

Hill to Lt. T. Pillarton in Charge, Laboratory & Shops, Tyler, Texas.

You will stop all other work in the Harness Shops and put the Harness makers to making sabre belts.

Hill to Capt. C. W. Wailey, Comdg., Arsenal, Shreveport, La.

Enclosed, please find receipts for 100,000 sporting percussion caps rec'd from you a few days ago.

Hill to Maj. Thos. G. Rhett, Chf. of Ord., TMD. Shreveport, La.

Please have the following men relieved from duty in this Dept. and ordered to their command or to the enrolling officer as the case may be: D. M. George—Col. Thompson's Regt., Robert Ward—conscript, Smith county, E. H. Blake—Co. I, Trans Miss. Vol., J. F. Shipp—Gould's Battery, D. L. Hoke—conscript, Smith county.

These men are neither of them of any sort of benefit to me, but only an encumbrance. George is entirely worthless. Ward has been in the Hospital ever since he 1st reported to me. Blake is trifling and worthless. Shipp is not the slightest use, being lazy and trifling, and Hoke has been sick for the last 9 months.

On this day the Hampton Roads Peace Conference was held on board the steamer *River Queen* and lasted four hours. President Lincoln and Secretary Seward represented the North. Vice-President Stephens, R. M. T. Hunter and James A. Campbell represented the South. The conference was informal and there were no secretaries or clerks to record the proceedings. President Lincoln seemed in a cheerful mood and told a number of funny stories. The commissioners parted in the best of humor, but were unable to reach any agreement. President Davis's only instructions to the Southern commissioners were to ask for the independence of the Southern States, and that was the one term which Lincoln was unwilling to grant.

At Petersburg, Va., men from both the North and South were dying. This at the same time Pres. Lincoln was telling his "funny stories," and the Southern Commissioners were in such "best of humor."

WEDNESDAY, FEB. 8, 1865

Hill to Capt. S. C. Faulkner, Comdg., Ord. Depot, Marshall, Texas.

Enclosed, please find receipts for 100 gross assorted screws etc. rec'd from you on Jan. 31, 1865.

Receipts for stores rec'd from you Jan 4th (250,000) musket caps, 25 boxes tin etc., has not been forwarded for the reason that the 10 gal. linseed oil mentioned in the invoices has not been rec'd. Everything else has. As soon as the oil is rec'd, I will send receipts.

FRIDAY, FEB. 10, 1865

Hill to Maj. Thos. G. Rhett, Chf. of Ord., TMD, Shreveport, La.

I lack about $35,000 of paying off the indebtedness of this Dept. up to 1st Jan. 1865, and this I owe for leather and lumber and the parties stand very much in need of the money. They are detailed men in the Dept., detached service, tanning leather, and sawing for the Ord. Works.

If you will arrange it so as to let me have that amount, I will be very glad, and shall feel greatly relieved.

Hill to Maj. Thos. G. Rhett, Chf. of Ord., TMD, Shreveport, La.

Your order for the 2,500 sabre belts has been rec'd and I am now at work on them. Have all the belts cut out and making as many as I can out of the leather I have on hand that is fit to make belts out of, but I am now nearly out of leather of any kind. I have sent a man down to Helm & Harrison tan yard to see if I can not get them to hurry me up leather. The weather has been very bad or I have no doubt but what I should have rec'd leather from them. I now have over 300 belts in process and shall

[159]

want the buttons and suitable buckles and hooks as soon as you can send them to me.

MONDAY, FEB. 13, 1865

Hill to Maj. Geo. D. Alexander, Comdg. Arsenal, Marshall, Texas.

Yours enclosing invoices and receipts for 2,000 lbs. musket and rifle powder is rec'd.

Enclosed, please find a certificate for loss of 1 keg (25 lbs.). I enclose also the invoices and receipts. Please correct them and return.

The head of one of the kegs was out, and the powder had entirely leaked out.

FRIDAY, FEB. 17, 1865

Hill to Capt. M. A. Harvey, Acting Chief Ord. Officer, N.S.D., Bonham, Texas.

I rec'd yours dated Feb. 3, 1865, through the Post Office. I did not see the Lieutenant bearing it, but am informed by Col. Bradfute, Comdg. Post that he called at my office several times but did not see me and did not feel authorized to deliver it to any of my clerks. I do not attach any blame to him.

If he had delivered the letter to me, it would have done little good as he had but one wagon, and I have a good many things to send. I have ready 475 guns, 475 cartridge boxes, cap boxes and waist belts for Col. Bourland Border Regt., all the magazines and 300,000 percussion caps. As soon as the wagons come, I will forward them.

Hill to Capt. S. C. Wailey, Comg. Arsenal, Shreveport, La.

Enclosed, please find invoices and receipts for 3 bugles sent to you a few days ago. Please sign and return receipts as soon as the bugles are rec'd.

I sent also by the wagon, ½ doz. chairs for Col. Ben Alston, Inspt. Gen'l which by seeing delivered to him, you will oblige.

Hill to Col. D. S. Martin, Comdg. Conscripts Dist. Texas, Brusk, Texas.

Enclosed, please find invoices and receipts for ordnance stores sent to you today to fill requisition approved by Maj. Rhett.

I could not furnish double barrel guns, not having them, and did the very best I could do, namely, to furnish Austrian and other Rifles, the calibres varying as little as possible, and sending ammunition to suit. Please sign receipts as soon as the stores are received.

Hill to Maj. Thos. G. Rhett, Chf. of Ord., TMD, Shreveport, La.

I rec'd requisition in favor of Col. D. B. Martin, Comdg. Conscripts, Dist. Texas today. I did not have the double barrel shotguns on hand in a condition to issue. The wagon was waiting and it would have taken sometime to repair the shotguns, almost all of them requiring new stocks and locks. I did therefore what I thought best under the circumstances and issued a lot of mixed guns with little difference in calibre with ammunition to suit.

I hope this meets with your approval.

MONDAY, FEB. 20, 1865

Hill to Maj. Thos. G. Rhett, Chief of Ordnance, DTM, Shreveport, La.

My cartridge boys are now doing nothing in the Laboratory for want of cartridge paper. During the last week, I have sent up a large number of Colts Pistol cartridges and now have made about 200,000 Navy and Army pistol cartridges on hand ready for boxing, if I had caps to go with them. All the sporting caps I have on hand are damaged and not serviceable, and I will have them condemned as soon as an inspector comes around.

My tinners are also doing little or nothing for want of block tin to make solder.

I now have the 2,000 cap and cartridge boxes and belts ordered for Indian Nation ready, excepting magazines. If I could get the solder, I could have them ready.

I am also very much pushed for want of transportation, having to haul corn 30 miles and next week will have to haul it 35 miles, and the roads are in such a condition that last week I was entirely without lumber. If you can in anyway supply me with 10 more wagons and teams, you would much facilitate the efficiency of my Works. I enclose you a short copy of a report just made to me by my AAQM in relation to my transportation and forage.

I am doing everything in my power to make as much in my Dept. as I can, but I am always in fear of running out of material, and I assure you Major, I am at times considerably exercised as to how I am to get along, for with my limited means of transportation, I find it almost impossible to make ends meet. I have been faithful in every way to get teams, but they are not in the county. The mules I now have are almost run down, for they are kept running all the time.

We know that Col. Hill was a faithful officer, and also an ingenious one, otherwise under the circumstances his works would not have operated as efficiently as they did. Nevertheless, he writes, "I am in need of solder," "If you would supply me with 10 more wagons & teams," "I can not make cartridges for lack of proper paper," "I lack soldering irons, and also lack copper to make new ones," "For lack of nails I can not make ammunition boxes," etc., etc. This lack of material was not peculiar to Tyler, Texas alone, it existed throughout the entire Confederacy. The letters Col. Hill wrote to Major Thomas G. Rhett, Chief of Ordnance, Trans Miss. Dept., were duplicated by each officer under his command. Although one can imagine the feeling of despair that beset Major Rhett as he opened letter after letter which began with the chilling words "because of the lack of so and so, I am unable to accomplish this and that"; how much greater must have been this feeling farther up the line of command. What must have been the feelings of General Josiah Gorgas, Chief of all Confederate Ordnance? A lesser man would have been overwhelmed

[162]

by impending defeat and disaster. If these emotions were known to Gorgas, they were carefully concealed. In reading the records written by men such as Gorgas, and others who in part shared his high place such as James Burton, Richard Cuyler, Thomas Rhett, etc., the feeling comes that these men never dreamed of defeat; they were too busy arming and equipping the Confederate armies to even consider such. Their accomplishments of making something from nothing must have been far more satisfying to the inner man than mere victory could ever have been.

TUESDAY, FEB. 21, 1865

Hill to Maj. Thos. G. Rhett, Chief of Ord., TMD, Shreveport, La.

I have just received 662 yards of bag cloth for my men, and I am having it made up into a uniform for them; that I may have every man in uniform, and I would like very much to have permission to issue 20 yards of red flannel to my AAQM to trim the pants and jackets, and respectfully ask that you give me an order to turn that much over.

Confederate uniform regulations called for a gray uniform trimmed with the corps colors, which in the case of artillery (or ordnance) was red. This trimming amounted to red cuffs, collar, piping, and for ranks of sergeant and above, a red stripe on the outer seam of the trousers. To have been properly attired, Col. Hill's men would have had brass buttons (7 to the jacket, and 2 on the cuffs) bearing the large letter "A" (for Artillery). The strict details of "regulations" were not adhered to, and the men in the field felt themselves lucky if they had any buttons, let along those bearing the initial letter of the corps to which they belonged.

SATURDAY, FEB. 25, 1865

Hill to Maj. George D. Alexander, Comg. Arsenal, Marshall, Texas.

Enclosed, please find receipts for musket and rifle powder rec'd from you Jan. 23rd, 1865.

MONDAY, FEB. 27, 1865

Hill to Maj. Thos. G. Rhett, Chf. of Ord., TMD, Shreveport, La.

I am almost entirely out of cap paper and it is necessary that I should have some. I am also nearly out of steel pens, and the letter paper on hand is hardly fit to make returns on.

Please send me 3 reams of cap paper, 1 ream of letter ditto and 2 gross steel pens.

Hill to Maj. Thos. G. Rhett, Chf. of Ord., TMD, Shreveport, La.

Enclosed, please find Report of Board of Survey, appointed by me to examine a lot of gun barrels on hand too small to make any Army guns. Please approve the same so that I may drop them from my papers as gun barrels and take them up as old iron and make use of them as such. They can be made use of in no other way.

Hill to Col. Ben Alston, Inspt. Gen'l, DTM, Shreveport, La.

Please write and let me know what is the line pay of soldiers in each arm of the service, and what changes have been made and when the same took effect?

The rate of pay per month in the Confederate Army was briefly as follows: Brig. General—$301, Colonel—$210, Lieutenant Colonel—$185, Major—$150, Captain—$130, 1st Lieutenant—$90, 2nd Lieutenant—$80, Sergeants—$34, Corporals—$20, Privates of 1st class—$17, Privates—$11. Master Armorer, Master Blacksmith, Master Carriagemaker —$34, Armorers, Blacksmiths—$20, Artificers—$17, Labor-

[164]

ers—$13, Military Storekeeper (MSK) pay and allowance of Captain. Note is made that a laborer got $2.00 per month more than a private soldier. It has always been thus. In today's wars for example, the riveter working amidst the dangers of the shipyard receives a great deal more than does the private soldier in his safe and comfortable foxhole within 50 yards of a steel jacketed bullet!

WEDNESDAY, MARCH 1, 1865

Hill to Maj. Thos. G. Rhett, Chf. of Ord., TMD, Shreveport, La.

Enclosed I send you a copy of an order from Col. Bradfute which requires that we haul our commissary supplies to this post.

With my limited supply of transportation, I am very much afraid I shall not be able to keep up my Department. Can you not do something for me?

The Richmond *Whig* said that the Governor of Louisiana had urged the employment of 200,000 negroes as drivers and pioneers with the Confederate army so that all the white men could take their places on the firing line.

A good idea, but too late in the war to really be effective. Had negroes been accepted directly into the Confederate army with promise of full freedom, at the start of the war (and there were many who would have welcomed the chance), the results would have been tremendous. Aside from the heavy advantage of having just so many more men, the psychological effect upon those crusading Northerners who fought the war "to free the slaves" would have been overwhelming.

FRIDAY, MARCH 3, 1865

Hill to Capt. C. W. Wailey, Comdg. Arsenal, Shreveport, La.

Enclosed, please find receipts for 4,965 lbs. English harness leather and 2,500 gun nipples rec'd from you today.

The leather was not weighed here because it was wet and there was no chance of making my weights agree with yours.

Hill to Maj. Thos. G. Rhett, Chf. of Ord., TMD, Shreveport, La.

I have been trying in everyway to get a man to cook for my men, and I have been unable to do so. There is a man here now, Pri. Elef Alberton, Co. "C", Johnson's Battalion at Fort Washita, C.N. He is here on leave of absence which expires 15th March. He is a 1st class baker and cook, and I would like very much to get him detailed and ordered to report to me, as his services are indespensably necessary, and I think that the Service would lose nothing by his being detailed as he would save to us a great deal and will be a public benefit to the post. If he is detailed I shall furnish my men entirely with good bread instead of flour, and I am certain that the health of my command will improve and I earnestly hope that you will do everything in your power to get him detailed for us.

A little band of Marylanders—the 2nd Battalion—fighting in trenches before Petersburg, hungry, dirty, cold and ragged, were made happy by the receipt of a new gray uniform and complete change of underwear each. The clothing was the gift of Col. George P. Kane of Baltimore, who was Marshal of Police at the time of the riots of April 1861, and who at that time had pikes manufactured to repel the Northern invaders, and who later became mayor of Baltimore. Col. Kane visited the Marylanders in February and was shocked at their condition. When he left, he promised each man a new outfit, and he kept his promise. The Second Maryland at that time had been reduced to 200 men under Capt. John W. Torsch.

Hill to Capt. C. W. Wailey, Comdg. Arsenal, Shreveport, La.

I sent by express 15 pieces, 228¼ yards flannel and 755 flannel cartridge bags 'ordered by Major Rhett to be shipped to you' to Capt. S. C. Faulkner at Marshall with the request that he send them to you immediately.

I enclose invoices and receipts. Please sign the receipts and return as soon as stores are rec'd. This will be mailed from Marshall.

Hill to Capt. S. C. Faulkner, In Charge, Ord. Depot, Marshall, Texas.

I send by Pri. Brock, 228¼ yards flannel and 755 cartridge bags flannel, all in two rolls which you will please send forward to Capt. C. W. Wailey as soon as possible. If necessary, send them by stage. I have orders to send them to Shreveport as soon as possible. By attending to the shipment of the above, you will confer a great favor on me, and promote the interest of the Ordnance Dept.

Hill to Surgeon L. T. Pim, Marshall, Texas.

I send you in care of Capt. Faulkner, one bit, and enclose voucher for same, which you will please sign and remit the money for same as early as possible.

Hill to Lt. H. B. Holmes, Ord. Dept., Tyler, Texas.

You will proceed without delay to Rusk, Cherokee Co., Texas, and procure if possible from Col. D. B. Martin, Comg. Conscripts Dist. Texas, 20 men for guard duty at Tyler Ord. Works.

If the colonel turns you over any men you will return with them to these works as soon as practicable.

If the colonel has men and has no authority to order them to report to me, you will find out from him through what channel I shall apply to get them. The men are absolutely necessary for the protection of these works and you will use all your exertions in trying to get them.

Hill to Col. D. B. Martin, Comd. Conscript Dist. Texas, Rusk, Texas.

Through ignorance or otherwise, the Enrolling Officers have furnished boys for guard duty at these works, and the reserve corps being ordered out, I must now give them up. It is absolutely necessary that I have a guard here on duty.

I have in my charge a large amount of Public property, valuable and extensive buildings etc., and if there is no other way to have them guarded, I will have to put my first class mechanics on duty, and if I was forced to do a thing of that kind, the Service would be greatly injured thereby, as there is at this time, great need of arms, ammunition, accoutrements, etc. & etc.

I send one of my officers, Lt. Holmes, down to receive any men that you may have to send me. If you can spare the men, please turn them over to him and very much oblige.

Hill to Maj. Thos. G. Rhett, Chf. of Ord., TMD, Shreveport, La.

I now have leather and am pushing the 2,500 sabre belts and have 7 or 8 hundred finished with the exception of hooks and studs for slings. I will have all the belts ready for the hooks and studs in a week, I think. Must I box them up and send them to Capt. Wailey and let him put the hooks and studs to them, or will you send the hooks etc. to me? I also will require about 1,200 7/8 or 1 inch buckles to put on the belts. I do not think I have enough. I am putting a billet at one end and a 7/8 or one inch buckle at the door, otherwise, they are made according to the ordnance manual.

THURSDAY, MARCH 9, 1865

Hill to Lt. E. Dupre, A AQM for Ord. Works, Tyler, Texas.

You will take receipt from the men in the Ord. Dept. to whom you issue clothing etc. and report to this office at the end of each month the names of those to whom you have issued, the amount of each article and cost of same, so that it may be correctly entered upon the records of this office.

MONDAY, MARCH 13, 1865

Hill to Maj. Thos. G. Rhett, Chf. of Ord., TMD, Shreveport, La.

Enclosed is a special requisition for Ordnance and ordnance

stores necessary to carry on these works. The Harness makers vises, awls, etc. should be supplied as soon as possible as they are very much needed. The block tin and borax are articles that we must have as it is impossible to get along without them. I make a large estimate for leather but when I get to work with all hands I shall use about 800 lbs. of leather per week. We have not a nail on hand.

Hill to Capt. S. G. Faulkner, Comdg. Ord. Depot, Marshall, Texas.

I send by wagon today, 311 lbs. iron (parts of Arty carriages) to you to be forwarded as soon as you can do so to Capt. C. W. Wailey, Comg. Arsenal, Shreveport, La.

Please attend to the same as the parts of arty carriages are very much wanted at Shreveport at present.

Hill to Capt. C. W. Wailey, Comdg. Arsenal, Shreveport, La.

Enclosed please find invoices and receipts for 311 lbs. old iron (parts of arty carriages) ordered by Maj. Rhett to be sent to you. I forwarded the same today by wagon to Capt. Faulkner at Marshall to be sent to you as soon as possible.

Please sign and return receipts when you receive the same.

Hill to Capt. C. W. Wailey, Comdg. Arsenal, Shreveport, La.

Enclosed, please find receipt for one pair of shoes to be charged to Private Clarkson.

Hill to Maj. Thos. G. Rhett, Chf. of Ord., TMD, Shreveport, La.

Enclosed, you will find a special requisition for clothing for 60 men ordered to report to me from the Army of Arkansas. They are almost naked and I do earnestly hope that the Comg. Gen'l will order the clothing issued as the men are actually suffering from the want of it. Most of them are recruits which came out of Missouri, and it is pitiful to look upon them. They claim that they have not changed their clothing since they left their homes in Missouri.

Hill to Maj. Thos. G. Rhett, Chf. of Ord., TMD, Shreveport, La.

Beeswax is now a considerable item and it is imposible to get it for Confederate money, but if I am allowed to trade caps and powder, I can very easily, I think, get all that I require. I propose to trade at the following rates:

For 15 lbs. of powder and 100 caps at this rate I think we will get the beeswax cheap. The caps I propose trading is a lot of damaged caps which I have on hand that are not fit for issue to the army. 15 lbs. of wax will go a long way and it is a thing that we need very much. As it is almost impossible to get along without it.

I send a specimen of the caps I propose to trade.

Col. Hill's works was not the only Confederate establishment forced to trade ordnance stores for necessities. The Augusta (Ga.) *Constitutionalist* carried the following advertisement; "Government Works, Augusta, July 30, 1864. For this date, Powder will be exchanged for Bacon at the store of Mr. W. H. Howard, Broad St., opposite Augusta Hotel at the rate of one pound of Powder for two and half pounds of Bacon. G. W. Rains, Col. Comdg." Caps for beeswax, powder for bacon! Clearly, this was no way to run a business.

Hill to Maj. Thos. G. Rhett, Chf. of Ord., TMD, Shreveport, La.

I rec'd day before yesterday from Capt. Faulkner, 2½ reams of cap paper and one ream letter paper. The cap paper has been wet and it is utterly worthless, and the letter paper is unfit for reports and returns, being too thin and light. My desire when I requisited the paper was to get a small quantity of good paper for returns. The paper sent by Capt. Faulkner in Jany. was the same kind of paper, damaged by wet and otherwise unfit for anything except the ordinary daily operations of the office. I do not know how I can make out my quarterly papers unless I can get some paper. If you can furnish me one ream of good cap and one ream of good letter paper, I shall be glad, and will keep it for reports, etc. and will use this I have on hand for office duties. If you can do so, please let me have also 1 gross of good steel pens. Those sent by Capt. Faulkner are the poorest sort of a pen.

Hill to Capt. S. C. Faulkner, Comg. Ord. Depot, Marshall, Texas.

Enclosed, please find receipts for stores all of which were rec'd Jan. 6th except the linseed oil which was rec'd yesterday in two cans instead of one. I have made the correction.

I rec'd from you yesterday 3½ reams of paper which is in miserable condition having been wet. I can not use it. Is it the best you have on hand? I must have some better paper from some quarter, or I shall not be able to make out my quarterly papers.

The caps and other stores with the papers were all right.

Hill to Maj. Thos. G. Rhett, Chf. of Ord., TMD, Shreveport, La.

I am compelled to have about 3 pr. cotton cards. These are not in town except a few and they are held by one man and he asks from 6 to 7 dollars in specie for them, or from 150 to 175 dollars in Confederate money, and I do not feel justified in paying that price for them. I want them in the Laboratory for carding cotton for spinning cut thread. I would like if you could do so to have me supplied with 3 pair.

On this day was hanged Marcus Jerome Clark, the famous Confederate from Kentucky. Better known as "Sue Munday" because of his escapades in woman's garb, Clark was captured in Meade County on Sunday, put in the Louisville jail on Monday, convicted on Tuesday, and hanged on Wednesday. Justice (?) was fast in those days. Clark was a very handsome man, 20 years old, and six feet tall. On the scaffold he said that he was a Confederate soldier, and that he was proud to die for his country.

On this date the Confederate Congress suspended the writ of habeas corpus.

Hill to Maj. Thos. G. Rhett, Chf. of Ord., TMD, Shreveport, La.

At the request of Col. Jimison, I enclose for your approval or otherwise, a special requisition for bayonets, gun wipers, etc.

The battle of Bentonville, N. C., between Sherman's army of 60,000 men and Johnston's army of 26,000 men ended with the retreat of the Confederates. The Union loss was 1,600 men; that of the Confederates about 2,200 men. A severe defeat to the Southern cause was only prevented by a desperate charge of a small body of Texas Rangers and Tennessee cavalry. In this charge, the 16-year-old son of General Hardee, commanding the Confederate rear guard, was killed. Young Hardee had joined the Terry Texas Rangers two hours before he fell.

Hill to Capt. S. C. Faulkner, Comg. Ord. Depot, Marshall, Texas.

Enclosed, please find receipts for 25 lbs. borax rec'd from you a few days ago.

Please correct and return the invoices sent with the receipts for 10 gal. linseed oil. 250,000 musket caps etc. were rec'd Jan. 6th, 1865. The oil was delayed but finally came and in two tin cans instead of one. I corrected and sent you receipts and enclosed also the invoices which you will oblige me by correcting and returning as the quarter is drawing to a close.

Hill to Capt. W. H. Lewis, Chief Ord. Officer, Dist. Indian Territory, Fort Towson, C. N.

Enclosed, please find invoices and receipts for 200,000 musket percussion caps and 100,000 sporting ditto, delivered to Lt. E. Q. Andrews Feb. 27th for your Dept.

I thought I should be able to send the remainder of your stores before the end of the quarter and intended to include the whole in one invoice, but the quarter is about closing, and you will oblige me by signing and returning the enclosed receipts at your earliest convenience.

The first battalion of Confederate colored troops paraded in Richmond today and attracted much attention. A few days later, President Lincoln reviewed the Union negro troops of the 24th Corps, Army of the James, before Petersburg.

FRIDAY, MARCH 24, 1865

Hill to Private A. Atkinson, (no address).

Yours of March 14th is rec'd. Your reason for not reporting is of a character not sufficient. It is your duty to report forthwith to this office in accordance with your furlough and you will accordingly do so or you will be sent for and treated as a deserter.

By remaining away after the expiration of your furlough you keep others here who desire furloughs, as leaves of absence will not be granted to others while there are any absent without leave.

The Richmond *Examiner* said of the seven hotels in Richmond, all except two—the Spottswood and the American—had been forced to close.

SATURDAY, MARCH 25, 1865

Hill to Lt. B. S. Tilley, En. Officer, Cherokee Co., Texas.

Enclosed, please find invoices and receipts for 4 lbs. powder etc. sent to you today by Sergt. Meadows. The caps are the very best water proof and I send a box of 250.

Please sign and return receipts as soon as convenient.

WEDNESDAY, MARCH 29, 1865

Hill to Capt. C. W. Wailey, Comdg. Arsenal, Shreveport, La.

Enclosed, please find receipts for 63½ gross gun nipples, gun locks, etc. rec'd from you a few days ago.

John M. Daniel, editor of the Richmond *Examiner*, died

at Richmond believing that the Confederates had won a great victory. All day the Confederate capital was thrilled by a strange report to the effect that Lee had broken Grant's line and captured thousands of prisoners. All the newspapers published the report, and John Mitchell, the Irish patriot, in his obituary of Daniel, expressed regret that the great Virginia editor had not lived to see the fruits of the Confederate success. There was not the slightest foundation for the report. Lee with 33,000 men, was holding 40 miles of intrenchments—about one man to every two yards, and the line was getting thinner every day, while Grant's daily reinforcements kept his army up to its full strength of 125,000 men. Besides this disparity in numbers, Lee's army was starving.

SATURDAY, APRIL 1, 1865

Hill to Lt. T. P. Martin, in Charge, Laboratory & Shops, Tyler, Texas.

The owners of the arsenal building complain that the windows of the 2nd & 3rd story are left open at night, thereby risking great injury to the building.

You will order, and see that your orders in this respect are executed, the shutters closed and the sash lowered both of the Harness Shop and Laboratory, so that no complaints of that kind can justly be made in the future.

The Richmond *Examiner* said editorially: "It is evident that the month of April will witness a decisive turn one way or another to Grant's grand converging campaign." Their prophecy was entirely correct, for 2 days later, (April 3rd), Richmond was in the hands of the Union forces.

FRIDAY, APRIL 7, 1865

Hill to Capt. C. W. Wailey, Comdg. Arsenal, Shreveport, La.

Enclosed, please find invoices and receipts for flannel cartridge bags and parts arty. carriages sent you 8th and 13th March.

Hill to Maj. Geo. D. Alexander, Comg. Arsenal, Marshall, Texas.

Enclosed, please find receipt for 400 lbs. pistol powder and 2 lbs. lamp black rec'd from you a day or two ago.

Between Col. Hill's letter of April 7, and that of April 10th, the Army of Northern Virginia, Gen. R. E. Lee commanding, was surrendered to the Army of the Potomac, Gen. U. S. Grant commanding. The Confederate Army of about 15,000 men, without food, and exhausted by days and nights of constant marching and fighting, was surrounded by Grant's Army of 106,000 men at Appomattox, Va. The terms of surrender were generous, and there was no demand by General Grant for General Lee's sword. The officers and men were paroled, not to take up arms again.

News of this of course had not yet drifted down Texas way, and it is doubtful if Col. Hill was even aware that the Confederate capital had fallen. About the time Hill was writing to Maj. Alexander acknowledging receipt of lamp black etc., General Lee sat wondering what to say to the 15,000 loyal men who had followed his banners and fortunes for so long. He wrote:

HEADQUARTERS ARMY NORTHERN VIRGINIA

April 10th, 1865

General Orders,
      No. 9

After four years of arduous services, marked by unsurpassed courage and fortitude, the Army of Northern Virginia has been compelled to yield to overwhelming numbers and resources.

I need not tell the brave survivors of so many hard fought battles, who have remained steadfast to the last, that I have consented to this result from no distrust of them. But feeling that valor and devotion could accomplish nothing that would compensate for the loss which would have accompanied a continuance of the contest, I determined to avoid the useless sacrifice of those whose past services have endeared them to their countrymen. By the terms of the agreement, Officers and men can return to their homes and remain until exchanged.

You will take with you the satisfaction that proceeds from the consciousness of duty faithfully performed; and I earnestly pray that a merciful God will extend to you his blessing and protection. With an unceasing admiration of your constancy and devotion to your country, and a grateful remembrance of your kind and generous consideration for myself, I bid you an affectionate farewell.

R. E. LEE, General

With the surrender of the Army of Northern Virginia, the fate of the Confederacy was doomed, but the war continued.

TUESDAY, APRIL 11, 1865

Hill to Maj. Thos. G. Rhett, Chf. of Ord., TMD, Shreveport, La.

Enclosed, please find receipt for $6,000 amount paid by you to Major Hill for hire of teams, negroes etc. in this Dept.

Hill to Capt. C. W. Wailey, Comdg. Arsenal, Shreveport, La.

Yours of April 5th asking for order to purchase lime is rec'd and then given in obedience to endorsement from Maj. Rhett. You will be informed when the lime is ready for you.

Hill to Capt. G. S. Polleys, In Charge Armory etc., Tyler, Texas.

You will order John McMillan detailed in this Dept. and on Detached service burning lime, to have and hold in readiness to be delivered on the order of Capt. C. W. Wailey, Comdg. Arsenal, Shreveport, La., 200 bushels of lime. This lime is to be delivered at the lime kiln on the order of Capt. Wailey and paid for by him. Report to this office when the lime is ready.

Hill to Capt. G. S. Polleys, In Charge Armory etc., Tyler, Texas.

You will at once try and make arrangements for more pine

timber for burning coal for this Dept. and will see Mr. Calloway Dean of Starville and see if you can not purchase of him the pine on the Chapin Tract of 640 acres on the Jim Town Road. See Mr. Dean and see if he will not let me have the pine that is on said tract of land.

There is another tract of pine on the Ross Road belonging to Mr. Isom Kindrick. You will also see it and try and purchase the pine on his land.

After seeing these two tracts of land, you will report to me what arrangements can be made for the purchase of the pine and which tract of land it will be best for me to get.

Hill to Maj. Thos. G. Rhett, Chief of Ordnance, Trans Miss. Dept., Shreveport, La.

The following is a report of operations in this Dept. for the 1st quarter of this year.

ARMORY

We have fabricated 194 Enfield rifles, 168 Texas rifles, 56 Austrian rifles, 2 Hill rifles and 28 smoothbore muskets, making in all, 448 new guns fabricated.

We have stocked 6 Enfield rifles, 1 Springfield ditto, 17 double-barrel shot guns, 2 musketoons and 43 smoothbore muskets, making in all 69 stocked.

We have also repaired 383 smoothbore muskets, 22 musketoons, 8 Texas rifles, 2 Spanish ditto, 2 Sharps ditto, 43 Austrian ditto, 18 Belgium ditto, 1 U.S. rifle, 5 Richmond ditto, 247 Enfield, 5 Arkadelphia ditto, 11 Springfield ditto, 24 Miss. rifles, 1 Colt ditto, 6 Whitney ditto and 3 double-barrel shot guns, making in all, 781 guns repaired.

In addition to the arms repaired and fabricated, we have kept all the tools in the other shops in order and made a complete set of harness maker's tools for 60 workmen. In the Armory we are doing good work and only want to be kept in material. The men are in good discipline and the officers and non-commissioned officers all attend strictly to their duties. We want more shop room and I now have a foundation in for a new shop but have no transportation to haul material and build with.

CARPENTER'S SHOP

We have suffered very much for want of material as it is impossible to keep the shop supplied with our limited supply of transportation at the Mill. We have fabricted 559 ammunition boxes, 28 arms chests, 34 ax helves, 57 saddle stretching horses, 60,700 shingles, 8 mallets. We have also built a large bridge over the Nochez River. The men in this shop all attend to their duties and work with a good will.

HARNESS SHOP

We have fabricated 4,825 cartridge boxes cavalry, 473 ditto infantry, 1,037 cap pouches, 1,898 waist belts, 6 saddles, 16 saddle trees, 2 halter bridles, 4 pairs bridle reins, 2 mule collars, 2 sets harness, 2 girths, 43 canteen straps, 18 pairs slippers for laboratory and 26 feet 3½ inch belting. All the men in this shop work well but I have been compelled from time to time to put some of the men on guard, as my regular guards were sick.

LABORATORY

We have done very little work for want of material. My boys I have kept at work cleaning up etc. We have fabricated 8,700 Enfield cartridges, Buck & Ball ditto—21,750, Army pistol ditto—1,311,952, Navy ditto—102,472, Enfield rifle double charged for testing—300, Enfield rifle balls—3,146 lbs., musket balls—665 lbs., Miss. rifle ditto—304 lbs., Army pistol balls—1,784 lbs., buckshot—339 lbs., buttons cartridge box—6,670, cap pouch buttons—4,022, thread cartridge—96 lbs., soap—72 lbs., envelopes official—112, ditto letter—200, and 54 lbs. of candles.

TIN SHOP

We have been very much in need of solder. The tinners have been cutting but have not completed much. We have fabricated: magazines cavalry—1,002, ditto infantry—1,290, burrs—20,500, guard plates—84, powder chargers—14, stencil plates—4, solder 47 lbs., bugles—3, funnels—2, glue kettles—2, sabre belt hooks—1,100, holtster tips—2, oil cans—3, plates for men's mess—10 and 36 tin ornaments.

My Dept. is now in a flourishing condition and all I ask is that transportation be furnished me. I now have my quartermaster off trying to hire, and am in hopes that he will succeed in getting me 10 or 15 more wagons and teams.

Besides the work reported, I have completed a work shop for repairs of wagons, etc. and am getting ready to build me a shed 200 feet by 40 feet for my animals in my horse lot, a thing very much needed to protect my animals from the weather.

I have been compelled to relieve my old guard and have been supplied with men from the invalid corps as they are no more use than so many babes. They are totally unfit for the duty and I respectfully suggest that if it is possible, that a detachment of 30 good men be ordered to me for guard duty.

From Col. Hill's quarterly report, it is evident that the Ordnance Works at Tyler, Texas, were in a flourishing state. Such was not the case elsewhere in the Confederacy. General Upton's troops of Wilson's cavalry corps were fast closing in on Columbus, Ga., there to destroy all the arms manufactories in that city. At Mobile, Ala., the last of the works defending the city, Forts Tracey and Huger, were blown up and evacuated by the Confederates, preparatory to retreating. Selma, Ala., with its large ordnance works, had fallen on April 2, and Montgomery, Ala., first capital of the Confederacy, was to fall on the 12th.

THURSDAY, APRIL 13, 1865

Hill to Maj. Thos. G. Rhett, Chf. of Ord., TMD, Shreveport, La.

All of the 2,500 sabre belts will be completed by the middle of next week excepting the studs. I have rec'd from Capt. Wailey 2,500, but it takes 2 studs to the belt, and I respectfully request that I be supplied with 2,500 more.

Hill to Maj. Thos. G. Rhett, Chf. of Ord., TMD, Shreveport, La.

I am very much in need of the grate bars that you promised to cast for me. Please cast them as soon as possible and let me know when I can get them.

I will send you by first wagon going to Marshall the old white walnut butts for stocks. I have a box of them put up for you.

Hill to Capt. I. Q. StClair, Q.A.Co., Tyler, Texas.

Will you please inform me what arrangements have been made for supplying this department with provisions on our requisitions? Our men up to this date have only drawn a half a pound of bacon to the man and my comm. sergeant informs me that he now has not three days rations of bacon on hand even at half a pound to the man.

Confederate General Johnston held a conference at Greensboro, N. C., with President Davis and other members of his Cabinet. As a result of which it was agreed that Johnston should propose a peace parley to General Sherman.

GOOD FRIDAY, APRIL 14, 1865

Hill to Col. W. R. Bradfute, Comdg. Post, Tyler, Texas.

It is just reported to me by my commissary sergeant that my men after tomorrow will be without meat. I asked him the cause and he reports to me that Capt. StClair gave Lt. Dupre (AACs for Ord. Dept.) last Friday an order for 3,000 lbs. on the agent at Athens, Henderson county, and he sent two wagons to that place for the bacon. My wagon master reports that there was no bacon there. From Athens, my wagon master went to Fincastle, same county, but could get no bacon there. Knowing that we were out of bacon he went from planter to planter and collected what bacon he could, and arrived here this morning. Up to this date, my men have been living on half a pound of bacon to the man. I hope you will investigate this matter and order your commissary to supply my Dept. with the proper rations.

My transportation is now all absent and it will be impossible for me to haul bacon in time to issue to my men, and I am afraid that it will be impossible for me to do any more hauling for the Post Commissary as my transportation is very limited and the mules are in such a condition that it is impossible for me to do the hauling required for my own Dept.

[180]

While attending a performance of *Our American Cousins* for the benefit of Laura Keene at Ford's Theater, Washington, D. C., Abraham Lincoln, President of the United States, was shot in the head by John Wilkes Booth. After shooting President Lincoln, Booth shouted; "Sic semper tyrannis" (thus always to tyrants), and jumped from the President's box to the stage, breaking his left leg. In the excitement, Booth escaped on a horse which awaited him at the stage entrance. President Lincoln was carried across the street to the humble home of William Peterson, a tailor, and was made as comfortable as possible. He died the following day (April 15th) at 7:22 A.M. Vice President Andrew Johnson was not at Lincoln's bedside although he was only three blocks away and knew that the end was near. A few hours after Lincoln's death Johnson took the oath of office as President of the United States.

SUNDAY, APRIL 16, 1865

Hill to Maj. Geo. D. Alexander, Comdg. Arsenal, Marshall, Texas.

I have an invoice from your office of March 18th, 1865 for: 198 bayonets, 51 gun bands, 34 breech butts, 49 guards, 24 locks. Thinking it time that these articles should have been rec'd, I deem it my duty to advise you that they have never been rec'd at this office, that you may explain how it was that invoices were sent and the stores never shipped. There must be a mistake somewhere.

Episcopal church-goers in Richmond, Va., were shocked to find all Episcopal Churches closed by order of General Ord, the Federal Commander, because the clergymen could not change the prayer for "the President of the Confederate States" to read "The President of the United States" without instructions from Bishop Johns, who at the time was in Canada.

[181]

Hill to Capt. C. W. Wailey, Comdg. Arsenal, Shreveport, La.

Enclosed, please find receipts for 101 Smooth bore muskets, 71 rifles, 2 Tower muskets, etc. & etc. Also receipts for 120 Enfield rifles, 120 bayonets, etc.

Hill to Capt. S. C. Faulkner, Comdg. Ordn. Depot, Marshall, Texas.

Enclosed, please find receipts for 4 cavalry sabres, 1 Sharps rifle, etc., received from you a few days ago.

Hill to Capt. C. W. Wailey, Comdg. Arsenal, Shreveport, La.

Enclosed, please find receipts for miserable arms.

These are the arms forwarded by you last Nov. and about which there has been some trouble.

I have endorsed on the receipts my certificate stating the actual number of guns rec'd by me, and the particular kind which fell short.

I also send attached the certificate copy of the certificate of Maj. Alexander which if you will send up with the papers and my certificate endorsed, will I think be sufficient to clear you in the matter.

I have made similar endorsements on the invoices and shall send up with them Maj. A's original certificate. I hope this will be satisfactory to you.

A treaty of peace was signed at Durham Station, N. C., by General Johnston of the Confederate Army and General Sherman. It is said that Sherman, who had heard Lincoln express his views as to the reconstruction in the South, tried to embody Lincoln's ideas in the treaty. When copies of the treaty were received in Washington, Secretary Stanton, South hater, hastily called a meeting of the Cabinet, at which the view was seriously expressed that Sherman was planning to seize the Government and declare himself dictator. General Grant was summoned and notified to inform Sherman that the treaty was disapproved. A sharp reprimand was also sent to Sherman.

Hill to Capt. T. P. Leavenworth, Ord. Off., Jefferson, Texas.

Sometime in last Sept. I rec'd from you 20 skillets and lids which I have never receipted to you for.
If you will send me invoices, I will return you receipts.

Hill to Capt. Q. M. Taylor, En. Off. Smith County, Texas.

I understand that you have ordered one of my men to Camp. I wish to know by what authority you issue orders to me in my Dept.? You have nothing to do directly with the men in this Dept. whether they are properly or improperly detailed. My men are under my command and under the command of no other person whatever. I control the affairs of my own Dept. and will not submit to any interference from you. Anything in regard to the men under my command must come through me.

Any violations in future of this very proper method of proceeding will be made the subject of the action of a court martial. Private Story will not be relieved from duty in this Dept. until he is properly ordered through me.

A conference was held at Millwood, Va., between General Chapman, representing General Hancock, and Colonel John Singleton Mosby, famous Confederate ranger. About 15 Union officers and a score of Mosby's officers attended. No agreement for the surrender of Mosby's command was reached, and the truce parley almost ended in a tragedy. One of Mosby's men discovered two regiments of Union cavalry nearby and believing there was a plot to capture the wily partisans while under a flag of truce, burst into the room where the conference was being held and shouted to Mosby what he had discovered. Every Confederate jumped to his feet and laid hold of his pistol, but at a signal from Mosby all filed quietly out of the room, mounted their horses and rode away. No attempt was made to stop them.

Hill to Maj. Thos. G. Rhett, Chf. of Ord., TMD, Shreveport, La.

The force in my Harness Shop has been greatly increased and will be still further increased and I have but two tinners and it will be impossible for them to make magazines as rapidly as they will be required to complete cartridge boxes. It seems to me therefore that it is necessary that I should have additional force in my Tin Shop. It is useless to have men to make cartridge boxes unless the cartridge boxes can be completed with magazines.

Sergt. A. T. Fones of Marshall's Ark. Light Battery, is a tinner (1st class) and a No. 1 workman and his services as such are indispensably necessary in my Dept. He is at present with his command. Please have him detailed in the Ordn. Dept. and ordered to report to me.

He is a sergeant, but it seems to me that he can better serve the country here than in the field as his place there can be filled by someone else, but here, it can not.

On this day, Col. John Singleton Mosby, commanding Mosby's Rangers, disbanded his command and took farewell of his men. With about 30 faithful followers Mosby set out to join Johnston's command in North Carolina, but upon learning of Johnston's surrender, they dispersed. With a price of $5,000 on his head, Mosby eluded the military authorities until the latter part of June, when an order was issued offering to parole him. Mosby then surrendered.

Hill to Col. W. R. Bradfute, Comdg. Post, Tyler, Texas.

I have this month only issued a half a pound of bacon to the men in my Dept., and I now have not enough by 300 lbs. to issue that amount to the end of the month. Capt. StClair tells my commissary sergeant that he can not issue any more bacon to him unless I haul it. That is impossible for me to do as I only have one four-mule team and wagon at the works. All the rest are away and if I stopped that wagon, my engine will have to stop and my work in hand cease, which will materially interefer with the Ordn. Dept.

You will oblige me by ordering your commissary to supply me the bacon required and to make arrangements for supplying us in the future for it will be impossible for me to haul anymore commissary stores, as I have not the transportation.

The above letter was returned with the following endorsement:

Office Post Commandant
Tyler, April 22, 7865.

Respectfully returned to Col. Hill with the remark that Capt. StClair informs me that Commissary Supplies are furnished your Dept. (upon orders from Gen'l Smith) as Dist. C.S., therefore I have nothing to do with the matter. You must apply to the authority that has the control.

Respectfully
W. R. Bradfute,
Col. Comg. Post.

Returned with the following endorsement.

Ord. Office, Tyler, Texas,
April 22.

Respectfully returned to Col. Bradfute with the remark that my orders are to draw my supplies in bulk, making requisition for the same on the Post Commissary, and every requisition for supplies. Since you have been in command of the Post, supplies have been approved and ordered issued to me by yourself. If I can not get supplies from the Post Commissary, I would like to be informed that I may correspond with Headquarters on the subject.

G. H. Hill, Lt. Col.
C. S. P. A., Comg. Ord. Works.

Hill to Maj. Thos. G. Rhett, Chf. of Ordn., TMD, Shreveport, La.

Your order of the 14th inst. has just been received, ordering me to issue to the Chief Ord. Officer, Indian Territory, 491 Texas rifles. I have 504 Texas rifles in store, but I have a requisition of Col. Bourland, approved by you of Nov. 7, 1864, for 475 cavalry guns, cap boxes, cartridge boxes and waist belts, and I have these arms and equipments (and I have had them) ready and marked ever since the receipt of the requisition, and Col. Bourland and Gen'l McCulloch have been notified time and again that the guns and equipment were ready for them to fill that requisition. I have put up 345 Texas rifles, 90 Hill rifles and 40 musketoons. I have on hand only 159 Texas rifles, as reported in my weekly report of the 15th inst. over and above the 345 marked for Col. Bourland. What shall I do? Shall I disregard Col. Bourland's requisition and issue the 491 guns to the Chief Ordnance Officer of the Indian Territory as ordered on the 14th, or fill this only with other guns? I now have on hand and ready to issue, 975 Enfield rifles besides the guns. I would respectfully request that you refer to my weekly report of the 15th for information as to what arms we have on hand over and above those called for on requisition. Since that report, I have repaired 120 Enfield rifles and a few other guns.

About 200 of Mosby's Rangers, under Lt. Col. Chapman, rode into Winchester, Va., and surrendered to the Union force there. They were paroled.

MONDAY, APRIL 24, 1865

Hill to General Hughes (no address).

In obedience to Circular Order from Office of Chief of Ordnance, DTM, dated March 28, 1865, I have the honor to submit the following with drawings of the shops with machinery etc. and ground plan of all buildings and contemplated buildings in our Arsenal grounds, viz:

1st—Harness Shop—two large rooms, 30 x 80 hired in the town of Tyler. I have no machinery in them. 30 hands are employed. Infantry and cavalry equipment manufactured exclusively. One man is employed as a saddler. The number of hands in this shop will be 3 times as great during this year, and we will be able to supply, I think, the whole army with equipments. I propose moving this shop from town next fall if I complete the contemplated building on the Arsenal grounds.

[186]

2nd—Laboratory—one room, rented, 80 x 80 with no machinery. 40 little negro boys and 3 white men employed. Small arms ammunition fabricated entirely. No changes contemplated except I shall move to the Arsenal grounds in a wooden building 70 x 30.

3rd—Tin Shop—small room rented, two tinners at work fabricating canteens, bugles and magazines for cartridge boxes. No changes contemplated, and no machinery.

4th—Blacksmith Shop—40 x 90 wooden building on Arsenal grounds. 16 forges running with one fan blast, 1 forge common (?) bellows, 30 hands employed fabricating almost everything—locks and parts of locks, screws, nails etc. No change contemplated.

5th—Carpenter's Shop—10 hands employed, a frame room 75 x 25 with no machinery. Ammunition boxes, packing boxes fabricated and all kinds of carpenter work done as needed in the Dept. No change is contemplated. We have suffered a great deal for want of nails. Nearly all nails were made in the Blacksmith Shop. The saw mill is 18 miles from the works and some of the time we have been out of lumber for lack of transportation.

6th—Armory—75 hands employed in a 2 story building 100 x 40. Machinery as in enclosed drawing. This operation is engaged in fabricating the Texas and Hill rifles—Texas rifle cal. .57 and Hill rifle cal. .54. All kinds of arms are repaired. Machinery is scarce, and nearly everything is done by hand. We can now put up 14 guns per day. Two aries (?) of stockers are constantly employed, the other hands doing repair work and fabricating spare parts. The foundations are in for another building of same size and in drawing of ground plan #4 with a cross #3 for an Engine room office, store room and inspecting room. The brick, shingles and lumber are all ready and we are now going ahead with the work as rapidly as possible. #2 in the drawing is a contemplated building 3 stories high which I have not estimated for. It is designed to be a store room, harness shop to the Armory for storing small arms. This will enable me to have everything together. As my works are now situated, I am compelled to keep my Office, Store rooms, Tin Shop, Laboratory and Harness Shop in town, and the other shops are a mile from town. We are so far from lumber and have had so little transportation that it has been impossible for me to do much building. Nails have been so scarce that I have been forced to put up mostly all my buildings with wooden pegs. All of my shops are well organized and I have some very excellent workmen and during the present year, we shall do a great deal of work. As to an estimate of it, it would be hard to specify any given amount in either shop. As soon as the hands that are ordered to report to me report, I shall be able to fabricate 300 cartridge boxes per day, and shall be able to stock and fabricate 15 guns, besides doing the repairing for the Dept.

Several news items of note appeared on this date.

The last meeting of the Confederate Cabinet was held at Washington, Ga., to discuss the proposed surrender of General Johnston. At the same time, General Grant arrived at General Sherman's headquarters in North Carolina with President Johnson's order, disapproving the treaty of peace between Generals Johnston and Sherman.

Farther South, the Confederate steamer *William H. Webb,* mounting three guns and commanded by Lieut. Commander Charles W. Read, which had been penned up in Red River by a fleet of Union gunboats, ran the blockade and made a dash down the Mississippi in an effort to escape to sea. In running past New Orleans, however, the little vessel was disabled by a shot from one of the Union ships and her commander then ran her ashore and blew her up. Read and his crew of 45 men escaped to the swamps, but were pursued and most of them captured. At the time, Read was only 24 years old.

TUESDAY, APRIL 25, 1865

Hill to Col. D. B. Martin, Comdg. Conscripts, Rusk, Texas.

W. M. L. Hurbough, a conscript from Anderson county, Texas, ordered to report to the camp of Instruction at Rusk, will hand you this in person.

He is a gunsmith, and used to work at Billips & Co. Works.

Please have him detailed in the Ordn. Dept. and ordered to report to me. His services are indispensably necessary in this Dept.

Hill to Col. Sam'l Roberts, Comdg. Labor Bureau, Bonham, Texas.

Mr. James Coltharp of Vanzandt Co. has a mill and is doing all the sawing for my Dept. Your agent has called upon him for the negroes that he has subject to the Govt. call. If his negroes are taken away from him, it will interfere very materially with my works. You will therefore oblige me very much by giving me an order exempting his negroes from conscription as their services are indispensably necessary to this Dept.

WEDNESDAY, APRIL 26, 1865

Hill to Capt. C. W. Wailey, Comg. Shreveport Arsenal

I enclose to you, two blank certificates of purchase which you will oblige me by obtaining the proper signatures to and returning to this office. You will please collect the money and send at the same time. I sent the saddles by Mr. Gunn's (wagon-master) train.

Col. Scymanski's saddle—$187.00

Maj. Dunlap's saddle—$175.00

You will oblige me also by delivering or forwarding them.

I sent by the same train, one box candles for Maj. Rhett. Please deliver it.

At Mr. Gunn's earnest request, I sent one of my men, J. L. Crelette with him with the express understanding that he was to return to this post after his arrival at Shreveport. Please see that he is sent back.

General Joseph E. Johnston surrendered the Army of the Tennessee to General William T. Sherman on the same terms granted to the Army of Northern Virginia by Grant. The total number of officers, men and non-combatants paroled was 30,000.

In effect, the war was over, but the Trans Miss. Dept. of the Confederacy ignored, as far as possible as it was to ignore, the events that transpired east of the Mississippi River and went ahead with their plans for the future—plans which evidently held no idea of surrender.

Hill to Gen. Ben Huger, Chief of Ordn. Bureau, Marshall, Texas.

I have just made a contract with the firm of Higginbotham Billips & Co. for supply of iron for my Dept. which is absolutely necessary for making gun barrels. Our agreement is this. They are to supply me with 1,000 lbs of iron per month until they get their works under full blast at which time they will supply me with all the iron that I may require to the full extent of their works, allowing them to sell outside a sufficient amount to procure necessary supplies and to keep successfully in operation, I paying schedule prices for what I get. I, on my part, agreeing to get them detailed, and ordered to report to me, and allowing them to work at their iron works in Anderson County viz:

Private G. G. Higginbotham—Co. "G", 13th Tex. Inf.
Private John H. Brown—Co. "D", 13th Tex. Inf.
Private David Mitchell—Co. "G", 13th Tex. Inf.
Private Andrew Alverson—Co. "G", 13th Tex. Inf.
Private I. D. Billips—Co. "B", Johnson's Battalion.

These men have all been conscripted in Anderson county and have selected these companies to be assigned to and are now at work in their iron works which is in successful operation on a small scale in Anderson county. It is absolutely necessary that these men should be detailed, for without them, we can get no iron, and one of the few iron establishments that are making iron in the TMD will be broken up. These men failing to supply me with a 1,000 lbs of good iron per month will forfeit their detail. I write General to you as you have Capt. Temple to inform you of what this company is doing, and if you get the men detailed, I am confident that with my assistance and patronage, that they will turn out considerable iron which will very much facilitate the wants of the Department and the surrounding country. I am satisfied that these men are working to succeed, and if permitted to go on with their works, that they will succeed.

Hill to Lt. E. Dupre, AACS, Tyler Ord. Works, Tyler, Texas.

You will issue to the mess at Armory, 102 lbs of bacon as a special issue, as they are entirely out of meat.

Hill to Maj. Thos. G. Rhett, Chf. of Ord. TMB, Shreve-port, La.

The men of my Dept. have been complaining all this month about the meat rations. I have tried to get the full rations from Capt. John Q. St.Clair, ACS, but he informs me that I will have to haul it from 30 to 40 miles. This month, my men have only had issued to them, one half pound of bacon to the man, and it is not enough. I see it cooked and it only gives a man a small piece for two meals a day. It will be impossible for me to have my commissary stores, and I think that Capt. StClair should be furnished the means of supplying me, and I would be very much obliged if you will lay this matter before the proper authorities to see if there is not some remedy possible, for men must be fed or they can not work.

FRIDAY, APRIL 28, 1865

Hill to Capt. S. C. Faulkner, Comdg. Ordn. Depot, Mar-shall, Texas.

I send one wagon down today for the following things which I am compelled to have, viz:

3 doz. files—single cut if possible
180 lbs of block tin
4 boxes of tin plate
2 reams of cartridge paper.

The other things I will get as soon as I can send for them. You will also please let me have if it has come, a pound or two of lamp-black. I will get an order for it as soon as I can. I understand that Rhett was looking for a quantity and I am very much in need of about 4 pounds.

The steamer Sultanta, carrying 2,100 sick and wounded Federal soldiers on the Mississippi River from Vicksburg to Cairo, was blown up by the bursting of her boilers near Memphis. Only about 700 of the men aboard the vessel were saved.

Hill to Capt. L. L. Horne, Chief of Labor Bureau, N.S.D., Bonham, Texas.

I was this morning informed by Mr. Durrough that 18 negroes would be ready for me in Hopkins county by the 14th of May, and I hasten to inform you in obedience to your request that I will send for them. I wish however that you would let me know at what point in Hopkins county I may receive them? Please answer this immediately so that there can be no mistake, and inform Mr. Russell, your agent of the facts.

The First Maryland Confederate cavalry, under Col. Gus Dorsey, which broke through the Union lines before the surrender at Appomattox (reached Cloverdale, Va., on its way to join General Johnston's army in North Carolina, and there met General T. T. Mumford, who informed the Marylanders that Johnston had surrendered. The First Maryland was then disbanded, the men dispersing. The great grandfather of the author, John William Albaugh, was a member of this group of men until he was killed near Winchester in the fall of 1864. His brother was one of those who broke through the Union lines and proceeded South to join General Johnston after Lee's surrender at Appomattox.

MONDAY, MAY 1, 1865

Hill to Maj. Thos. G. Rhett, Chf. of Ord. TMD, Shreveport, La.

Enclosed, please find receipts for $50,000 rec'd by Lt. Dupre.

Hill to Maj. Thos. G. Rhett, Chf. of Ord. TMD, Shreveport, La.

I am now about to run out of coal and unless I have permission to take pine I am certain I shall be entirely out in six weeks or sooner. I have tried in every way to purchase of those having it and none would sell the land. I have been up to this time, getting coal off of land belonging to a person who is now in the enemy's line, but the pine is entirely exhausted. I have selected a tract of land belonging to a land speculator in Nachagdoches, a Mr. Ragie. It is entirely unoccupied, has 300 acres in the tract and a good road leading to it which is passable all the year, and is the most convenient pine to the Armory I know of, and I would like very much to have permission to impress the pine on this piece of land to make coal for my department. It will be the only chance I see of getting it, for no one will sell for Confederate money.

It being May 1, 1865, it is not hard to believe that Confederate money was getting somewhat difficult to pass, and in most parts of the country, South as well as North, it was worth less then than it is today.

John Wilkes Booth, the slayer of President Lincoln, and David Herold, one of his accomplices, were surrounded on the farm of Richard J. Garret, in Caroline County, Va., on Wednesday, April 26. Herold surrendered but Booth refused to do so. The barn in which he had taken refuge was set on fire. Sergt. Boston Corbett, of the 16th New York Cavalry, saw Booth by the light of the flames and shot him. This was about 5 p.m. and he died 2 hours later. His body was taken to Washington and buried temporarily. Later it was disinterred and delivered by the Government to Booth's brother, Edwin Booth, and reburied in the Booth family lot in Greemount Cemetery, Baltimore. The New York papers of April 30th, published sensational stories regarding the disposition of Booth's body. The *Times* which then, as now, had little use for anything Southern, said the body had been dismembered and the pieces wrapped in canvas then thrown in the Potomac. It was also said that Edwin Booth, the brother, had asked for, but had been refused the body.

TUESDAY, MAY 2, 1865

Hill to Lt. H. B. Holmes, In Charge Armory etc., Tyler, Texas.

Mr. Wilfing, Disbursing Clerk will begin paying off the detailed men in this Dept. this afternoon at 2 o'clock, beginning at the Harness Shop.

Each commissioned officer in charge of a Dept. connected with these Works will be required to be present and witness the paying off of the men in his Dept.

Orders similar to the above were sent to Surgeon Mc-Gregor, and Lts. Martin and Dupre.

From the above, it is evident that the word was finally getting through to the Tyler Ordnance Works that the war was coming fast to a close. Nevertheless, Col. Hill seemed to retain a "business as usual" attitude.

THURSDAY, MAY 4, 1865

Hill to Maj. Thos. G. Rhett, Chf. of Ord., TMD, Shreveport, La.

Confederate money at this place is worth nothing. The citizens will not take it and it is impossible to purchase provisions with it. Some of the families of our men are now suffering for something to eat and I shall have to commence issuing rations to them or have trouble with the men. Please see if the Comdg. Gen'l would not, under the existing circumstances, allow my AACS to sell to the married men of my Dept. rations to the amounts according to the size of the men's families?

General Richard Taylor surrendered the troops under his command in Alabama, Florida and Louisiana to General E. R. S. Canby at Citronelle, Ala. The Confederates were granted the same terms as were granted Lee's army. This was the last Confederate army east of the Mississippi. There remained of the once vast Confederate military might, only the Army of the Trans Mississippi Dept., commanded by General E. Kirby Smith.

Hill to Maj. Thos. G. Rhett, Chf of Ord. TMD, Shreve-port, La.

About the 20th of last month, I was arrested by the Civil Authorities on the charge of misapplication of public transportation, in that I did, on such and such a date, have hauled to the public grave yard near this place, 5,000 brick with a public team, for my own private use. I was carried before Judge Hill and was asked if I had any counsel. I told him I had none and wanted none. He then asked me if I was prepared to give bail. I told him I was not, but that I was ready for trial and as the charge was false, I would like to have a hearing. He told me that I could not be tried now, and would have to give bail or go to jail. I asked him what amount of bail I would have to give, and he told me $5,000. I then consulted with a lawyer and I gave the required bail and am now bound to appear from day to day at the call of the C. S. Court.

The Court is to meet again I understand in October next, and my trial may come off or it may not, just as the Dist. Attorney feels whether he will try the case or not. If there was any foundation for the charge, I would not then complain, but would willingly submit, but to be persecuted in the way that I consider I am without any help for it, is in my opinion shameful. Here I am compelled to employ a lawyer at great expense to myself, and forced to give bail of $5,000 or go to jail and there lay incarcerated for 6 months, and for what? For simply hiring a wagon from a private citizen and having brick hauled to a grave yard to have a wall built around a brother officer's grave, for the facts are as follows:

On the 20th of March, 1865, Capt. George Polleys and myself hired a wagon to have brick hauled to the grave yard to build a wall around the grave of Lt. Clark and his and my child, who are all buried near each other. The wagon was hired of Private J. W. Story, a conscript of Smith county, Texas, who is on a surgeon's certificate and was at that time doing nothing. After he got through hauling the brick for myself and Capt. Polleys, I hired him and his team in the Ordn. Dept., promising to try to get a detail for him, and applied for a detail which I am now expecting from the Chief of the Conscript Bureau. The papers having been returned for some correction. The man is still in my Dept. driving his own team. These facts I can establish and hope something may be done that I may be enabled to have a speedy trial or be entirely relieved. I will also state that it has been the custom of service since I have been in the Army for an officer to use (when it is not otherwise engaged) a wagon for doing any little hauling of this kind that he might want. But this was a private team and hired privately and if it had been a public team I would not have known that I was doing anything against the law, but would have thought I was doing what was, and has always been, customary, for I nor none of the Lawyers have ever heard anything of any such as having been published or enacted until after Judge Hill's charge to the grand jury. I should not think that officers, or anyone else should be punished for an act which they knew not to be in violation of any law, but men simply doing what they had always seen to be the custom of the service.

After the lapse of almost 100 years it is difficult to say with certainty who "put the finger" on Col. Hill, so to speak. The likeliest suspect however would be Col. Hill's old friend Col. Bradfute, Comdg. Post, Tyler, Texas.

MONDAY, MAY 8, 1865

Hill to Capt. Walter Caruth, AQM, Tyler, Texas.

I have 30 boxes weighing about 7,000 lbs., containing cartridge boxes, cap boxes and waist belts that I was ordered to turn over to you for transportation for the Chief of Ordn. Dist. of Texas. Will you receive them and store them in your store room, or will you ship them from mine?

You will please inform me how soon it will be before they can be sent off?

Hill to Maj. Thos. G. Rhett, Chief of Ord., TMD, Shreveport, La.

Enclosed, please find communication from me to the Post Quartermaster with his endorsement thereon, stating that it will be impossible for him to forward the stores alluded to, to the Chief of Ordn. Dist. Texas, unless he is furnished more transportation. The stores are all ready except about 500 infantry cartridge boxes for which magazines will be made this week.

Hill to Maj. Thos. G. Rhett, Chf. of Ord., TMD., Shreveport, La.

Yesterday, one of McMurty & Atkinson's trains left with the Post Quartermaster at this place, the following list of Ord. Stores, viz:—150 shovels, 148 spades, 149 picks, 20 boxes tin, 7 kegs spikes, 12 kegs nails, 12 rolls harness leather, 8 rolls kip hides, 46, 5-gal. cans linseed oil, 26 boxes of glass, 484 sides sole leather, 6 large casks oil and 19 pigs of copper.

I would like very much to get of the above things, the 12 rolls of harness leather to make the 2,500 gun slings. The leather I have on hand is very inferior and I am afraid that I shall be out of leather before I can get more. I would also like to get 10 shovels, 10 spades, 10 picks, and one 5 gal, can of the linseed oil, and I would like to retain one of the pigs of copper. All these things I need, and if you could turn me over all the leather, I would feel greatly relieved, for I am afraid all the time that I will run short.

Hill to Maj. Thos. G. Rhett, Chf. Ord. TMD, Shreveport, La.

I am now out, or nearly out of engine wood, and I must have some or my engine and works must stop. There is adjoining and east of the Armory Tract, a body of 70 acres of good wood land, sufficient on it to answer for a considerable time to come. It belongs to a man by the name of Edwards who lives at Nachadoches, and is one of the largest land holders in Texas, and the wood in that tract could be used by the Govt. without injury to the interests of the owner. If I can obtain an order to impress the timber on said tract, I can make arrangements with the agent of the owner by which I can purchase the same, but he will not sell or make any contracts with me unless I can get an order to impress. I suppose he wishes to be justified in entering into an arrangement by an order for me to impress.

Hill to Capt. S. C. Faulkner, Comdg. Ordn. Depot, Marshall, Texas.

I send a wagon down to day for the following list of stores which I am needing particularly, viz: 22 doz. files (assorted as follows if possible)—3 doz. 14 inch, 3 doz. 12 inch, 3 doz, 10 inch (or 2 doz. 8 inch flat bastard files), 3 doz. 10 inch, 2 doz. 16 inch (or 2 doz. in half round bastard files), 1 doz. 10 inch smooth flat finishing files, 1 doz. 8 inch half round finishing files, 1 doz. 12 inch cabinet wood rasp, 1 doz. cabinet finishing wood wasps, 1 keg of 6 D, one of 8 and one of 10 D nails, 15 yards enameled cloth for Gen'l Huger's ambulance which I understand Maj. Rhett was to send to you.

Capt., you will oblige me if you will pick out the files and send me as near as possible in accordance with the above list.

These stores will not load the wagon, and you can fill up with anything else you have for me.

Hill to Maj. Geo. D. Alexander, Comdg. Arsenal, Marshall, Texas.

Enclosed, please find receipts for 198 bayonets, etc. (parts of guns) rec'd from you a few days ago.

I sent by the return wagon in charge of Mr. Greer, wagon master, the box of timber for pistol stocks.

And so once again we have mention of pistol making at the Marshall Arsenal.

Today, whatever remaining Confederate forces there were in Florida, surrendered at Tallahassee, Fla., and the troops in Arkansas surrendered at Chalk Bluff.

Hill to Capt. W. H. Lewis, Chief Ordn. Off. Dist. Indian Territory, Fort Towson, C. N.

I rec'd from you yesterday evening, invoices for 200,000 musket caps and 100,000 sporting ditto, which I sent to you sometime ago.

This was evidently a mistake, as I sent the same invoices to you requesting you to send me corresponding receipts, at the same time enclosing blank receipts, and instead of sending me the receipts, you have returned me the invoices. Please send me the receipts. I have just rec'd from the Chief of Ord. an order in favor of your Dist. for 491 guns. They are ready for you at anytime you may send for them.

Hill to Surgeon J. F. McGregor, in Chrg. Tyler Ord. Works Hospital.

I am perfectly satisfied that some of my men now on sick report have simply reported sick that they may be able to do private work at their rooms. You will order all men to remain in hospital who you have the least doubt about, and make them remain there all the time, not allowing them to leave the hospital for anything.

SUNDAY, MAY 13, 1865

The last battle (not engagement) of the war was fought today at Palmetto Ranch, Texas, between 600 Union troops under Col. Barrett, and 350 Texas Rangers and other cavalry under General Slaughter and Col. Ford. The Union force was defeated.

Col. Hill's Day Book is silent for a week, and what went on at the Tyler Ordnance Works, we can only surmise. What goes on in men's minds and hearts when the stone house in which they live comes slowly tumbling down—with them on the inside?

Although it is impossible to determine what went on inside of Col. Hill, it is not impossible to establish what was transpiring inside the Confederate Department of the Trans-Mississippi, only portion of the Confederacy that yet remained.

Composed of Missouri, Arkansas, Louisiana and Texas, the Trans-Mississippi Dept., because of its geographic location, had, remained in isolation as regards to the devastation that had been wrought throughout the balance of the

[199]

Southern States. The conqueror's heel had not been felt, the enormous physical resources of this fertile area were yet unspoiled. Although Missouri, Arkansas and Louisiana had known and seen the march of friendly and unfriendly troops, and suffered accordingly, the great State of Texas had heard scarcely a gun fired in anger within her borders. Certainly the area was not invulnerable—nothing ever is— but it was as invulnerable as any geographic location could be. True, its eastern waterways of the Mississippi and Red River were controlled by the Federals, still it realized that farther venturing west on the part of the Union army would be an expensive procedure, both from the standpoint of men and supplies. Roads were primitive, railroads practically nonexistent, while the west boundry of this area was protected by almost unexplored lands known variously as the "Indian Territory" or "Choctaw Nation," inhabited by Indians who had sworn their allegiance to the Southern Cause. The South border of the Trans-Mississippi consisted of the Gulf of Mexico, and Mexico itself, the latter in the process of violent civil upheaval between the "Liberals" and the "Imperialists" represented by Maximilian. Little wonder the Trans-Mississippi felt secure. They had every reason to feel such.

The news of the evacuation of Richmond, and General Lee's surrender drifted slowly to the people of the Southwest, and was received as had been the news of Gettysburg, and the fall of Atlanta, with somewhat shocked disbelief, but nevertheless still plainly with the air of "it can't happen here." The surrender of Johnston's Army of the Tennesee was somewhat more of a stunning blow, in that it left the door wide open for the hords of Yankees who would now most certainly turn their united attention towards this last remaining portion of the Confederacy.

Too late came the realization that the 60,000 men composing the military might of this area should have been sent to the assistance of either General Johnston or Richard Taylor.

The people became uneasy at once and disheartened too, though a great effort was made to stimulate their drooping spirits. A mass meeting at Shreveport was ordered, and speakers were appointed to address the soldiers and citizens from each State. General Harry Hays spoke for Louisiana, General Hawthorne for Arkansas, Colonel Flournoy for Texas, and Colonel Musser for Missouri. According to *Shelby and His Men,* "The speeches were in favor of further resistance, and expressed hopes that the army would keep the field—as Texas was vigorous with supplies —and be joined by numerous soldiers from the disbanded armies of the Cis-Mississippi Dept. (those east of the Mississippi). The meeting consumed the greater part of a beautiful spring day—there was flutter of laces, clatter of drums, and the undulating, dim, nebulous swing of burnished bayonets."

Despite this meeting, "the political and military horizon lowered black and gloomy now, with not one single ray of sunshine anywhere all over the rough and rugged sky. Weakness, trembling, indecision and imbecility made headway in the army fearfully, and—a paralysism unaccountable and wanton, because so unnecessary, settled down upon officers, soldiers and citizens." (*Shelby and His Men,* page 434).

Another meeting was held at Marshall, Texas, attended by the Governors of the States involved. Here, Gov. Reynolds (of Texas) openly and firmly advised the blending and concentrating of every element of resistance. The others temporized and asked time to consider.

Still another meeting was held by the ranking military

-officers concerned, and after much talk, General Shelby finally proposed that General E. Kirby Smith be informed frankly that his commanders had lost faith in his ability to successfully wage war, and that a change in command was therefore necessary. It was proposed that he turn his troops over to General Buckner, who would send General Preston to Mexico to learn how matters stood between the Liberals and Imperialists; order the concentration of the entire army on the Brazos river, and fight step by step to the Rio Grande, when, in the event of everything else failing, he was to take service with one or the other of the contending parties in Mexico, and to establish either an Empire or a Republic.

The suggestion was not a bad one, and looking back upon it with all the advantages of "hindsight," might well have succeeded.

After persuasion, General Buckner, Smith's Chief of Staff, accepted the proposition. Smith was called upon, and —the conference ended with a full and complete understanding on the part of all, that no surrender would be resorted to, and no steps whatever looking to an abandonment of the contest.

However, following this meeting on April 19th, a request was sent to General E. Kirby Smith, Comdg. Confederate Forces, Trans-Miss. Dept., by the Federal Army suggesting that a surrender, on the same terms as offered General Lee, was in order. After conferring with the Governors of the four States involved, Smith declined this offer on May 9th, and on the same date, issued a circular letter to the four Governors as follows:

Gentlemen—The surrender of General Lee and the perilous situation of the armies in North Carolina and Alabama, seem to preclude the probability of successful resistence in the States east of the Mississippi. The army under my command yet remains strong, fresh and well equipped. The disparity of numbers, though great between it and our enemies, may be counterbalanced by valor and skill. Under these circumstances it is my purpose to defend your soil and the civil and political rights of our people to the utmost extend of our resources, and to try to maintain untarnished the reputation which our soldiers have so nobly won in many fields. In order, however to accomplish this great object, it will require the perfect concord of the civil and military authorities, the application of all our energies, and the united and devoted support of the people.

The Trans-Mississippi Dept. is so separated from the States on the eastern side of the Mississippi that communication is suspended. Since the evacuation of Richmond the seat of Government of the Confederate States has not been fixed, and it may be transferred to the western side of the Mississippi.

It is impossible to confer with the President so as to meet the exigencies of the times, and questions of grave political importance beyond my military authority may arise, and require prompt decision. Intending to uphold the authority of the Confederate Government by arms to the utmost, I yet feel that I should carefully avoid any appearance of usurping functions not entrusted to my discretion. Under these circumstances, I esteem it my duty to consult you in the absence of the President, as the chief magistrates of the States within this department, touching such important matters as are not embraced in my powers as commanding general, and as may conduce to the common defense and welfare. I therefore desire to confer with you in order that I may furnish any information in my power which may be useful in your deliberations; and without proffering suggestions, ask you to indicate such a policy as you may deem necessary to maintain with honor and success the sacred cause in which we are engaged.

The conference which ensued, carefully weighed all possibilities and the document that was drawn up as a result, amounted to little more than that a cessation of hostilities between the United States and the four States involved be considered. This was wishful thinking, and as might have been expected, no such offer was accepted by the United States Military.

Between the rejection of this proposal and the actual surrender of the Department on May 26th,

The Texas infantry first felt the pressure, met among themselves, resolved to disband and go home, and openly made preparations for a general break-up. A few honorable exceptions occurred, however, and some regiments and brigades stood by their colors until—(the formal surrender). The cavalry went next, and entire squadrons left in the night, plundering the country of everything on the line of march. Anarchy reigned supreme in Texas. Government stores, warehouses, manufactories, and treasury offices were sacked, destroyed, or fired. Quartermaster and commissary trains were charged in regular line of battle, and mules, wagons, tents, and even the baggage of the officers, plundered or carried away. Private dwellings and private stores were rifled remorselessly, and no citizen dared expose his horse or mule to the eyes of the greedy ruffians. Vast parks of artillery, imported at enormous cost, stood abandoned upon the prairies by officers and men, stripped of every animal, and pitiful in utter desolation. Arsenals were entered and their previous contents scattered wantonly over the country or fired off to celebrate drunken and infernal orgies. A mania for plunder and pillage seized upon the minds of all classes, and the women attended in crowds to urge on the robbers and quarrel among themselves about the spoils. Organization, discipline, pride, honor, manhood, dropped speedily away, and the country was filled with innumerable bodies of armed men without leaders and without restraint. History must damn to all eternity these last days of the Trans-Mississippi army, when it tells how sixty thousand well-armed, well-appointed, well-fed, healthy and well-officered men, with not an enemy nearer than two hundred miles, spontaneously gave way to a universal desire for desertion, and disgracefully surrendered everything, without the exhibition of a single heroic impulse or the exercise of one manly virtue with which to crown their previous honorable endurance and well-earned reputation. (*Shelby and His Men*, page 445-446.)

In short, there was chaos.

Hill to Maj. Thos. G. Rhett, Cf. of Ord. TMD, Shreveport, La.

I rec'd your telegram and about 120 of my men are now here. I found so much grumbling, growling and disaffection that I was compelled to protect the public property, to allow all that wanted, a furlough to go home. The men that I have left, I have organized into a company and am now simply guarding the stores. The reason that I was compelled to do this was that the transportation quartermaster had furloughed his men, and a report had gotten out that all the ammunition, arms and everything was to be turned over to General Shelby, and you never in your life saw such excitement. I am now trying to close up everything. The persons owning teams and negroes I have, are demanding them, and I will discharge them next week. It will be very hard to keep the men together long, as it will be almost impossible to feed them. Men now in charge of Depot, supplied of corn, wheat, etc. are distributing it to the citizens. You never, or no one else, ever did see such a time. If you can, I would like very much to get a good officer to help me close things up.

MONDAY, MAY 22, 1865

Hill to Sam'l D. Gibbs, Chf. Justice of Smith County, Texas.

I answer to yours of this date. I will state that the powder, lead and caps will be turned over to any one you may designate when ever you send transportation for same, authorizing the person who receives the supplies to receipt for same.

Hill to Major General J. O. Shelby, Comdg. Cavlry Div.

Everything here is in a complete state of confusion, and I would most respectfully suggest that you would send a strong guard and some good officer to command the post. All of my men have left except about 100 and some of them are not to be depended upon. My Works are in danger and all the stores here are at the mercy of a mob. The Qtr. Mst. was cleaned out last night of anything. He has not a mule left and it was with the greatest trouble and activity that I could guard my Works from being sacked and everything taken. If you want what stores are left I would advise a strong guard to be sent to protect them. The grab game is now the order of the day, and I think that a guard and a strong one should be sent here at once. I hope that you will send one with all possible haste, and send a good officer to command it.

Hill to Maj. Thos. G. Rhett, Chf. of Ord. TMD, Shreveport, La.

Enclosed, please find report of work done etc. at these Works during the week ending May 22nd, 1865.

Force of habit is strong. With his world crashing around him, Col. Hill still managed to send out his weekly Work Report.

Hill to Maj. Gen. J. O. Shelby, Comdg. Cavlry. Div.

I would advise a strong force sent me at once and a good officer. It is necessary to protect ord. stores, and should be sent at once. Some beef, and considerable flour is on hand in the commissary store. It is reported that a large body of marauders will be here this week to sack the town, and I fear there is some truth in it. Col. Bradfute has left. Capt. Barratt of Swert's Regt. now commands the Post.

Yours just rec'd—5 o'clock.

WEDNESDAY, MAY 24, 1865

Telegram from Hill to General E. Kirby Smith, Houston, Texas, via Henderson.

I am without orders. The most of my men have left me. Every department near this place has been robbed. Several attempts have been made upon me, but so far, I have defeated them. A great many things have been stolen. I asked Gen'l Shelby for a guard, and he sent Col. Blackwell and 150 men to guard what stores he has in my Department. Col. Bradfute has left. Col. Blackwell has assumed command of the Post. All my tools and material I am paying out to the men and creditors of the Dept. I have on hand about 1,200 stand of arms and about 800,000 rounds of ammunition, and some powder, caps and equipment. Had I not better turn over all these things to Gen'l Shelby's Comg.? Please send me orders.

Hill to Gen'l Joe Shelby—no address.

Much to my satisfaction, Col. Blackwell has arrived, and the presence of his noble person and the soldierly bearing of his brave Missouri boys has put a quietus upon the most shameful state of affairs ever heard of in the known world. Last Sunday night after placing a guard over my stores, etc. I was going the rounds when one of my men came and reported to me that the QuarterMaster Dept. had been forcibly entered and that they were taking everything. I immediately called on a few of my men and went over to see if I could not disperse the raiders. I had only 6 men with me and I at once put the whole party to flight. I soon found that they had removed the most of the stores. I got what I could together, called for the QM, and made him have the things put back excepting about 20 barrels of whiskey which I had dumped in the street. The raiders then charged my horse lot and stable, about 30 in number. I went into the lot with 6 men, ran the raiders off excepting 2 men which we took in charge. I found about 20 of my mules and horses saddled. I captured the saddles which I now have. Capt. S. C. Kirby's Dept. was charged and everything was taken. Dr. Johnson, in Charge of the Medical Laboratory was charged and everything he had was taken. These last two Departments are about 3 miles from town.

On Tuesday morning the women made a raid on the Post. Commissary Dept. but I went to his assistance and so disbursed the raiders without the effusion of blood. The women were very much exasperated at their defeat, and returned here today very largely reinforced, and their motto was: 'Blood or Sugar!', but on Col. Blackwell's arrival, they concluded they were not strong enough to accomplish anything and so dispersed.

Things are in a devil of a state, but everything is now quieted and I am very glad that you sent Col. Blackwell, for if he had not of come, I am certain that I would have had to use some stringent means for putting a stop to the warfare forced upon me.

If I was in your place, I would, I think, come down here in person with my Quarter Master and Ordnance Officer and make immediate arrangement for the removal of all the stores I needed.

[207]

I will give you what stores you want and I have. The stores you
have at Marshall and Jefferson, I do not think you will get. I send
you a copy of a letter which I have just sent to Henderson to go
to Gen'l Smith. Come down and bring more men. Forage and
subs. can be had. Come to my house as soon as you come. I will
take care of you. Capt. Watkins has just arrived from Marshall.
He reports that on last Monday night the Federals were in Shreveport, that the Army below has broken up—make haste and send
for your ammunition.

An eye witness to all this turmoil was John N. Edwards,
one of Shelby's men. In *Shelby and His Men,* his account
of the affair bears out the statements of Col. Hill.

The large arsenal and gun manufactury at Tyler was threatened
by some disbanded soldiers, and he (Shelby) sent Colonel Blackwell with a hundred men to defend it as he would against the
Federals. Blackwell took his stand, as he always did, firm as a
rock, and the country around about and the disbanded soldiers
coming up from below gathered in his front to demand surrender. "We have yet to understand that word," replied the heroic
Blackwell; "these are Joe Shelby's soldiers and therefore you are
mistaken," The robbers insisted. Blackwell formed his veterans for
the attack, his men girting him around with forms unused to
fear. Then, with all the courtesy of his calm, staid manner, Blackwell addressed them: "You have been soldiers, and you wish to
deter soldiers of your own cause from doing their duty. It is
a long time since we tasted blood, and you are welcome to Tyler
and all its contents, if a man among you dare to march five
paces forward to an attack. Steady men!" Not a skulker moved.
Shrill female voices from the outside of the mob urged on the
cowards, but one by one they dropped away, no doubt heartily
ashamed of their conduct, and influenced in a great measure also
by one hundred desperate soldiers, with weapons bare and eyes
to the front. After quiet had been restored, Major Lawrence
commenced work in earnest. Wagons were impressed, teams
hired, and even mules bought to carry to Shelby's camp great
loads of shell and canister, grape and shrapnell, Enfield cartridges, revolvers, caps, and accounterments of all kinds.

FRIDAY, MAY 26, 1865

On this day appeared the last entry in the Day Book of the Tyler, Texas, Ordance Works. It is addressed to Col. Blackwell "Comdg. Post, Tyler, Texas," and is of course signed by "Lt. Col. G. H. Hill, Comdg. Works."

I find my men leaving me so rapidly that I shall be unable to keep anykind of a guard on duty more than today. All my ammunition, arms and equipment are at the Armory and Magazine, and Major Lawrence has concluded to receipt for them. I will turn everything over to him and you can do with it as you please.

In the morning, I will publish an order disbanding the Ordnance Works at this place.

While Col. Hill was writing the above, and taking his farewell of Tyler, in New Orleans, La., the surrender of the Confederate Department of the Trans Mississippi was being signed, and the Confederacy no longer existed.

May 30, 1865, E. Kirby Smith, former commander of the military of the Trans Miss. Dept., wrote Col. John T. Sprague, U.S. Army, with whom he had discussed terms of surrender prior to the actual signing thereof. Says General Smith:

When I gave you at Shreveport a memorandum which I hoped might be the basis of negotiations with the United States Government, I commanded an army of over 50,000 men, and a department rich in resources. I am now without either.

The Army in Texas disbanded before my arrival here (Houston). From one extremity of the department to the other, the troops except Shelby's heroic division of Missouri cavalry, with unexampled unanimity of action, have dissolved to their homes. Abandoned and mortified, left without either men or material, I feel powerless to do good for my country, and humiliated by the acts of a people I was striving to benefit.

The department is now open to occupation by your Government. The citizen and soldier, alike weary of war, are ready to accept the authority and yield obedience to the laws of the

United States. A conciliatory policy, dictated by wisdom, and administered with patient moderation, will insure peace and restore quiet. An opposite course will rekindle the flames of civil war with a fierceness and intensity unknown even in this sad and unfortunate struggle.

I myself shall go abroad until the future policy of the United States Govt. towards the south is announced, and will return to my family only when I can do so with security to my life and person.

Thanking you for your kindness to my wife, I remain Colonel,

Your friend,

E. KIRBY . SMITH.

P.S.—Since writing the above, I have information that the Missouri and a portion of the Arkansas troops still retain their organization.

General Smith was right. A portion of the Missouri and Arkansas troops did still retain their organization—under General Joseph Orville Shelby, and it is General Shelby with whom we are now concerned as a possible lead to the ultimate disposition of the weapons made at Tyler.

PART III

EVENTS AFTER THE FALL OF THE CONFEDERACY

SOLDIERS OF SHELBY'S DIVISION!

The crisis of a nation's fate is upon you. I come to you in this hour of peril and gloom, as I have often come when your exultant shouts of victory were loud on the breezes of Missouri, relying upon your patriotism, your devotion, your heroic forti- tude and endurance. By the memory of our past efforts, our bril- liant reputation, our immortal death, our wrecked and riven hearthstones, our banished and insulted women, our kindred fate and kindred ruin, our wrongs unrighted and unavenged, I con- jure you to stand shoulder to shoulder and bide the tempest out. In union there is strength, honor, manhood, safety, success—in separation, defeat, disgrace, extermination, death. I promise to remain with you until the end. To share your dangers, your trials, your exile, your destiny, and your lot shall be my lot, and your fate shall be my fate, and come what may, poverty, misery, exile, degradation, Oh! never let your spotless banner be tar- nished by dishonor. If there be any among you who wish to go from our midst when the dark hour comes, and the bright visions of liberty are paling beyond the sunset shore, let him bid farewell to the comrades whom no danger can appall and no disaster deter, for the curse of the sleepless eye and the festering heart will be his reward, as the women of Missouri, the Peris of a ruined Paradise, shall tell how Missouri's braves fought until the Confederate Flag "by inches was torn from the mast."

Stand by the ship boys, as long as there is one plank upon another. All your hopes and fears are there. All that life holds nearest and dearest is there. Your bleeding mother-land, pure and stainless as an angel-guarded child is there. The proud imperial South, the nurse of your boyhood and the priestess of your faith is there, and calls upon you, her children, her best and bravest, in the pride and purity of your blood, to rally round her altar's shrine, the blue skies and green fields of your nativity, and send your scornful challenge forth, "The Saxon breasts are equal to the Norman steel."

Meet at your company quarters, look the matter fairly and squarely in the face. Think of all you have to lose, and all you have to gain. Watch the fires of your devotion as you would your hopes of heaven. Stand together, act together, keep your discipline and your integrity, and all will be well, as you strike for God and humanity. I am with you until the last, and Oh! what glad hosannas will go up to you when our land, redeemed, shall rise beautiful from its urn of death and chamber of decay; the storms of battle and the anguish of defeat floating away forever!

If Johnston follow Lee, and Beauregard and Maury and Forrest all go; if the Cis-Mississippi Department surrender its arms and quit the contest, let us never surrender. For four long years we have taught each other to forget that word, and it is too late to learn it now. Let us meet as we have met in many dark hours before, with the hearts of men who have drawn the sword and thrown away the scabbard, and resolve with the deep, eternal, irrevocable resolution of freemen, that we will never surrender!

If all the regiments in this department go by the board, if coward fear and dastard treachery dictate submission, we will treat every man who leaves his banner now as a base recreant, and shoot him as we would a Federal. *This Missouri Division surrender*—my God! Soldiers, it is more terrible than death. You, the young and the brave of Missouri, who have so often marched away to battle, proudly and gayly, with love in your hearts and light in your eyes for the land you loved best, you who are worshipped by your friends and dreaded by your enemies; you who have the blood of Cavaliers in your veins—it is too horrible to contemplate.

No! No! We will do this: We will stand together, we will keep our organization, our arms, our discipline, our hatred of oppression, until one universal shout goes up from an admiring eye, that this Missouri Cavalry Division preferred exile to submission—death to dishonor.

Such read a circular distributed throughout Shelby's men by their Commander, General Joe Shelby. Cheap theatrics? Sentimental trash? Sincerity can be neither, and

Shelby was sincere—terribly sincere. He meant every word he said, and proved them by his later actions. His command, as such, remained together until June 2, 1865, when at Corsicana, Texas, it was disbanded, not surrendered.

Then, surrounded by 500 officers and men determined to follow his fortune, Shelby turned his face to the West and to the South. Out of the rubble that was once the Confederacy, but now the land of dead hopes and deader promises, he marched his followers across the great State of Texas, unpursued by the Federals. From time to time his band was increased by men whose nature would not permit them to defeat or surrender. As far off as the yet smouldering battlefields of Virginia they came, men eager to join the banner of Joe Shelby. The dreams of these men as they rode through the vastness of Texas towards they knew not what? Some dreamed of a new Empire or Republic carved from the Southwest, others of forming an alliance with either Emperor Maximilian or President Juarez for a breathing spell and a base from which to launch a new blow for a Confederacy they could not believe dead. All of them dreamed of freedom, that intangible something that men must have to hold head high and be a man. Visionaries or adventurers? Who can say, but in either event, without backward glance towards the land of their birth and children, the land they had helped to defend for so long, they followed their chief into exile, into a foreign land whose tongue and customs they knew not.

Shelby had in his little camp of five hundred, four splendid new rifled cannon; one large train loaded with flour and bacon; two thousand new Enfield muskets; forty thousand rounds of small-arm ammunition; six hundred rounds of artillery ammunition; bushels of gun caps, pistol cartridges, and five hundred heavy dragoon sabres. The men from the leader down had a splendid Sharpe's carbine and four navy revolvers each—with one hundred and twenty rounds for both to the man. (*Shelby and His Men*, page 453.).

Having already noted that the stores at the Tyler, Texas, Ordnance Works had been accepted by Shelby's Quartermaster, Major Lawrence, on May 26, just one week before, it seems reasonable to suppose that the greater portion of the above equipment had previously been under the command of our friend Lt. Col. G. H. Hill.

We recall that on April 22nd, in a letter to Maj. Rhett, Lt. Col. Hill advised having on hand; 345 Texas rifles, 90 Hill rifles, and 40 musketoons—all of which were packed and ready to ship to Col. Bourland. In addition to this, Col. Hill advised having 159 Texas rifles and 975 Enfield rifles.

As there is no letter to Col. Bourland advising that the 475 requested cavalry guns had been sent him, we must assume that all the above, a total of 1,609 new rifles, were on hand at the Armory when Col. Hill closed out accounts on May 26, 1865. Might not these be the "two thousand new Enfield muskets"?

If our reasoning be correct, then the "two thousand new Enfield muskets" which were a portion of General Shelby's armament, 1,609 were from Tyler and of these, 604 were "Texas rifles," and 90 were "Hill rifles." These guns, for the moment, followed Shelby South.

From Corsicana to Waco, to Austin, to San Antonio, to Eagle Pass, Texas, the horsemen traveled, a distance of about 400 miles. Over this route, many adventures befell them, but which do not concern this story.

Eagle Pass is a little town on the American side of the Rio Grande, and Piedras Negras is a little town on the Mexican side. In Eagle Pass Shelby therefore bivouacked, threw his guns into battery bearing upon the Mexican shore, stationed his pickets, and went comfortably into camp. By and by a little skiff shot away from the shore at Piedras, bearing two greasers and a white flag to the American side. The bright yawning James (cannon) had terrified the Liberal garrison over the way greatly, and the commander sent a polite request asking time to remove the women and children, fully intending doubtless to remove himself at the same time. His fears, however were soon explained away, and General Shelby with a few of his escort crossed over to negotiate for the sale of the arms and ammunition. The governors of the States of New Leon and Coahuila came to Piedras Negras; runners were sent post-haste over the surrounding country for the prominent rancheros, and for two days the powwow went interestingly on. There the uninitiated had ample opportunity to thoroughly understand the remarkable ease and rapidity with which Mexican hands squeeze the last dollar from plethoric and horrified Dons. After much pressing and assessing—threatening and expostulating—eighteen thousand silver dollars were at length concentrated. For safe keeping they were deposited in the office of the collector of customs. Engaged in this office as a clerk, translator, spy—anything required in fact—was a Louisiana Creole who had served on Union General Canby's staff in New Mexico, but who had in all probability deserted the service when the work became heavy and hot. He was a rare polyglot. French, Italian, Spanish, German and English rattled off from his tongue in soft persuasive accents, and his bows and studied politeness were as seductive as Chesterfield's. However, the night before the eighteen thousand dollars were paid to Shelby this amiable interpreter very coolly abstracted one bag containing two thousand of the bright silver dollars, and was the most uproarious the next morning in denouncing robbers in general and Mexicans in particular. He certainly was the most finished scoundrel ever encountered, and deserved the bag of money for superb affability with which he ingratiated himself into the confidence of the Confederates.

So for the cannon, the arms, the ammunition and accounterments, Shelby received sixteen thousand dollars in cash and some sixteen thousand more in 'Juarez script' which never brought a farthing and perhaps never will. The money received was divided out among the officers and men pro rata, and with it—small as the amount was to each man—they started their march of a thousand miles into a strange and foreign country (*Shelby and His Men,* page 456.)

And now a sad scene occurred before the Confederates marched southward from this Mexican city. The old tattered battle-flag of the division was brought from its resting-place and given once more to the winds. Rent and bruised, and crimson with the blood of heroes—it had never been dishonored. Missouri breezes had felt the flapping of its silken folds; woman's imperial hand had decorated it with battle-mottoes; sweet, coy victory—her locks heavy with the dust of conflicts and red with the blood of martyrs —had caressed it often and tenderly; ambition had plumed it with the royal crest of triumph; fate and dear dauntless hearts had borne it flashing like a meteor upon the rough, stormy waves of battle waters, shining like the face of a struggling king, it had gleamed grandly through the smoke and the sorrow of two hundred desperate fields; and still broad barred, but worn, and old—it was displayed once more to its followers before the swift waves of the Rio Grande closed over it forever. It was yet early morning of the 4th of July, 1865. The picturesque mountains of El Paso del Aquilar were in full sight, and imparted additional grandeur to the ceremony thus solemnized by the romantic chief, whose exploits with his Missouri cavalry have shed the luster of renown upon the pages of his country's history. With bare, bowed heads, Shelby's soldiers gathered around the dear old banner. It had been all to them, and they worshiped it. Colonels Elliott, Williams, Gordon, Slayback and Blackwell held it up for a few brief moments above the rushing tide; the sun shone out broad and good upon the upturned faces of these engaged in silent prayer— and at last, with not a dry eye among all those five hundred stern soldiers, the Battle Flag of Shelby's division was lowered slowly and sadly beneath the water. (*Shelby and His Men,* page 457.)

From Piedras Negras the troop journeyed to Monterey, and there the command separated. Some went to Sonora to join the Liberal chief Corona; some went to California; some to British Honduras; some to Brazil, and many joined the French contra-guerrillas under Col. Dupin. Shelby however, with fifty of his men marched on to the City of

[218]

Mexico, finally settling in the Cordova Colony of Carlotta. While it is possible that some few of the Tyler arms and ammunition accompanied Shelby and his men even so far as Carlotta, it would appear that the great bulk of such arms and accoutrement were among those sold at Piedras Negras, and which went to supply the Liberals of the States of New Leon and Coahuila, and somewhere in that country South of the Border are 604 "Texas rifles" and 90 "Hill rifles" waiting to be discovered by some collector.

As to the disposition of the Tyler Armory itself, the Tyler Daily *Courier Times* of Oct. 3, 1928, gives the following account:

After word came that the war was over, Capt. James P. Douglas, of Douglas Battery fame, and H. V. Hamilton, were delegated to go to this arsenal (Tyler) and destroy the gunpowder and munitions there. Arriving at the scene, they debated as to how best accomplish this. Near the arsenal (armory) was a running stream, so it was decided to dump the powder and munitions into this stream, and calling to their aid other men, they packed out this war material, and dumped it into the branch, but it was soon evident that the water would not quickly destroy the tons of powder. As there were threats of a negro uprising, they did not want the negroes to have access to this powder. So after a parley, it was decided to run a train of powder over a nearby hill and fire a rifle into the powder (train) and thus blow up or burn up the powder. They did not figure on the consequences that followed. Watching the hissing powder as the fire wormed its way down the hill and then seeking protection behind the hill, a tremendous explosion followed that shook the whole country roundabout. The arsenal building itself was shaken to its foundation. The men were knocked unconscious, but soon rallied. When Mr. Hamilton faced Captain Douglas, who was still dazed from the shock, Captain Douglas said:

"Van, we've played hell."

And they had. Soon the entire population began to arrive on the scene. They found the men about the place bleeding at mouths, ears, and noses. All were badly shaken, many wounded, but none killed. But the lights (glass) in every window in Tyler were gone, and so were the supplies that had been packed out of the arsenal, and in place of these was a hole in the earth big enough to plant a battleship.

APPENDIX

Notes taken from Vol. 148 and Vol. 149 "Chapter IV of the Captured Rebel Records," National Archives, Washington, D.C., and consisting of various "Summary Statements of Work" and disbursements at the Tyler, Texas, Ordnance Works for the months of October 1863 through April 1865. The first three months (October, November and December, 1863) are given verbatim, as they are not covered in detail by Lt. Col. Hill's quarterly returns in his Day Book. The balance have been skeletonized as their salient points appear in the Quarterly Reports of the Day Book. Abbreviations and spelling, as taken from the records have been retained.

SUMMARY STATEMENT OF WORK DONE AT TYLER ORD. WORKS IN THE MONTH OF OCT., 1863.

Articles Fabricated

7,520 Buck & Ball cart.
18 tables
4 drawer
6 desks
1 rule
1 stool
1 frame and post for bell
1 pr. steps
1 well curb
3 gates for Gov. stable
1 shelf for clock in guard house
1 set gate hinges
1 buggy stirrup
4 benches for laboratory
8 spit boxes

Articles Repaired

90 muskets
2 sporting rifles
1 Sharps pistol
1 Colt's pistol

Tools

2 work benches for carpt. shop
1 pr. trustle benches for carpt. shop
2 hatchet handles
4 saddlers stitching horses
3 treddles for stitching horses
4 springs for stitching horses
1 hand mallet
1 tool rack
20 chisel handles
24 boxes for laboratory
4 binding blocks for laboratory
4 ax handles.

Other Work done

Government stable repaired
1 crutch made
Hired men*****cartridge makers, 14
Enlisted men—Master workmen 4, mechanics 19

SUMMARY STATE OF WORK DONE AT TYLER ORDNANCE WORKS DURING THE MONTH OF NOVEMBER 1863.

ARMORY

Articles Fabricated

100 new rifles with bayonets
  4 hooks
  2 pr. dog irons
  1 pr. butt hinges
 12 block hooks
  1 round ⅜ inch bolt
  1 piece 1 X 15 inch ⅝ hole
  1 rod for bullet shop
  1 bolt for bullet shop
  1 door latch.

Articles Repaired

 12 prs tongs
  1 cock swedge
  1 lock & key
  1 lock & key
158 perc. muskets
  4 pistols
 12 DB guns
  6 SB guns
 11 Enfd. rifles
  1 pr. bullet moulds
  1 sporting rifle
  1 Savage pistol.

Tools

 12 prs nippers
  2 pr dyes
  1 round knife
  1 claw tool
  1 crease iron
  1 edge tool
  1 pr. compasses
  2 hollow punches
  6 saddlers awls
  1 guage knife
  4 grub hoes
  1 saddlers hammer
 20 test breeches
 82 steel rods
  1 pr pincers
  1 reamer
  5 iron wedges

  2 froers
  2 plug cutters
  1 —⅜ bitt
  1 rivet sett
  4 screw drivers
  6 ferrels for harness shop.

Men employed in Armory—Detailed.

1 Master Armorer, 1 foreman, 40 armorers, 19 blacksmiths, 6 laborers.
Hired men 1 laborer, 1 blacksmith.

LABORATORY

22,292 buck & ball cartridges
 6,803 Enfield Rifle cartridges
12,564 Miss. Rifle cartridges
   500 test cartridges—double charge.

Hands employed—Detailed men—1.
Hired men—Part of the time, 23 hands employed but a greater part, no work done for want of lead.

Other work done

  12 barrels filed up
  42 barrels taped
  33 barrels squared
  14 rifles stocked and partly finished
  23 barrels taped and ready for breeching
   3 guns finished except locks hardened
   1 auger handle ironed
   2 keys made
   1 wheel barrow ironed
  65 strap swivels forged
   6 snails forged
  29 lock plate screws forged
  88 cock screws forged
  29 breech screws forged
  36 barrel screws forged
1,056 lock screws forged
   1 chain to arty trace
   1 band for auger handle
   2 breech pins made
  19 cocks forged
 195 swivels forged

36 screws made
572 tubes forged
72 main springs forged
3 band springs forged
102 sights forged
6 sear springs forged
110 rivets for belting
1 tumble made
2 arty traces ironed
35 nails made
4 window hooks
9 axes upset
1 large work Bench made
11 axe handles
5 sets hinges for lead shop
4 stamping letters made.

Material expended
137 lbs of steel
437 lbs iron
500 bushels charcoal
12 cords wood
3 gals oil
12 musket cocks
1 steel rod
45 tubes
11 main springs
12 swivel springs
1 sear spring
44 screws
30 musket springs
9 sights
2 tumblers
42 S. rods
1 pr. moulds
4 B. Springs.

In Laboratory. Other work done
1,200 Miss. Rifle Cart. bound &
    crimped
900 B & B Carts. Boxed
3 doz. Official & 6 doz. Letter
    envelopes made

Material Expended
476½ lbs buck shot
1,151 lbs musket balls
470 lbs Enfd Rifle balls
197 lbs Musket powder
220 lbs Rifle Powder

844½ lbs Miss. Rifle Balls
23½ lbs cart. paper
3½ lbs spun cotton.

TIN SHOP
Article Fabricated
150 tin magazines
1 quart measure
1 ½ gal oil can
6 tin cups
15 stencil plates
22 canteens
5 candle sticks
1 sprinkling pot
700 burrs
1 wash pan
1 paper file.

Articles Repaired
123 magazines
Other Work
1 bugle repaired

Material Expended
106 sheets tin (12 X 18)
4½ lbs zinc
3 lbs solder
3 lbs wire
1 oz. muriatic acid.

Hands employed—2
Hired men—1

CARPENTER SHOP
Articles Fabricated
2 trussel benches
57 amm. boxes
5 tables
1 grind stone frame
1 hatchet handle
5 arm chests
1 small box for lead shop
2 rakes
3 benches
1 rolling barrel
9 binding blocks
1 rule for office
2 desks
13 spit boxes.

Articles Repaired
13 arm chests
1 amm. packing box
1 bullet sweage
1 saddlers stitching horse
1 crimping machine.

Other Work
   1 partition for storekeepers Office
   1 filling room for Laboratory
   4 window frames made
   4 window shutters made
   1 door frame made
   1 door shutter made
   6 axe handles made
   1 slack box for Armory made
   1 lead shop completed
   Furnace for lead shop completed.
   2 gates made
   1 sett shelves
   1 cover for stairway made
   1 bullet press
   1 double tree made
   1 chest made
2,955 wooden pegs
   1 house for qtrs in progress
   1 wagon bed repaired
   1 door frame & shutter made.

Material Expended
4,046 feet lumber
56½ lbs nails
   1 lock & key
   lot of iron for repairing
   1 bullet swedge
   2 drawer locks
   2 butt hinges.

Hands Employed—Detailed
1 foreman, 8 carpenters.

HARNESS SHOP
Articles Fabricated
   1 saddle, 1 halter
   4 arty tuggs

157 cart. boxes
   2 single setts arty harness
   2 setts driving reins
   2 straps, 1 bridle
   2 stay straps for buggy
   1 bridle, 50 setts arty harness, 11 arty tuggs
   3 leg guards
   6 blind bridles, 1 saddle
   2 single setts traces
   1 pr. martingales
   1 single sett ambluance harness
   2 setts buggy harness

Material Expended
30 lbs harness leather
45 lbs sole leather
22 sides (300 lbs) leather
142 burrs for cart. boxes
142 buttons for cart. boxes
   2 paper tacks
   9 buckles

HANDS EMPLOYED—Detailed.
1 foreman, 14 workmen part of the time, but a great part but 5 hands employed.
Hired—1 workman

LEAD SHOP
Fabricated
414½ lbs buck shot
926 lbs Miss. Rifle balls
501 lbs Enfd Rifle balls
350 cap box buttons
400 cart. box buttons.

Material Expended
1,592 lbs lead.

Hands Employed Detailed, 1 foreman
1 moulder
Hired—4 hands employed part of the time, but a greater part no work done for want of lead.

Negroes Employed and Work Done

113 cords wood cut & corded, 8 posts made for plank kiln, 25 sleepers made for ditch at Armory, 1150 bushels charcoal burnt, 1500 boards made and other work done at Armory.

Hands employed—6 burning coal, 6 cutting wood, 1 employed at Stable, 1 cooking, 1 in storeroom, 2 teamsters.

SUMMARY STATEMENT OF WORK DONE AT TYLER ORDINANCE WORKS IN THE MONTH OF DECEMBER 1863.

ARMORY

Articles Fabricated

43 bands for guns
84 new guns
20 horse shoes
21 heel plates for new guns
21 wipers for new guns
33 bayonets for new guns
238 front sights
21 cups for screw hears
322 strap swivels
21 triggers for new guns
21 tubes for new guns
21 trigger plates for new guns
56 breech pins for new guns
21 gun guards for new guns
1 lock key, 5 halter rings
1 halter swivel, 1 trace
1 pr. spurs, 1 tube wrench
64 main springs, new guns
40 belt hooks
11 screws for vice
56 hind sights
281 front sights
1 DB gun for Major Rhett
1 lathe now made set
12 bolts for lathe
22 buckles
2 staples & kings
2 slides or engine
2 bullet moulds.

Unfinished work

170 steel rods forged
1,196 lock screws forged
416 cock screws forged
150 breech screws forged
190 cock screws forged
687 band swivels forged
603 lock swivels forged

59 stocks for new guns turned
64 blls for new guns turned
11 main springs forged
1 sear spring forged
111 hind sights forged
921 front sights forged
2 cylinders forged
167 breech pins forged
18 wipers
3 sear springs
713 tubes forged
1 Snail forged (term for screw to pull loads also called worm)
137 tumbles forged
36 gun blls welded
39 gun blls finished with the exception of case hardening.

Repaired

73 Miss. rifles
23 Enfield rifles
114 percussion muskets
11 DB guns
1 Colt pistol
10 Austrian rifles
12 bullet moulds
1 ladle
1 morticing machine
1 monkey wrench
2 lathes repaired & set up
1 upright drills.

Other Work Done

6 axes upsett & steel put in
1 wagon tire shrunk
75 gun blls tested & fitted for stock
17 bayonets filed
3 butt screws, head turned, gro(unded)
1 sledge hammer upsett
59 lock screws milled

81 wrench screws milled
185 gun blls fitted or made ready for rifling
8 bearings turned on shaft, Dr. Johnson
26 gun blls swedged
265 main springs reset
281 gun blls tested or sound
78 gun blls tested—unsound or busted
60 scalps drawn
17 gun stocks returned
32 gun barrels rifled
1 pr hinges made.

Tools Fabricated
6 brace bits
3 awls
2 ribet sets
10 drills
1 peg cutter
2 stocking chisils
1 stocking bitts
13 screw pins
1 chissel
6 seat awls
4 round knives
6 clan tools
5 hollow punches
1 burr or rint set
1 plan bits
1 screw driver
1 gunners bitt
6 edge tools
1 main spring sett
2 belt punches
2 vice sockets
1 milling tool
10 centre punches
2 reamers, 3 tongs pr.
3 iron wedges, 2 slicks
1 hammer springs
6 saws for rifling machine
1 swedges, 1 tongs gouges.

Tools repaired
4 welding rods
2 long handle shovels
1 cold chisel

1 swedge for lead shop
1 clan togs pr.
1 shoe knife
2 cherries.

MEN EMPLOYED IN ARMORY
detailed.
1 master armorer
2 foremen
41 armorers
21 blacksmiths
Hired
1 armorer
1 blacksmith
Total—67.

Material Expended
284 tubes
112 hind sights
109 front sights
100 main springs
107 tumblers
110 sear springs
129 cocks
109 tumbler screw
150 heel plates
159 gun guards
170 band springs
170 bands
110 (bruck?) screws breech
85 lock
157 steel rods
199 strap swivels
86 lock dogs
52 lock & breech screws
88 lock plate screws
85 breech pins
84 gun blls
84 bayonets
84 gun stocks
84 lock plates
84 trigger plates
84 triggers
84 cups for screw heads
118 trigger plate screws
84 heel plates screws
84 breech pins screws
344 inside lock screws
84 bridles

84 lock swivels
1,732 iron llbs.
60 steel llbs.
10 lead llbs.
2 bavit metal llbs.
¼ spurr gaiss llbs.
1,360 coal—bushels
53½ wood, cords
12 sand paper, quires
7 emory paper, quires
5 glue llbs.
5¼ potach llbs.
11 borax llbs.
500 blank cartridges
1,000 balls.

CARPENTER'S SHOP

Articles Fabricated
9 small boxes for lead shop
2 small boxes for harness shop
1 ladder for Carpenter shop
1 bed stead
1 gun case
2 sentry boxes, 5 ax helves
1 wood frame for Ord. Dept.
1 cutting board for Lab.
3 targets, 1 table for Ord. office
1 wheel barrow for lead shop
1 wheel barrow for Armory
1 large box for MSK
1 house for quarters
7 ammo. boxes
4 rough boxes for MSK
1 table & desk for Cpt. King's Off.
2 shoemakers benches.

Tools Fabricated
2 slickers
12 ctgr box formers
13 cap box formers.

Hands employed
detailed
9 men.

Articles Repaired
1 bench for lead shop
1 bullet mould
1 axe with new handle
10 gun boxes

1 chair for Cpt. Clark
1 table for Col. Hill
1 bed stead
1 wash stand
1 bullet swedge.

Other work done
7 large packing boxes
1 plank kiln
1 small table—Col. Hill
1 wash stand—Col. Hill
1 house for lead shop unfinished.

Material Expended
16,177 ft of lumber
1 lock & key
45 llb nails
1 paper 10 oz tacks
15 coffin screws
½ quire office paper
1 doz nuts & bolts
5 prs butt hinges
3 chest locks
5 ceawer locks
2 doz ½ in. screws
4 doz. ⅝ in. screws
5 doz. 1 in. screws.

HARNESS SHOP

Articles Fabricated
483 cartridge boxes
365 cap boxes
557 waist belts.

Articles Repaired
1 single set artillery harness.

Other work done
1 halter rein & collar
2 hame straps
33 ft of 2 in. **leather belting**
28 ft of ½ in. leather belting

Hands employed
Detailed—17, hired 1. Total 18.

Expended
861 llbs leather, 58 sides, 7½ llbs thread
4½ paper tacks
1,014 burrs for ctges & cap boxes

467 buttons for cap boxes
485 buttons for ctge boxes
1,230 hookswst bitts, 1 1/16 doz.
buckles
5/12 doz rings, ½ pt. neat foot oil
16 artly tups, 1 swivel
½ doz. needles
1/3 doz. awls
1 sheep skin with wool.

TIN SHOP

Articles Fabricated
520 magazines
500 burrs
1 lantern
6 small sht iron pins for MT
58½ llb solder
1 tin cup.

Articles Repaired
2 joints stove pipe
1 smitter.

Other Work Done
24 elevators for Col. Bocage
1 funnel for Col. Bocage.

Hands employed
1 man hired.

LABORATORY

Material expended
12 llbs solder
8 llbs sheet iron
64½ llbs old roofing tin
164 sheets tin 14 X 20
1 oz. muriatick acid
3 bushels charcoal
1 sheet tin 12 X 18.

Articles Fabricated
42,356 Missi. Rifle Ctges
42,356 Enfld. Rifle Ctges.

Other work done
500 blank test ctrdgs.

Hands employed
1 detailed
from 2 to 18 hired.

Material expended
723 lbs rifle powder
66½ lbs ctgr paper
1917 llbs Enfield rifle balls
4251 llbs Missi. rifle balls
12 llbs thread.

LEAD SHOP

Articles Fabricated
2774 llbs Enfld rifle balls
4435 llbs Missi. rifle balls
281 llbs musket balls
381 llbs buck shot.

Other work done
500 cartridge box buttons.

Hands employed
5 detailed
2 hired.

Material expended
9443 llbs lead
20 prs Enfield moulds worn out
1 ladle.

Work done by negroes
2020 bushels coal burned
144 cords coal wood cut
128 cord engine wood cut."

Skeletonized Summaries of Arms Made at Tyler, Texas.—
J. C. Short, Master Armorer, J. J. Hamilton, Foreman.

January, 1864—130 New Texas rifles.

February, 1864—39 bayonets, 92 Texas rifles, 92 Hill rifles, 195
lock plates forged. (33 Hill rifles tested sound, sec'd on testg.,
28 Hill rifles tested sound, 1 Hill rifle tested—bursted).

March, 1864—36 Hill rifles (long), 40 Hill rifles (short), 283 lock
plates forged, (43 Hill rifles tested sound, 79 New rifles tested
sound, 11 Texas rifles tested sound, 2 New rifles—bursted).

April, 1864—95 bayonets, 107 lock plates, 133 Texas rifles, 26 Hill
rifles (long), 1 Hill rifle (short).

May, 1864—111 Texas rifles, 64 bayonets.

June, 1864—118 New Texas rifles, 54 Hill rifles (long). For the
quarter ending June 30, 1864, George Yarbrough was paid
$1,350 for the rental of a three-story brick building in payment
of rental for the fourth quarter of 1863, and the first and second
quarter of 1864. S. H. Boren, also received the same amount on
rental of a three-story brick building. J. C. Rogers, was paid
$300 for rental of house for Carpenter Shop for the same quar-
ters. J. C. Fowler, was paid $54. for rent of stables from Jan. 1,
1864 through June 30, 1864.

July, 1864—7 Texas rifles, 46 Texas rifles (short), 80 Hill rifles.
148 patent breech for rifles were also made.

August, 1864—24 Texas rifles (short), 13 rifled muskets. 25 patent
breech for rifles were also made.

September, 1864—181 Enfield rifles, 60 Hill rifles (long). 60 patent
breech for rifles were also made.

October, 1864—71 Enfield rifles, 40 Hill rifles (long). 40 patent
breech for rifles were also made.

November, 1864—62 Enfield rifles, 57 Texas rifles (caliber .57), 2
sporting rifles.

December, 1864—123 Texas rifles, 16 Hill rifles.

January, 1865—28 Enfield rifles, 57 Texas rifles.

February, 1865—156 Enfield rifles, 74 Texas rifles, 4 Hill rifles, 9 Austrian rifles.

March, 1865—47 Austrian rifles, 10 Enfield rifles, 1 Hill rifle, 37 Texas rifles, 28 muskets.

April, 1865—No rifles were made. Work in Armory consisted of repair of 418 Enfield rifles, 32 B & Austrian rifles, 3 Richmond rifles, 49 Springfield rifles, 10 Texas rifles, 8 Hill rifles, 4 Whitney rifles, 8 Spanish rifles, 7 Mississippi rifles, 2 Arkadelphia rifles, 127 muskets, 10 musketoons, 4 muskets rifled, 1 double-barrel shot gun, 94 bayonets.

The reader has undoubtedly noted the number of "Enfield" rifles, and "Austrian" rifles made at Tyler. No clue is given as how these differed from the Hill rifles (made of Hall's rifle barrels) or the Texas rifles which were evidently made from sporting rifle barrels and barrels actually made at the Armory. It is the writer's opinion that the name of "Enfield" or "Austrian" was given to those rifles whose barrels were made from old Enfield or Austrian rifle barrels, possibly to show source of supply. As these barrels would have been turned on a lathe to meet the standards of the new rifle, old and foreign proof marks might have been obliterated. This however is only conjecture as to date, no "Austrian" nor "Enfield" Tyler rifles have appeared.

Guns Made at the Tyler Works by Month and Quarter from October 1, 1864, Through March 31, 1865—Eighteen Months.

Last Quarter of 1863 (October, November and December).
October, 1863—no firearms made.
November, 1863—100 Texas rifles with bayonets.
December, 1863—84 Texas rifles with 33 bayonets.
Quarterly total of 184 Texas rifles, 133 bayonets.
First Quarter, 1864 (January, February and March).
January—130 Texas rifles.
February—92 Texas rifles, 39 bayonets and 65 Hill rifles.
March—76 Hill rifles.
Quarterly total of 363 rifles, 39 bayonets.
Second Quarter, 1864 (April, May and June).
April—133 Texas rifles, 95 bayonets, 27 Hill rifles.
May—111 Texas rifles, 64 bayonets.
June—118 Texas rifles, 54 Hill rifles.
Quarterly total of 443 rifles, 159 bayonets.
Third Quarter, 1864 (July, August and September).
July—53 Texas rifles, 80 Hill rifles.
August—24 Texas rifles, 13 rifled muskets.
September—60 Hill rifles, 181 Enfield rifles.
Quarterly total of 411 arms. (no record of bayonets made after
    May 1864).
Fourth Quarter, 1864 (October, November and December).
October—40 Hill rifles, 71 Enfield rifles.
November—57 Texas rifles, 2 sporting rifles, 62 Enfield rifles.
December—123 Texas rifles, 16 Hill rifles.
Quarterly total of 371 arms.
First Quarter, 1865 (January, February and March).
January—57 Texas rifles, 28 Enfield rifles.
February—74 Texas rifles, 4 Hill rifles, 156 Enfield rifles, 9
    Austrian rifles.

March—37 Texas rifles, 1 Hill rifle, 10 Enfield rifles, 47 Austrian rifles, 28 muskets.
Quarterly total of 451 arms.

During the eighteen months covered, the Armory made: 1,009 Texas rifles, (of which 70 were the "short" variety), 423 Hill rifles, 2 sporting rifles, 13 rifled muskets, 508 Enfield rifles, 56 Austrian rifles and 28 muskets. 292 bayonets were made from November 1863 through May 1864. This gives us a grand total of 2,223 guns and 331 bayonets.

Only one question now remains—what happened to the guns?

BIBLIOGRAPHY

PRIMARY SOURCES

Captured Rebel Records, Chapter IV
General Orders, Confederate Army
Laws of Texas
Official Records, War of the Rebellion
Various Newspapers, North and South, of the Civil War Period

SECONDARY SOURCES

Bradbeer: *Confederate and Southern Currency*
Brokenburn
Confederate Military History
Dexter: *A.R.C.A. Arms Quarterly*
Edwards: *Shelby and His Men*
Fuller and Steuart: *Firearms of the Confederacy*
Greg: *History of the United States*
Handbook of Texas
Pollard: *The Lost Cause*
Steuart: *Fifty Years Ago Today in the Civil War* (column in the Baltimore
    American)
Wise: *Long Arm of Lee*
Woldert: *A History of Tyler and Smith County, Texas*